Contents at a Glance

Table of Contents

Mindfulness-Based Cognitive Therapy

FOR DUMMIES®

A Wiley Brand

Mindfulness-Based Cognitive Therapy For Dummies®

Published by: **John Wiley & Sons, Ltd.,** The Atrium, Southern Gate, Chichester, www.wiley.com

This edition first published 2013

© 2013 John Wiley & Sons, Ltd, Chichester, West Sussex.

John Wiley & Sons Ltd, The Atrium, Southern Gate, Chichester, West Sussex, PO19 8SQ, United Kingdom

For details of our global editorial offices, for customer services and for information about how to apply for permission to reuse the copyright material in this book please see our website at www.wiley.com.

For general information on our other products and services, please contact our Customer Care Department within the U.S. at 877-762-2974, outside the U.S. at (001) 317-572-3993, or fax 317-572-4002. For technical support, please visit www.wiley.com/techsupport.

A catalogue record for this book is available from the British Library.

ISBN 978-1-118-51946-2 (pbk); ISBN 978-1-118-51943-1 (ebk); ISBN 978-1-118-51944-8 (ebk); ISBN 978-1-118-51945-5 (ebk)

Printed in Great Britain by TJ International, Padstow, Cornwall

10 9 8 7 6 5 4 3 2 1

Introduction

*W*hen I was young I learned to sing and read very early on but, my mum tells me, I refused to learn how to read the time. Clocks and watches were my enemy. They spoilt my games and forced me to do things I wasn't ready to do at that moment. I resisted until I was seven years old, and then the world got me!

Little children are naturally mindful. They don't want to look at a clock to determine whether playtime is over or whether they're hungry or not; they just play until they're tired or until their stomach rumbles. They enjoy sweets without worrying whether the next portion is going to taste just as good as this one; they climb onto climbing frames and roundabouts in the park because doing so is exciting; they build sandcastles even though they're going to be washed away by the sea. They don't feel guilty about just being and not doing much. They live in the moment completely.

Unfortunately, most adults have lost this immediate experience of life. Mindfulness-based cognitive therapy (or MBCT as you'll see throughout this book) may be a way to return, at least temporarily, to these moments of joy, these moments of simply tasting life.

MBCT was developed to help people help themselves. It features in-depth training in meditation and moment-to-moment everyday awareness. More precisely, you can see mindfulness as bringing your awareness deliberately to the present moment and accepting what you find, as opposed to judging it or wanting to change it.

I can't stress enough the importance of being able to just experience life, rather than rushing through it. When you look at your life, do you find yourself being calm and centred, joyful and relaxed? If so, congratulations! The majority of people find that they've less and less time for being, despite all the technological advances you can dream of. In fact these are often your bane rather than your saviour. Perhaps you too find yourself using your mobile or computer tablet while eating, travelling, crossing the road or even when having a conversation.

If you belong to this latter category of 'human doings' (rather than 'human beings'), this book is for you. I demonstrate numerous ways of stepping out of autopilot and moving back into moments of simply being alive. My hope is that this book reminds you that being alive is special and that every moment counts and is precious, because it's all part of your life experience.

About This Book

Everybody's talking about MBCT: newspapers and magazines are writing about it; books are being published on it; YouTube is bursting with short videos explaining how to do it. Perhaps a well-meaning friend even gave you this book as a gift. The purpose of *Mindfulness-Based Cognitive Therapy For Dummies* is to introduce you to the concept of MBCT, the whys and hows, and whether it may be a life skill that can benefit you. Being a *For Dummies* book, you can choose to pick up a couple of useful tools and meditations or a whole bag full of them, depending on what you choose to read and how much you feel you want to experiment with mindfulness.

This book is helpful for the beginner, who wants a taste of mindfulness and maybe to take things further step by step, as well as for the more experienced meditator, who may find a number of new insights and perspectives on the subject.

I want you to read this book in the way that helps you most. I've done my best to create something that gives you the insights and tools to help you cope better with the various upheavals that life may throw at you. I sincerely hope that you don't need to read all the chapters. You may, however, gain deeper insight into MBCT and the human condition if you skim-read what the different chapters are about: go on, take a peep.

I include many anecdotes, stories, examples, poems, and so on, but place these in grey-tinted boxes called sidebars so you can choose to read or skip them. They enrich your experience (stories and poems have this great way of unfolding complicated facts so that you can feel the truth rather than just know it), but these sidebars aren't essential to practising mindfulness so skip them if you want to.

Foolish Assumptions

In my line of work I meet many individuals who struggle with aspects of their lives, including clients and therapists alike. So I assume that every person can benefit to a larger or smaller degree from this book. I also assume that you're genuinely interested in finding out what MBCT is and how it may help you.

I certainly don't assume any existing knowledge about MBCT, mindfulness, cognitive behavioural therapy, meditation or Buddhism.

I lead you gently through the subject and hope that this book becomes a good companion to you over the next few months or years.

Icons Used in This Book

If this book is your first *For Dummies* one, you may not be familiar with the icons used throughout the book. Even if this is your umpteenth *For Dummies* experience, remembering what they stand for is still useful:

This icon points out ideas to help you make your mindfulness voyage smoother.

This icon features essential pieces of guidance that you may want to note down in your diary or read a few times until they sink in.

Sometimes, you have to watch out for specific problems, and I provide advice on avoiding the pitfalls that other people have fallen into beside this icon.

Beside this icon you find exercises, practices and meditations that lead you through something new and inspiring.

Here I demystify therapy language that you may not have come across before.

This book comes with a selection of guided MBCT meditations and exercises. This icon draws your attention to those meditations and exercises for which you can download accompanying audio tracks.

Beyond the Book

As you walk your journey of discovery into the world of MBCT, you can augment what you read here by checking out some of the access-anywhere extra goodies I've hosted for you online.

You can find the book's e-cheat sheet online, at www.dummies.com/cheat sheet/mindfulnessbasedcognitivetherapyuk. The at-a-glance ideas and tips I offer in this cheat sheet can help you to make room for mindfulness in your life, and to bring mindful attitudes to everyday activities.

I've also recorded a selection of guided meditations and exercises to go along with some of those I've included in the book:

- **Track One:** Introduction
- **Track Two:** Making yourself comfortable, Chapter 4
- **Track Three:** The body scan practice, Chapter 4
- **Track Four:** Ten-minute sound meditation, Chapter 5
- **Track Five:** Mindful breathing exercise, Chapter 5
- **Track Six:** Allowing awareness of sound, breath and body meditation, Chapter 6
- **Track Seven:** Sitting with difficult thoughts meditation, Chapter 7
- **Track Eight:** Sitting with spacious awareness exercise, Chapter 10
- **Track Nine:** Mindful walking exercise, Chapter 12

You can access these audio tracks online, at www.dummies.com/go/ mindfulnessbasedcognitivetherapyuk.

Additionally, you can also find bonus content online, at www.dummies.com/ extras/mindfulnessbasedcognitivetherapyuk, which includes an extra Part of Tens chapter: 'Ten (Plus One) Tips for Developing Mindful Attitudes'.

Where to Go from Here

I've been leading MBCT courses for more than a decade, and over the years I've discovered plenty about what works and what doesn't. I do my best to convey this knowledge to you, so that you can make practical use of it in your own time and at your leisure.

You can read this book in any order you like. I suggest, however, that you read Chapter 1 initially and then skim through the Table of Contents to pick out what seems most interesting to you. If you have a specific issue you want to tackle quickly, you can turn to the relevant chapter in Part III, such as Chapter 12 for depression or Chapter 16 for handling retirement, for example.

My guess is that when you understand how essential mindfulness is for surviving mentally and physically in this frenetic world, you may feel inspired to engage more deeply and start the eight-session voyage into mindfulness that forms the core of this book in Chapters 4 to 11. Whether you choose to take eight weeks or eight months, these sessions are the best way of getting your head round the topic and installing enough mindful ways of being into your brain and daily life.

If you get infected with the mindfulness bug, you may even set up a group with others and meditate together. Sitting in a circle can be particularly powerful and unifying; connecting with others and experiencing kindness. Be well!

Part I

Introducing Mindfulness-Based Cognitive Therapy

getting started

with

mindfulness-based

cognitive therapy

Part I

Introducing Mindfulness-Based Cognitive Therapy

In this part...

- Grasp what purpose mindfulness-based cognitive therapy has and how it is used as a treatment tool, and discover how it can enable you to tackle and live with problems, struggles and challenges.

- Know the importance of experience and of being in the present moment as central aspects of mindfulness-based cognitive therapy.

- Understand yourself and the problems you face in your life today, and get motivated to make a real change for the better.

- Learn how to use mindfulness-based cognitive therapy to let go of pointless ruminative thinking and to help you focus on *now*.

- See the benefits of regular mindfulness-based cognitive therapy practice, and prepare yourself for and successfully personalise an eight-week voyage into mindfulness to suit you.

Chapter 1

Improving Your Wellbeing with Mindfulness

In This Chapter

▶ Introducing MBCT

▶ Perceiving its purpose

▶ Focusing on the benefits

*T*he person who's never worried, faced challenges, suffered pain or struggled with life has never existed. Every single person (however rich or materially successful) experiences difficulties, simply as a part of being alive. So don't worry – you're not alone! Therefore, the issue isn't to try and avoid or run away from problems (that's futile), but to find a healthy way to tackle or live with them, without adding to your original suffering.

I believe that mindfulness-based cognitive therapy (MBCT) is a great technique for doing just that, first because it worked for me and second because research proves that mindfulness can convey a sense of meaning and purpose to life, based on the understanding that everything in life is interconnected.

In this chapter I introduce you to the basic concept of MBCT, how it works and how you can use it to improve your life and wellbeing. I describe two central aspects of MBCT that crop up throughout this book: the importance of experience and of trying to be in the present moment. I also provide a brief taster of some of the useful skills you can pick up as you practise the meditations and exercises in this book.

Although the term may seem a bit forbidding at first glance, MBCT isn't something reserved for academic experts or an elite group of super-dedicated Eastern monks. Quite the reverse: MBCT is a practice for you to use in your own way and integrate into your personal life to help combat your personal demons. Whatever your background, culture, religion, experience, age, and so on, MBCT can work for you. After all, if suffering is a universal fact of being human, the world needs a universal approach to dealing with it.

Placing the Power in Your Hands: Discovering MBCT

In this section I introduce you to the nature of MBCT practice, which helps you overcome personal problems by increasing your understanding about the reality of the world you live in and your own thoughts and behaviours. I describe the term MBCT, break down its components of Eastern philosophy and cognitive behavioural therapy (CBT), and explain how these aspects integrate so effectively in MBCT.

The essence of MBCT is discovering how to let go of negative thinking and behaviour patterns.

You certainly don't need to know anything about the historical development of MBCT to practise it successfully but if you're interested, check out the nearby sidebar 'A brief history lesson: East meets West' for a little background.

A brief history lesson: East meets West

MBCT is a fusing of two distinct techniques: the Eastern, Buddhist philosophy of meditation and everyday mindfulness and the Western psychological treatment called cognitive behavioural therapy. First created and used as a group-intervention tool to prevent relapse into depression, MBCT is used today as a path of healing for loads of mental and physical health issues.

MBCT was developed by three clinical psychologists: Mark Williams, John Teasdale and Zindel Segal. They all studied mindfulness-based stress reduction (MBSR), a programme based on mindfulness meditation and yoga that Jon Kabat-Zinn created in the US to help people with chronic pain and illness. For more on Jon

and on MBSR, turn to the later sidebars 'The work of Jon Kabat-Zinn' and 'MBSR: The forerunner to MBCT', respectively.

These early practitioners discovered that even negligible increases in sadness reactivated depressive thinking patterns in formerly depressed people. But an experiment showed that MBCT significantly reduced the recurrence of depression in people who had experienced clinical depression more than twice; in fact it halved the recurrence of depression in this group. To confirm its effectiveness, the experiment was repeated a few years later and the positive results were repeated.

Encountering the term MBCT

Don't let the apparent jumble of consonants of MBCT put you off! Its meaning is pretty straightforward.

The 'M' stands for *mindfulness,* which you can see quite simply as the practice of bringing your awareness deliberately to the present moment in time and experiencing it without judgement or expectation. Mindfulness isn't about intense concentration or effort. In fact, most little children are quite naturally mindful, such as when they're absorbed in flying a kite and being amazed, eating a delicious ice cream or building sandcastles. Children have the enviable ability of living in the present moment without any reason for doing a particular thing. In this sense, they live life to the full.

Although adults often lose this natural ability as they mature, mindfulness can reconnect you to this sense of pure living without constantly feeling that you need to create purpose.

And the other letters? Well:

- ✔ B stands for *based,* as in 'derived from' or 'connected to' (but you knew that, didn't you!).
- ✔ C stands for *cognitive,* which refers to the thinking, planning and measuring part of your brain.
- ✔ T stands for *therapy:* the treatment of disorders and illnesses. (Interestingly, *therapia* is a Greek word meaning 'walking a path together for a while', so you can see me as walking with you for these eight weeks. The rest of your life then continues to deepen your practice.)

Essentially, MBCT is about becoming more aware of how you think and behave in order to help improve your life.

Drawing on Buddhist philosophy

Although MBCT draws on techniques from Buddhist mindfulness meditation, Zen, yoga, Taoism and Christian mysticism, MBCT isn't a spiritual path in itself. It's a secular form of meditations and exercises aimed at reducing your suffering.

That said, traditional Buddhist philosophy is a central part of MBCT. This philosophy emphasises the importance of direct personal experience, as opposed to just studying a theory. Meditation, therefore, is the path that connects theory with practice. The goal of mindfulness is to observe your mind in depth. In order to develop profound insight into the unfolding of life and the meaning you give it, you need to observe your mind deeply and regularly, and question what you find out.

Awareness, as seen in the Buddhist context, refers to a certain kind of focusing in the present moment: with alertness, openness, objectivity and non-judgement.

When practising mindfulness, try as best as you can to observe everything that arises; experience thoughts without adding emotional memories from the past that may taint them as positive or negative. Furthermore, try to experience awareness of the present moment as an unbroken progression, coming and going, without being censored or interpreted, or held on to or pushed away.

In this book's eight-week course (which I introduce in Chapter 3 and cover week-by-week in Chapters 4 to 11), I encourage you to experience mindfully every single moment of your life (however apparently mundane) as something special and almost miraculous – to allow life to unfold itself moment by moment. In other words, when you eat, just eat; and when you walk, just walk!

One practical example that's a central part of Buddhist meditation is just focusing your attention on your breath. By this simple act of anchoring awareness on the breath, you start breathing more deeply, which leads to a more peaceful and focused awareness moment to moment. In a sense, meditation is a way of befriending yourself, because with practice you tend to experience life with less anger and more acceptance.

The work of Jon Kabat-Zinn

The vision of molecular biologist Jon Kabat-Zinn made the application of mindfulness to medicine and psychotherapy possible. A keen practitioner of yoga and Buddhist meditation for more than a decade, he was inspired by the benefits these traditions brought him. He was convinced that others could improve their own wellbeing as well, by adopting these practices in their own lives.

His goal was to make mindfulness available as a life-enhancing skill for all and to 'translate' parts of Buddhist wisdom and philosophy. He hoped to reduce suffering where it was mainly caused by unhelpful thinking, expectations and behaviours. He wrapped the wisdom of the East into a digestible form for people in the West.

For more on Jon Kabat-Zinn, flip to Chapter 19.

Working together

Dr Aaron Beck, a psychiatrist and the founding father of CBT, was frustrated with his attempts to treat patients suffering from major episodes of depression with psychoanalytical therapy in the 1960s. He concluded that the notion and motto of the analytical approach that patients need to suffer was simply unnecessary and even damaging at times. He applied psychoanalysis to patients, at times for more than six years, without seeing significant changes. In some cases, they responded so negatively that they attempted suicide.

In contrast, in CBT the therapeutic relationship is extremely important and focuses on empathy, genuineness, respect, warmth and unconditional positive regard. The client and therapist work as a team to resolve problems and two-way feedback is encouraged. Goals for change are identified and agreed upon. Even the therapist's mistakes are admitted and the client suggests solutions when therapy gets stuck. In fact, you could say that clients are trained to become their own therapists.

Keep a look out for these aspects that I revisit repeatedly throughout this book. They're central to the exercises I provide and to the attitude I invite you to have when practising mindfulness: bringing awareness to this moment you've selected and doing so without judgement. So, if you choose to focus on your breath and your mind flits off occasionally, you just kindly and patiently bring it back and start over.

Developing from CBT

Cognitive behavioural therapy (CBT) is one of the most highly recommended and respected talking therapies of the 21st century (for some background, see the nearby sidebar 'Working together'), and can be defined as an active, directive, time-limited, structured approach used to treat a variety of mental problems such as depression, anxiety, phobias, stress, pain, and so on.

CBT mainly focuses on the here and now, and the therapist accompanies the client towards chosen goals. In this sense, CBT (and MBCT) is *client driven* and you choose what you want to work on throughout the whole therapy. As with MBCT, you're also advised to use a notebook to record insights, just as I do in this book (check out Chapters 3 and 4 for more about creating your personal mindfulness diary).

MBSR: The forerunner to MBCT

MBSR is a group-based programme, designed and developed by Jon Kabat-Zinn and colleagues at the University of Massachusetts, for people with a wide range of physical and mental health problems. It comprises an eight-week course and has been used to treat patients within a large traditional American hospital since 1979.

By 1999 over 10,000 patients had completed the course and it was extended into prisons, deprived inner-city areas, schools, and professional sport and corporate environments. MBSR is now a recognised part of behavioural medicine and general healthcare. Its potential lies not only in treatment, but also in prevention of 'dis-ease'!

MBSR uses the ancient tradition of mindfulness in an accessible, secular format and helps participants to conquer their difficulties when suffering from a variety of physical and psychological illnesses. MBSR research shows positive results for participants with chronic pain, fibromyalgia, multiple sclerosis, psoriasis, generalised anxiety disorder and panic attacks, and some forms of cancer, among other ailments. The programme involves intensive training in mindfulness meditation, yoga movements and discussions on stress and life skills.

During CBT treatment sessions, problems are uncovered and assessed constantly. Problems are identified and therapy helps you to shed light on how your thoughts and emotions, physical health, relationships and general daily functioning, are interrelated. The treatment plan is created early on but constantly reviewed and expanded; plus a specific timeframe is set and adhered to.

Integrating mindfulness and CBT into MBCT

MBCT is based on an integration of CBT components with Eastern mindfulness meditations (check out the preceding section and the earlier 'Drawing on Buddhist philosophy', respectively), as well as mindful movement skills. It aims to increase your understanding about your particular difficulty (such as anxiety, chronic fatigue, chronic pain and illness, depression, eating disorders, post-traumatic stress disorder, sleeping difficulties, stress, and so on).

For example, in the case of depression (to which I devote the whole of Chapter 12), you're given information about the universal characteristics of depression to help you recognise your personal *relapse signatures* (behaviours and thinking patterns peculiar to you – when you know the signals that indicate you may be slipping back into depression, you can nip it in the bud). The pattern of behaviour that makes people vulnerable to depressive relapse is called *rumination*. When ruminating, the mind repetitively reruns negative thoughts. The core skill that MBCT develops is intentionally to shift mental gears. It doesn't so much attempt to change unhelpful thoughts into more helpful ones, as encourages the insight that focusing repeatedly on negative thoughts and how to change them can accentuate and highlight them, possibly deepening them rather than alleviating them.

Key themes of MBCT include learning by experience (see, for example, the body scan meditation in Chapter 4 and mindful movement in Chapter 6), and the development of an accepting, open attitude, in which you deliberately face problems and uncomfortable feelings.

Through increased mindfulness training, you become more aware, moment by moment, of physical sensations and of thoughts and feelings as merely experiences rather than absolute truths. This insight helps you to become less convinced and bothered by your negative thoughts, and allows you to notice much earlier on when you're moving towards the blues.

Thus, you discover how to take the stand of an observer looking at your thoughts but not believing them or acting on them. You slowly but surely understand that you *aren't* your thoughts!

MBCT is relatively cost- and time-effective and is now included in the National Institute of Health and Care Excellence (NICE) Guidelines for the prevention of recurrent depression.

Here's a quick exercise to demonstrate an important truth about thoughts. Please sit down in a comfortable position and think of yourself as being a green frog jumping about and croaking. What do you feel? Most likely, you feel silly or even ridiculous – you know that you aren't a frog (if you're not sure, I'm afraid you need more than mindfulness!). Don't worry, just keep an open mind and enjoy the silliness.

Now, with the same open mindedness, think of yourself as a failure, remembering all your lost relationships, failed job interviews and other things that didn't work out as you hoped. Does that sound more like you? Is this how you think of yourself at times?

But nobody is a 'complete failure', because no one fails at every single action in their life! See how easily you slip into believing your negative thoughts and pessimistic self-talk?

When you were thinking that you're completely inadequate, I bet you felt low, raw and vulnerable. Yet when you visualised being a green frog, you may have felt giddy with laughter, imagining yourself leaping and making strange noises. Sigmund Freud, the founder of psychoanalysis, apparently advised his patients to *regress* (be childish) at least twice a day. So come on – fool around!

This frog-versus-failure experiment shows how much easier you believe the suggestion that you aren't good enough, whereas the 'frog' suggestion doesn't stand a chance of being taken seriously. Human beings are much more easily convinced of their flaws rather than funny or positive things, because the human mind is more inclined to believe negative suggestions. Unfortunately, negative thoughts are like Velcro and positive thoughts are like Teflon!

Recognising the Need for a Mindful Approach

Although CBT (see the earlier section 'Developing from CBT') is often effective in treating depression, one particular client group (whose members had suffered three or more episodes of depression) continued to relapse, almost as if CBT can turn off negative thinking but not fully delete it from the mind's hard disk. The more often a person experiences a major episode of depression, the more likely they are to relapse.

For this reason, clinical psychologists Segal, Teasdale and Williams started searching for a therapeutic way to prevent or at least reduce depression relapse (turn to the sidebar 'A brief history lesson: East meets West' for the background). The result was the eight-week MBCT course, during which you acquire the necessary skills to improve your wellbeing and *joie de vivre* in the here and now (see the chapters in Part II of this book).

Addressing the shortcomings of CBT

In contrast to CBT's focus on recognising unhelpful thoughts and replacing them with helpful ones (which often gives the negative thoughts too much power and simply reinforces them), MBCT states that thoughts aren't facts and therefore you don't need to focus on them more than necessary. In Buddhist philosophy, thinking is seen as an additional sense, no more or less important than seeing, smelling, tasting, touching or hearing.

MBCT endeavours to show you how to focus your awareness on all your senses. Meditations regularly use one anchor for your awareness. Without an anchor, you can just end up thinking, planning, worrying, day-dreaming and so on. As a result, MBCT really makes you aware of how busy your mind is and how it tends to stick to negative thoughts.

By giving your mind one single anchor of attention (such as your breath or body, a sound, and so on), you can truly be and experience the present moment.

Get meditating, quick!

Modern technology and hard evidence prove what people who practise mindfulness meditation have known for a long time: MRI scans show without doubt that MBCT is like a mental workout for your brain. Areas of the brain connected to compassion and calm tend to increase, whereas areas to do with the stress response and anxiety become less activated.

The brain's amygdala plays a key role in the processing of emotions, memory and emotional reactions. Buddhist monks who meditate intensely on a regular basis have (unknowingly) modulated their amygdalas to the extent that they experience less anxiety than non-meditators.

Going beyond traditional therapy

Choosing to practise MBCT is more than choosing a therapy: it's about engaging in a lifestyle change (as I explain in Chapter 2). If you decide to give it a go and slowly but surely harness yourself with its skills, it doesn't end after you're familiar with the practices. MBCT becomes part of your everyday life and affects not only your existence, but also that of all people you're connected to or are in touch with.

Enjoying the Benefits of MBCT

In this section I lay out just some of the many benefits that MBCT can bring to you, whether combating problems such as anxiety, depression and fear or generally improving your life and relationships by making you more aware and attentive and able to live in the present. For more benefits, check out Chapters 2 and 3.

Seeing the evidence of success

MBCT has managed to improve the lives of many people with diverse problems. Here are just a few examples of such problems (with appropriate chapters if I mention these issues directly):

- Anger management (Chapter 10)
- Bipolar disorder with a history of suicidal thoughts
- Cancers, including breast and prostate

- Chronic fatigue syndrome
- Chronic pain and illness (Chapters 6 and 15)
- Coping skills for parents and carers of children with autism
- Depression (Chapter 12)
- Eating disorders (Chapter 13)
- Fibromyalgia (an autoimmune disorder causing physical aches and pains)
- Generalised anxiety disorder (Chapter 14)
- Health anxiety
- Living healthily after retirement (Chapter 16)
- Psoriasis
- Psychosis
- Relationship difficulties (Chapter 17)
- Sleep disturbances (Chapter 14)
- Stress (Chapters 7 and 14)

To help you appreciate the importance of application and regular use of MBCT, consider this comparison: using MBCT is as important and useful as brushing your teeth. Just as regular dental hygiene improves how long you can keep your own teeth, reduces stomach cancer and digestive disorders (and has even been linked to reducing heart disease), implementing the MBCT exercises in this book is sure to have a positive effect on your internal and mental wellbeing.

Depression

Depression is the subject of Chapter 12, but here are some of the proved benefits (published by the Mental Health Foundation):

- MBCT is more successful than maintenance doses of anti-depressants in preventing depression relapse.
- Three-quarters of people engaging in an MBCT programme alongside anti-depressants were able to come off their medication within 15 months.
- MBCT can reduce the severity of symptoms for people who are currently depressed.

Anxiety

Although I discuss anxiety in detail in Chapters 7 and 14, here are some of the Mental Health Foundation's published results for anxiety:

✔ MBCT can reduce sleeplessness in people with anxiety disorders.

✔ Mindfulness promotes greater self-acceptance in practitioners.

✔ Mindfulness can reduce dependency on alcohol, caffeine, prescription medication and illegal drugs (Chapter 13 focuses on addiction in detail).

Fearing past and future experiences

Dealing with events from your past and expectations or fears of the future can be extremely difficult. These fears even have the power to hold you back from the life you want to lead in reality. MBCT can help you overcome and find a way of coming to terms with those unhelpful thinking and behaviour patterns.

As you gain more and more insight through the practice of MBCT you may comprehend that whatever your plans for the future may hold you have no guarantee that they'll unfold as you hope they will. The only certainty is the fact that everything changes, and sometimes too soon. This is why this moment is so precious; it represents your life right here and now.

MBCT helps you enhance your ability to be aware in the present moment. You find out how to be less attached to pleasant experiences and less worried about unpleasant ones, because when you realise that life changes moment by moment you truly understand a central slice of MBCT wisdom: everything is impermanent for everybody. Nothing's wrong with enjoying the moment, but you need to avoid fixating on it over and over or keeping it alive forever, because that's when you create disappointment and suffering for yourself. Nothing lasts forever!

Knowing where the fear comes from

Your past experiences shape you and your thinking. Some aspects of your beliefs about the world may have been formed when you were a young child. They may have helped you to survive then, but over time they may well become an obstacle for enjoying the present moment.

For example, people who were bullied at school, or who have been neglected by adults who should have cared for them, can become overly self-sufficient people who barely ever seek the help or company of others. This behaviour can become a real obstacle at work, when they're seen as recluses who refuse to delegate or communicate, and in their private life, when they're unable to open up to friends. Intimate relationships suffer too: the perfectly independent and self-sufficient person can never trust or commit fully, because their underlying belief is that other people are going to hurt or disappoint them.

Mindfulness can help you uncover such fears and negative underlying beliefs and so free you to start again in the present moment. The memory of your suffering doesn't disappear, but you can file it away so that it doesn't constantly interfere with your experience.

Knowing what the fear can lead to

Fears about the future are partially due to how the human brain evolved. The brain is amazing, but alas it is primed to watch out anxiously for potential dangers. Mother Nature never worried about you having a peaceful life, but instead how your species can survive.

Thus, you and all other humans have a tendency to worry about the future, because your cave-dwelling ancestors never knew what threat lurked around the corner. Neuropsychologist Rick Hanson calls this feeling 'an ongoing internal trickle of unease. This little whisper of worry keeps you scanning your inner and outer worlds for signs of trouble.' (You can read more about Rick and other inspiring people in Chapter 19.)

Mindfulness works out your brain and builds 'thinking roads' that enable you to be less fearful of the future and the now, and fully immerse yourself in truly living life. The more you practise, the more your brain structurally changes and engages your self-soothing system.

Choosing to live in the now

The meditation master Thich Nhat Hanh says that 'if we are not fully ourselves, truly in the present moment, we miss everything.' How true that is! Check out Chapter 19 for more on Thich Nhat Hanh.

Please carry out this simple exercise to experience the sense of relief that comes from focusing on the present moment. I invite you to bring your awareness to this moment: are you aware of any immediate danger or threats? If not, you can safely adopt an attitude of 'right now, in this very moment, everything is okay'. You're obviously reading this chapter, and your mind is trying to digest this information, which is great, because it proves that right now you have no need to feel anxious.

Continue to check in with yourself every hour or so and see whether you're still okay. In all likelihood, more often than not, the answer is 'yes'. So think to yourself: 'I'm fine, all is okay right now'. Feel into your body; what are you aware of when you just soothe yourself this way? Maybe it feels more than okay, perhaps even good. You may not have everything you want or desire (who does?), but think about the things you do have and the parts of your body that are well and not in pain.

As an experiment, write down in your diary (I describe setting up a mindfulness diary in Chapter 4) all the things that are okay, good or wholesome in this very moment. The list may well get quite long.

Here are a few ways you can live in the moment in everyday practice:

- ✔ Drink and talk more slowly.

- ✔ Eat nuts, raisins, chocolate buttons and the like one at a time, instead of scoffing a whole handful!

- ✔ Don't read or watch TV while eating.

- ✔ Don't look at your mobile phone when meeting with friends and family, or just before you go to bed.

When feeling stressed, ground yourself, feel your feet rooted to the floor and connect deeply to your breathing.

Perusing even more ways that MBCT can help you

Here are some more key aspects of MBCT (in no particular order), along with the chapters where I discuss them, so that you can turn straight to any location that seems particularly relevant to you:

- ✔ Responding wisely and kindly rather than acting rashly or unthinkingly. I discuss the importance of wisdom and compassion in Chapter 11.

- ✔ Accepting what is, even if that's challenging. When you know what you're dealing with, you can discover what can be mindfully changed and what has to remain as it is ('*Que sera sera,* whatever will be, will be'). (Flip to Chapter 8 in particular for more on this aspect.)

- ✔ Discovering all about your thoughts, how they affect you, how you can observe them and most importantly that thoughts are only mental events, not facts (check out Chapters 5, 7 and 9).

- ✔ Developing meditation practice, in particular the 40-minute body scan and 3-minute breathing space exercise (check out Chapters 4 and 6, respectively).

- ✔ Harnessing your aptitudes of childlike curiosity, trust and kindness (read Chapters 9 and 10).

- ✔ Reading mindful poems and stories that help to deepen your understanding of mindfulness. (I scatter such poems and stories throughout the book).

✔ Seeking out other mindfulness resources to maintain your motivation and expand your experience (I provide ideas in Chapter 18) and visiting mindful locations (see my suggestions in Chapter 20).

✔ Getting back in touch with your body, so that you learn to notice the little signals it gives you before having a panic attack or a full-blown episode of depression (see Chapters 4, 12 and 14).

✔ Keeping your body moving; challenging the idea that you can no longer enjoy movement because aspects of your body are no longer fully functioning (see Chapters 3 and 15).

✔ Motivating you to experience another new way of living every day in the present moment (I describe an entire mindful day in Chapter 11). Step out from autopilot and really engage in regular activities by fully experiencing them. When you eat an orange, for example, take your time and sense deeply how you peel the fruit, how you break it up into individual slices, eating one at a time, enjoying the sweet taste and being truly present when doing so (see Chapter 4 for more on performing everyday activities mindfully).

Autopilot refers to functioning without awareness (being 'mindless'): for example, entering a room and forgetting why you went there, driving home and being clueless about what happened during the journey and how you got safely from A to B, or having a shower without remembering how it felt (being unaware of the sensation of water on your skin or the smell of the soap because you were busy making plans for the day). The concept of *not* living on autopilot is central to mindfulness and so occurs throughout this book.

Autopilot, however, does have a place in your life. If you had to learn everything daily over and over again, you wouldn't learn very much and wouldn't fulfil your potential. Life would become very repetitive. So what you're aiming towards is the middle ground: using autopilot and also bringing awareness to special moments throughout the day.

Chapter 2

Deciding to Lead a Mindful Existence

In This Chapter

▶ Gaining an insight into your personal troubles

▶ Getting to know yourself better

▶ Understanding the potential difficulties ahead

▶ Appreciating the benefits of MBCT

I invite you to open your heart and mind to accepting and understanding a central truth of human existence – all humans suffer and suffering is part of living – while also realising the deep change that mindfulness-based cognitive therapy (MBCT) can bring about in you. The insights and exercises I offer in this chapter really can reduce your suffering. They help you to let go of pointless ruminative thinking and to focus on each individual moment with such detail that you experience gladness and gratitude for those moments.

Going through the journey that leads you from simple beginnings, such as mindfully eating a piece of fruit, you discover that MBCT provides the tools to help you become a deeply aware and conscious person. I encourage you to discover yourself and your personal issues anew and give you an insight into the required mental preparation and commitment of MBCT, as well as its benefits. I train you in the discipline of meditative practice so that you can see just how much of suffering depends on the frame of mind you're in. You also find out how to create a more helpful mindset through the various practices offered on your mindfulness voyage.

Understanding Your Problems

One of the hardest challenges you can come across in life is to develop an honest understanding of your own issues from an objective standpoint so that you can begin to help yourself. This element is the first step of mindfulness practice – you don't necessarily need to put a name to it, just let yourself know that something is wrong and that you want to change it.

Knowing precisely why you're reading this book is a great start to uncovering your issues. Take a minute to think about your responses to these questions:

- ✔ Did you make a conscious decision to buy this book or did somebody choose to give it to you as a gift?

- ✔ Have you come across mindfulness in the news or heard about it from friends who say it changed their lives and who've whetted your appetite?

- ✔ What specifically got you interested in MBCT and in this book?

- ✔ What do you think engaging in this book/course will entail?

- ✔ Who or what will benefit from you having read this book? Yourself? Your partner? A friend? Your work?

- ✔ Right now, what would be the most important outcome you could hope for as a result of becoming more mindful?

- ✔ Could becoming more mindful make a difference in your life, health and relationships?

Setting out on a journey through MBCT will certainly be an adventure, and like all good adventures you will find some obstacles. Whatever your reasons are for setting out on this journey, I suggest that you read Chapter 1 (if you haven't already) to get an inkling of how the ideas that MBCT promotes can help you.

To get motivated and apply real changes to your life, you need to develop the strong desire to overcome what's holding you back, causing you pain and making life troublesome and difficult.

Feeling that you can't cope

Perhaps all you can say is that, for whatever reason, things aren't working out for you. But can you identify the problem more closely? Are you overly tired/stressed/angry/lethargic/sad? Do you have problems being intimate or talking to people or motivating yourself? What's troubling you?

Please sit down and put on soft background music, maybe light a candle and take a few deep breaths. Now open your diary (I describe setting up a mindfulness diary in Chapter 4), or simply use a sheet of notepaper, and start to write down all the things in your life that feel out of balance: the thoughts and feelings that cause you pain and dissatisfaction. You don't need to organise them into any categories. Simply connect as best as possible to the wounded or frightened part inside you and let it speak.

Here are some examples to help you start uncovering the thorn in your side:

- My life is such a lonely experience.
- I'm tired all the time and feel numb.
- Why am I here? What is this life all about?
- I've been feeling so listless and uninspired lately.
- I feel ugly, unattractive and unloved.
- Why didn't I go for the adventure of life? Why did I go for the safe option instead?
- I still miss 'X'. We had this stupid argument about nothing and now we've not talked for three years. It's so sad, but I'm frightened that he won't reply to my call or message. It would hurt even more if he rejected me now.
- I constantly feel that I'm on the verge of bankruptcy. There's never enough money and I'm working my socks off.
- I'd like to do something crazy, but what if something goes wrong?
- When will I meet my Prince Charming? I'm fed up with superficial relationships.
- I'm retired, the children are grown up with their own lives, the pension barely covers my living costs and I wonder what I'm still doing here. What now?
- I'm so frightened since my diagnosis; I don't want to die, but what if there's no cure? Should I end my life now?
- I'm always in pain . . . 24/7. Why did I draw this bad lot? I don't deserve this. I hate my life.
- I look at the state of the world and I feel disgusted, with so much suffering, cruelty and so many wars. Humans never change. This planet is a despicable place.

All the statements above signify that the people uttering them are suffering to some degree. Perhaps a few of them would go as far as to say that life is only filled with suffering. But is that true?

I invite you to consider what would need to change for these individuals. Would they be happy if they had more money, better health, their Prince Charming? People often attach themselves to particular hopes and desires and tend to believe that if only these desires would come true they would live happily ever after. The truth of the matter, however, is that as soon as you have attained the desired object or outcome, your mind tends to find another object of desire or, alternatively, starts fearing the loss of what you've obtained. Do you identify with any of the above statements, or perhaps several of them? Think about what has to *change* in your life for you to feel less suffering and more contentment, rather than the short-term solution of obtaining something specific that you desire.

Wanting to make a change

When you've gained an idea, however basic, of what appears to be wrong in your life (from the preceding section), you need to decide whether you want to go on a journey that may free you from a lot of your suffering. After all, you may discover that the way this journey is going to happen is rather different than you may hope or predict. Be assured that no one else can force you or convince you to do anything – the decision has to come from you.

Often, making a real change in your life requires several attempts. Here are a few suggestions to bolster your self-confidence ahead of trying to make this change:

✔ Posting positive messages around the house.

✔ Looking at YouTube recordings about mindfulness.

✔ Reading how much others have benefited from mindfulness.

Also, kindly remember that the more specific you can be with your desired goal, the more likely you are to feel motivated to strive for it.

Please write down a few reasons that will remind you, in times of future need and procrastination, why you set off on this mindfulness journey. Be as precise as possible. Instead of saying 'I want to be better', write down 'I want to enjoy my job more', 'I want to make time for nature photography again', 'I want to find out how to play the lute', 'I'd like to stop smoking and have a weekly massage with the money I save' or 'I'd like to spend time with myself and after I reconnect, start dating again': whatever works for you and your situation.

Breaking the cycle of mental anguish

Getting motivated, particularly when you're having a bad time, is extremely challenging. Mindfulness is all about moment-by-moment awareness training, moment-by-moment letting go of unhelpful thinking patterns, and moment-by-moment allowing change to enter your life.

 Let yourself off the hook now and again. By reading this book you're allowing yourself the time to make a positive change, so try as best as you can to let go of being angry at yourself when things go wrong or not as well as you hope. You're already doing something about it! The good news is that you can never fail by being mindful. Even when you forget about mindfulness, the moment you notice your wandering mind is the moment you start your practice all over again.

Here's an example of the cycle of mental anguish and deepening mental imbalance. Imagine that you're really uncomfortable about the thought of having to go to a wedding in Mexico. It's not the destination that worries you, but a whole array of other things: what to pack, what gift to buy, when to start preparing, how to get to the airport and how to endure sitting on a plane for tens of hours. You hate leaving the comfort of your home, being in large crowds of people, getting on any form of public transport and, most of all, giving up your freedom by flying long haul.

So every time you try to get ready for any of the above activities, one thought triggers the memory of all the others and you enter a never-ending cycle of fear. No wonder you don't book your ticket, buy gifts or do any preparation. Here's the story of your life – everything is just too difficult and painful. Fear takes over so many aspects of rational thinking that the ability to plan goes out of the window, along with the ability to look at the benefits. Even though nothing bad has happened yet, you're already feeling guilty for once again having to opt out at the last minute (guilt is an excellent way to prolong mental anguish).

I'm sure that you can think of your own personal version of this cycle of negativity. But MBCT shows you how to break down the individual aspects that comprise this rollercoaster into small digestible bites; it also shows you that feeling fear is no indication that something bad is ever going to happen. It may, but equally it may not.

 Many famous actors have experienced stage fright and yet when they're in front of their audience and let go of fear, they experience and pass on a sense of wonderful exhilaration.

So, for now, please prepare to embrace the idea of stepping out of old patterns and experimenting with living your life totally differently.

Living moment-to-moment with compassion

This short verse takes a glimpse at a moment and conveys the uniqueness that life offers to you moment by moment, if only you can see and consider it.

This ONE

Only one day

Only one hour

Only one moment

One song or poem

One smile or kiss

One touch of ice cubes

One smell of rose tea

One lick of ice cream

One biscuit dunked in tea

One glimpse of your smile

One glimpse of your eyes

One tenderness

One and one

One

By Patrizia Collard

Do you know any poems, stories, films or songs that inspire you to open up to the moment? (I provide a favourite of mine in the nearby sidebar 'Living moment-to-moment with compassion', because feeling the touch of the sun on your face after a long winter can be like a miracle.)

What else gives you a sense of wonder? Kindly write or draw the things that touch you deeply. If you want, you can use stickers or cut images out of magazines. Creativity is one sure way to leave sadness and fear behind.

Developing an Understanding of Yourself

The movement towards mindfulness starts with taking time to get to know yourself better; not just what you think you know, or what others think about you, but listening deeply to yourself and what you can be like if you park self-judgement for a while and simply be.

Imagine developing the compassionate, kind side of yourself. Look for those aspects that others love about you, admire in you or get drawn to. Don't worry: you won't get too full of yourself, unless you do this for years and years!

Opening up to yourself

You can open up and get to know yourself better in all sorts of ways:

- ✔ Go for a long walk and observe what attracts your attention – you may be fascinated by things you never thought would interest you.
- ✔ Read an unusual book, watch a new film or listen to unfamiliar music.
- ✔ Draw a self-portrait from memory (that is, without looking in the mirror first) so that you can see how you see yourself. Your self-portrait doesn't have to be a masterpiece, but may well reveal the things that stand out most strongly about yourself in your mind.

Please sit quietly for a few minutes and consider what other ideas arise in your mind that could help you discover yourself more deeply. Being fully present in this very minute and finding out more about yourself is a beautiful gift you can give yourself.

Studying your personal thought patterns

Please take a look at the sad statements in the earlier section 'Feeling that you can't cope'. Would you say that they reflect anything that was happening at the moment they were uttered? Mostly they don't; they tend to go into the past or the future or focus on one aspect of life and overgeneralise it.

I now ask you to become a detective of your own habits of thinking. Take your mindfulness diary (see Chapter 4) and simply note down how you think about things – or, more precisely, your usual train of thought in certain situations. Don't try to make any changes yet – just use this exercise as an experiment to note stuff down that you can look back on in the future. Doing so helps you see more clearly how certain thinking patterns hook you into a sad, angry or desperate mood, and so forth. See yourself as Sherlock Holmes, Brother Cadfael, Inspector Frost or any other favourite detective analysing a situation.

Here are two contrasting examples of the same scenario, which show you how negative as against open and positive thought processes can completely change your perception of a day:

- ✔ **Example 1 – negative response:** Your train to work is delayed in the morning and you're angry with the transport system. You arrive late for work and a colleague looks at you and smiles. You're absolutely certain he's thinking, 'She's late again'. You don't sleep well from worrying if people at work now think of you as unreliable.

✔ **Example 2 – open, positive response:** Your train to work is delayed. You're annoyed because this happens so often, but you switch on your favourite piece of music and lose yourself in it, forgetting your anger. You arrive late for work and a colleague looks at you and smiles. You say, 'Hi, guess what, the trains'. He nods sympathetically and tells you that half the staff are late today. You appreciate the support. You sleep well; the train is forgotten. It was so long ago.

These examples reveal how thoughts, feeling and actions are connected, and how simply turning away from negativity can affect the rest of your experiences (at least some of the time).

Analysing your responses in this way is fascinating, and helps you to see patterns emerging in how you deal with certain situations, people, work, and so on. Don't make judgements: just look at these connections and patterns with a childlike curiosity, noticing how your mind works and creates situations.

I now want to use a more serious example from the earlier section 'Feeling that you can't cope', where the person says 'I'm so frightened since my diagnosis. I don't want to die, but what if there's no cure? Should I end my life now?'

I wonder what you imagine had occurred to the person who said this statement. Perhaps they're talking about a malignant tumour? In fact, the person had been recently diagnosed with pre-diabetes. Her doctor warned her that it can lead to diabetes, in which case she'd have to go on medication, and encouraged her to consider a few lifestyle changes. She wasn't even overweight, though she did love chocolate and wine in large quantities. The thought of having to give up or at least reduce her severe use of these two substances made her feel that her life was no longer worth living. On top of this, she read up a lot on the Internet and found horrendous tales about what can potentially go wrong if diabetes remains untreated.

I hope that you're getting an insight into how her mind created a monster out of an insect. Of course, finding out that you can't continue doing everything you want without consequences is somewhat alarming. This person, however, thought only of the worst-case scenarios, along the following lines:

✔ 'I'll have to live without the things that I love most.' True or False?

✔ 'If I don't, I'll get so sick that I'll die young.' True or False?

Please look at whether you can answer these two questions in a more subtle, proportionate manner. I suggest that things would appear quite differently if this person thought:

Well I'd prefer to eat a big bar of chocolate and have two big glasses of wine every day. But I'll try to see whether I can mindfully and with awareness eat just a small bar and reduce my wine intake by half. I'm positive this will make a difference. After my next blood test I'll see whether I need to put the brakes on even tighter. One step at a time!

If she had been able to apply a more balanced way of thinking, which is something that mindfulness training helps you to do, she may well have felt less desperate and less fearful.

Here are two more examples of black-and-white, jumping to the worst conclusion, thinking errors, plus two corresponding positive suggestions:

✔ All the homeless are addicts and no good. I'm not going to give this person a penny. Let him work like ordinary people.

Versus:

This poor guy, having to sleep in the road, even when it's so cold. I wonder what happened to him to end up in such an unfortunate situation. I'll give him a cup of tea and a sandwich.

✔ All these immigrants deplete this country's system, why should I pay for their doctor's appointment.

Versus:

I feel privileged to live in a country where every human gets treated when they're sick or have an accident.

Ask yourself whether you have any similar thinking patterns that are unnecessarily negative (and thus potentially damaging to you), and whether you can think more compassionately.

Preparing for the Challenges Ahead

When you decide to make a change in your life, such as taking up regular mindfulness practice, making yourself aware that things may not go entirely smoothly is a good idea. At times you're going to feel great, but you do have to maintain a certain amount of discipline. Practising MBCT meditation regularly isn't for the fainthearted.

Changing your thinking patterns – from mental rat-racing to awakened, aware human being – requires persistence, trust in the practice and the research that supports it, patience with yourself and determination. Don't worry if you think you don't 'have what it takes', because all you need right now is the intention to start and restart, and the curiosity to see what happens.

To help prepare yourself for the challenges to come, make time in your schedule to read the various chapters in this book calmly and, without feeling rushed, give yourself the time and space to practise the exercises and allow yourself to try things out.

Please don't feel overwhelmed, because you're in control. Take your practice as slowly as you like: you aren't hindering anybody by taking your time. Go with the flow. Read mindfully, and see which exercises are doable at this stage of your life. If you want, you can take six months or a year to complete this book. Just remain open to how your journey unfolds.

Facing your fears

Sometimes, truly engaging with yourself and feeling deeply can cause you to experience a sense of rawness and upheaval. Often, you have to confront your fears and discover how to cope with them being in your mind, which can be difficult and painful to begin with. Ultimately, however, you'll be able to feel whatever exists in the present moment, knowing full well that the feeling is going to pass sooner or later. Plus, as an antidote, mindfulness helps you to become much more in touch with the experience of life – for example, really tasting that strawberry, its juiciness and sweetness. You'll be like the child who jumps into puddles not worrying about getting wet, and come to realise that life is precious, every single second.

Please consider making a list of the fears that have surfaced since you began reading this book, such as:

- ✔ What if I don't have the time?
- ✔ What if I fail?
- ✔ I'm scared about confronting my past.

Now write down what you feel about that fear – not judging it, but asking yourself what it's based on, why you think that this fear has surfaced and whether you feel that you can put it behind you . . . or at least allow yourself to deal with it slowly but surely. Be as open as you can; remember that you're the only person who ever needs to read what you write. Here are a few suggestions:

- ✔ Maybe I can just watch a little less TV for a week and see what happens.
- ✔ Ah, there you are again, you little 'fail devil': I'm not getting everything right, but I'm going to give it a go anyhow.

> ✔ I'd rather not relive any of my past or even think about it. But maybe I can just register that a certain fear or thought first appeared in my past and not go into the finer details of it, at least for now.

Jumping over hurdles

You may well erect certain barriers for yourself that you have to overcome, such as: 'I have no time', 'This is too difficult', 'I can't be bothered anymore', and so on. If so, this is where discipline comes in.

Start thinking of ways in which you can maintain your motivation now. Consider writing down a promise to yourself. The one I stuck on my PC is: 'Just take care of now.' This promise is a wonderful reminder. Rumi puts it succinctly in the poem in the nearby sidebar 'Poetic persistence'.

Recognising the importance of everyday practice

Like everything else worth doing in life, making mindfulness part of your everyday existence doesn't just happen from one day to the next. Practising MBCT exercises and techniques regularly is a must, just like regular hygiene and food and water. Mindfulness is nectar for your soul, the force that makes you stop and relish the moment.

Meditation master Jon Kabat-Zinn puts it clearly: 'Mindfulness practice is like a parachute you weave day and night, and when you need to jump out of the plane it will hold you.'

Poetic persistence

Come, come, whoever you are

Wanderer, worshipper, lover of leaving,

It doesn't matter

Ours is not a caravan of despair

Even if you have broken your vows

A thousand times it doesn't matter

Come, yet again, come.

In this poem, Rumi spells out for you in no uncertain terms that you will from time to time forsake the importance of the journey you're beginning ('lover of leaving') and yet that doesn't matter because you can start over a thousand times. So, come and forgive yourself (your 'broken vows') because every moment is the moment to start all over.

However, you don't want to start weaving while you're already in mid-air! Of course, you may forget to practise or not get round to doing it, but kindly remember that you're trying to redevelop your way of living for the better. Mindfulness practice is just like any other skills that you may have developed, which needed a lot of input at first but are now second nature to you, for example:

- ✔ Using a new computer or mobile phone
- ✔ Finding out how to ski, ride a motorbike or play a musical instrument
- ✔ Studying a foreign language or flying a plane

Add your own list of skills you've developed to your mindfulness diary (for tips on starting your diary, check out Chapter 4), particularly the ones that you kept on pursuing and mastered.

Looking Forward to Long-Term Balance

Ultimately, the aim of your mindfulness practice is to find balance and purpose in your life. You can see it as a wake-up call if you've fallen into the traps of chasing success and acquiring more and more. After all, how do you know when you're good enough or have sufficient possessions?

This book isn't about how to be a massive success story, make loads of money, find love, and so on. My aim is to help you exist in each individual moment and thus get the most out of a balanced life. Talking to people who only wake up near the end of their lives and realise how much they've missed is sad. I remember my own father, when he was near his death, saying to me how he always focused on providing for the family but missed out on 'being a father'.

In a balanced life, you have time for:

- ✔ Working and looking after yourself and those you love
- ✔ Learning and growing as a human being
- ✔ Simply being alive
- ✔ Following your dreams
- ✔ Relaxing and rebalancing
- ✔ Searching for your deeper purpose

How many of these items can you tick at present?

Living in the moment

Really being in this moment means connecting totally to what you're experiencing here and now, good, bad or neutral, because all experiences can show you something about yourself and life. How often in a day are you truly present in whatever action?

> *Learning how to say no is the most exciting, liberating thing I've learned to do in my whole life. To not worry about what I might be losing out on, and just have an hour of silence to myself.*

These words by actress Debra Messing signify that sooner or later you no longer have to struggle to create time, but instead make sure that nobody is able to claim the time you've set aside for MBCT.

Regular mindfulness practice gives you a greater understanding of the concept of living in the moment. Here are a few examples of things that you can experience if you just let yourself:

- Feeling the rain on your face
- Biting into a fresh apple
- Listening to a piece of music
- Having a relaxing shower
- Stroking your pet
- Holding the hand of a loved one
- Drinking your first cup of tea/coffee in the morning
- Breathing in fresh air
- Watching clouds in the sky
- Smelling fresh flowers, fresh coffee, warm bread, and so on

> *To the mind that is still the whole universe surrenders.*
>
> —The Buddha

Accepting reality

Mindfulness and awareness help you to come to terms with and accept things in life that aren't so wonderful. As I discuss in the earlier section 'Studying your personal thought patterns', things do go wrong at times (this is reality), but with MBCT you can prepare yourself and find ways to cope with them in a way that allows you to move on.

My personal story

I started practising mindfulness meditation 22 years ago when I found out that one of my children was autistic. I can't explain how terrified and wounded I felt when I was told the news. Total panic grabbed me by the throat and twisted my heart. I feared that my child would never be able to have an independent life, felt guilty that I had done something wrong and, I suppose, not only did I feel sorry for him, but also for myself. Would my son ever be able to speak?

Exactly at this time I met a meditation and yoga teacher and I threw myself into the practice to stay sane and composed. During my son's struggles, I often lost my temper and would shout, and still do at times. I haven't become a saint or a perfect practitioner of mindfulness, but I wonder where I'd have ended up without the wonderful guidance and support through my practice.

Also, I'm sure that my child wouldn't have made the wonderful progress he did if I hadn't been patient enough to continue repeating many words and tasks thousands of times until he eventually got them. Mindfulness held me up, kept me going and fed my soul.

Acceptance doesn't mean being a doormat for other people to trample on, simply that you're giving yourself the time to understand and process what happens. When you accept what is, you can decide mindfully what action to take, if any.

Reducing suffering

MBCT can always help you to reduce your suffering. By understanding where pain (both mental and physical) comes from and why you experience it, you can develop coping mechanisms and find ways of dealing with it more effectively, leading to a more adventurous and individual everyday existence. No single right way exists to practise MBCT, just your way of doing it. The aspects of you that you want to shine through will do so, and this creates the best recipe for you.

Here are just a few of the many areas in which MBCT has helped people to cope with physical pain (for more details and loads of practical tips on coping with pain, check out Chapters 6 and 15):

- Chronic pain
- Migraine
- Stomach ache
- Tension pain

Becoming your own best friend

When you practise mindfulness regularly, you come to feel the authority and responsibility to be good to yourself, to understand yourself deeply and to rely on yourself – in short, to be your own best friend. Trusting yourself fully is a tremendous gift, which MBCT can help you to attain.

> *Steer clear of anyone who's uncomfortable with you being you. I'd take that further and say stay clear of anyone who's not proud of you, your accomplishments as a human being, and the things you have yet to accomplish. They should be excited about seeing all of those things unfold.*
>
> — Ellen Barkin

 Kindly sit down and take time to recall the insights about yourself that you've gained by reading this chapter and engage in some of the exercises. Even if you don't engage with all the suggestions, write down in your mindfulness diary (which I introduce in Chapter 4) what you may want to try out in the near future – just for fun and out of curiosity! MBCT is constantly encouraging you to experience the effects of practicing it for yourself, not to just believe what you're told without trying it out in person.

Chapter 3

Putting Mindfulness into Practice with the Eight-Week Course

In This Chapter

▶ Tailoring MBCT to suit you

▶ Getting rid of false preconceptions

▶ Maintaining a practical and pragmatic attitude

▶ Realising how beneficial MBCT can be

The cornerstone of practising mindfulness-based cognitive therapy (MBCT) successfully is to practise regularly. In this chapter I introduce you to the core of this book – the eight-week course that comprises Chapters 4 to 11. Over this period you discover how to be more present and to experience your life now, while it's happening, to help alleviate worry, fear and any number of other problems. I help you to understand gradually the importance of a regular personal mindfulness practice and what this decision may lead to for the rest of your life.

You discover in this chapter how to personalise the course to your requirements and maintain your motivation. I also dismiss some erroneous preconceptions you may have and spell out the benefits that you can expect to gain. Please bring a childlike curiosity to the eight-week course – the willingness to taste life moment by moment, even the ones that leave a bitter taste behind.

Life is an ongoing series of changes and a constant adventure. Explorers find out and discover wondrous things, but during their journey they also experience challenges, pain and loss.

Creating a Personal Practice that Works

I'd like to emphasise the importance of creating time and space for MBCT in your life, over these eight weeks and for the rest of your life. Only if you commit personally to it (the more the better) can you experience the power of this tool for better living. In the end, I intend this book to be practically useful for you. You know how it is when you make a New Year's resolution, such as buying a membership for a gym: come March, those people who are still going are the long-timers, the ones who already committed prior to Christmas.

Speaking of gyms, when you first start exercising in a gym, you may well have one of the personal trainers checking in with you and helping you to create your own highly unique exercise programme. In the same vein, you can decide after tasting the eight-week course how you want to continue your own regular practice of mindfulness for the future. You can stick to the routine I describe in this book or change and adapt it according to your needs or wants.

Good news! Mindfulness is far less expensive than an annual gym membership and you've no time restraints when the mind gym is open. You don't have to travel to it and if you do ever lapse, rest assured that every morning is a new beginning. Even better: every moment is a new start.

Although practising MBCT may sound relatively straightforward at this stage, it's certainly not effortless. In fact, unless you discipline yourself, your early enthusiasm can become swamped by old habits that are so automatic you may not even be aware of them. You may find yourself resorting to:

✔ That gin and tonic when you arrive home and put your feet up

✔ That automatic cup of tea and reading of the newspaper

✔ Sitting down just to watch the news briefly (and then finding yourself asleep a couple of hours later)

To prevent any backsliding, I suggest that you make a firm appointment with yourself for your mindfulness sessions in your diary or always do them first thing in the morning.

Also, consider finding a friend who wants to practise with you – experimenting with others can help avoid procrastination. You can perhaps exercise in pairs and make observations about each other or even make recordings of instructions for exercises.

Setting yourself goals

If you prefer to build up to something in baby steps, you can choose to do so with the course.

Perhaps start small and pick one of the shorter practices, such as the Breathing Space (see Chapter 6), but regularly set yourself little goals. For example, say: 'for one week I'm going to meditate for ten minutes at a time and try to eat the first spoonful of my cereal mindfully.' Please don't be annoyed or disheartened if you don't manage to achieve these ten minutes every day! Just do the practice whenever possible and give yourself the encouragement and motivation to carry on.

At the beginning you may need to see a little success to keep going. You can say to yourself: 'I want to practise for ten minutes every day.' You may find that this amount of time is achievable despite the fact that you may have many other commitments. After you timetable 10 minutes, perhaps you end up doing 12 or more minutes. You're most likely going to feel gratitude and joy when you achieve this goal, and when rooted in this ten minutes you can slowly venture out into longer practices. When you taste the sweetness and tender gravity of mindfulness, the wonderful gift of simply being without having to do something, you start to look forward to it – as a time just for you and your rebalancing.

Please set a do-able goal for yourself right now and write it down in your mindfulness diary (see the later section 'Keeping a practice diary'). Here are a few examples:

✔ 'I will practise ten minutes of the breathing meditation (from Chapter 6) in my allocated meditation spot. I will also eat one fruit daily with true awareness.'

✔ 'I will practise a brief walking meditation every day and two body scans (from Chapter 4) at the weekend. I will also play the guitar for a few minutes a day and really be present when doing so.'

✔ 'I will listen to bird song and other nature sounds first thing in the morning. I will drive mindfully to work and be patient when stuck in traffic. I will take a mindful lunch break three times a week.'

Making the practice part of your daily routine

As I mention in the preceding section, practising mindfulness over these eight weeks is more convenient than going to the gym: you don't need to go far or have to take a shower afterwards. You can, however, choose having a shower as one of your daily routines. The idea is to let all everyday activities become a natural mindful experience.

When you're having a mindful shower, feel the water, the temperature, the smell of your soap or shower gel and be fully present in mind and body.

Patiently let mindfulness become part of a daily routine. When you dry your body, notice the feeling of your towel soaking up the pearls of water.

Another idea for experiencing everyday awareness is preparing a meal mindfully. You can start when you shop for the meal, looking for the ingredients, appreciating their colour or packaging and their smell (such as the fresh coffee or fresh baking smell). When you pick up an item, say a melon, really feel its weight, shape and texture. When you start the cooking process at home, notice how you mindfully cut vegetables, for example, paying attention to their texture and their smell in particular and also enjoying the variety of colour. You may even taste different pieces of vegetable prior to cooking and after cooking and compare taste and texture.

Let your whole experience of life become an ongoing experiment, with mindful actions slowly but surely being introduced until you're living mindfully (check out Chapter 4 for more everyday mindfulness suggestions).

One important aspect of mindfulness is compassion and self-compassion. Part of integrating MBCT with your daily routine is remembering to act with compassion, but also recognising where you're already letting compassion influence your relationships with other people and yourself. Please write down a list of all the different roles you fulfil in your life. Work, for example, is also divided into many sub-roles. A teacher, for example, can also be head of a department, a figure of parental support, a figure of peer support and even a student when attending professional development courses, whereas a mother can be a protector, an organiser, a pacifier, a household maintainer, a close confidante and so on. Creating this list may well reveal how challenging creating a space for MBCT is in such a busy life. On the other hand, each role benefits hugely from a little more awareness, patience and gratitude.

Making time, not finding time

I make a distinction between finding and making time. You need to be disciplined and *make* the time for MBCT practices to happen! Here are some tips for doing so, and don't worry, I remind you repeatedly of this fact throughout the book:

- ✔ If you like watching the TV, make a conscious decision on which programmes you choose to watch and create at least 30 free minutes by reducing your couch time.

- ✔ If you record your favourite programmes on the commercial channels, you can often shorten your viewing time by fast-forwarding through the adverts to save 10 to 15 minutes an hour (shush: don't tell the advertisers).

- ✔ If you read a daily newspaper, perhaps you don't have to watch the news as well. Just choose one or the other, or perhaps alternate.

✔ If you check your emails regularly, write down how many minutes you spend on the computer or smartphone daily. Can you devote 20 per cent of your computer time to mindfulness?

When I was young, computers and mobile phones didn't exist, People survived (and yes, we did survive quite well!) by writing letters and cards. Maybe once a week you can write a mindful card to someone instead of replying by email.

✔ If you're worried about offending friends and family, just tell them what you're endeavouring to do so that they understand that you're going to be unreachable for a whole half hour a day.

Drawing up a schedule

Pencilling in a mindful appointment with yourself in your diary is helpful. Mindfulness is a crucial part of staying well, and is as important as going to see friends, to the movies or out to dinner. By the way, you can take MBCT with you wherever you go and apply it to almost every life experience. Therefore, I suggest drawing up a schedule, whether daily or weekly, of what kind of things you want to focus on in your mindfulness training.

Keeping a practice diary

Starting and continuing with a mindfulness diary is an *essential* part of your journey through MBCT and I refer to it throughout this book – kindly get the sort of diary to write or draw in that you find inspiring! After all, it constitutes your private practice journal, so make it look special.

Employ a little creativity when designing and filling in your diary. Choose something with a beautiful cover or even create the cover yourself out of personal photos, cuttings you selected from magazines or your own drawings. Making your mindfulness diary can be a really inspiring and mindful act in itself!

I discuss logging your reactions in your mindfulness diary in Chapter 4.

Dispelling the Myths

Many myths and false ideas exist about mindfulness, meditation, yoga and so on that may hold you back from fully committing to MBCT. They're often based on lack of knowledge, and on missing or misunderstood information, as follows:

✔ **Myth:** 'Mindfulness is an Eastern practice and you have to become a Buddhist or yogi to practise it.'

Not true: this book trains you in a secular way. Even if you do become interested in spirituality, you certainly don't have to give up whatever religion, if any, you believe in.

✔ **Myth:** 'By practising mindfulness meditation, you become so relaxed and peaceful that nothing ever hurts or bothers you again.'

Not true: bad things happen, now and then, but by focusing merely on one single object of attention you may feel very much at peace and even relaxed. You don't float above the ground, however, and you need to remember that each exercise session is different and has different outcomes. Each practice is a new experience – moment by moment.

In fact, MBCT encourages you to take a different stance in relation to difficult thoughts and sensations. You find out how to observe early warnings signs of an assault (of say depression, migraine, panic attack, and so on) and handle them competently.

✔ **Myth:** 'You have to stop eating meat, chocolate, sweets, drinking alcohol, smoking, and so on.'

Any of these habits are absolutely your choice. Whether they give you pleasure or grief, again, only you can decide. The more mindful you are, the more you notice which foods and drinks serve you well and which are causing you discomfort or even pain. You become so in touch with your body that you simply know what to do gladly and what to let go of, if anything.

✔ **Myth:** 'Mindfulness is just another thing the media wants people to spend money on.'

Perhaps partly true, but unavoidable in a consumer society where the media is so pervasive and so many things are promoted and sponsored. However, mindfulness meditation has been around for a long time (close to 3,000 years). When you stop referring to written texts about mindfulness and start remembering how you experienced life when you were a young child, you remember moments of just being alive. Furthermore, you can read up on thousands of research studies that show that it's a proven method of healing from within.

Children can be so much more mindful than the most trained meditator. They haven't been corrupted yet by expectation, rules, guilt and resentment. Watch a toddler for a day, or a cat for that matter, and you see unrehearsed mindfulness at its purest (or should I say purrrrest!): the joy of being alive!

Feeling that you lack the necessary experience or knowledge

If you've never participated in any sort of self-help programme or experienced these kinds of exercises before, you may think that you've no idea what you're doing. Fear not, for all you need to know is already seeded within you. This book is more like the manual to help you look after the seeds and water and feed them so they can flourish and bloom.

This book isn't a volume for experts, yogis or people who want to teach MBCT to others: it's very much designed for the curious beginner. From your first exercise of week one (in Chapter 4), you find yourself invited on a voyage. The journey takes you logically and gradually through eight chapters that open your mind and heart to being alive, helping you to take in the goodness that you can find in life and giving you options on how to deal with the painful and difficult experiences in life.

You can't lose your way, because I provide 'Getting Your Bearings on the Course' and 'Reviewing Your Accomplishments This Week' sections in each chapter for orientation.

To see how the course progresses and how each of the eight chapters focuses on a specific aspect, flip to the later section 'Introducing the Eight-Week Course'.

Assuming that mindfulness is all spiritual mumbo-jumbo

Cynicism can be a big mindset to get over. Cynicism is quite understandable, with so many fake prophets telling people how to lead better and more spiritual lives. But MBCT isn't some pseudo-religion – it's simply a way of uncluttering your mind and allowing your mind and body to function better.

MBCT encourages you to feel a bit of kindness, patience, awareness, acceptance, empathy and emotional intelligence. Research shows that you can have a more fulfilling life and more rewarding relationships if you practise these skills. (For a long list of the mental and physical ailments that mindfulness meditation has been proved to improve, turn to Chapter 1.)

Research is ongoing and ever-expanding. Everything you encounter is based on scientific research and decades of experience, and I hope that helps you to let go of worry and try it out. Only you can judge whether MBCT works for you.

Unless you give it a good and regular go, you'll never know for certain whether MBCT is for you. So try the eight sessions before you judge the outcome.

For more on the Eastern aspects of MBCT, read the later section 'Practising oriental disciplines'.

Distinguishing between meditation, mindfulness and awareness training

You may well have heard these terms before, and similar ones too, and may now be wondering what they mean in the context of MBCT. The following list should clarify some issues for you:

- ✓ **Meditation:** A general term for any practice that involves sitting or kneeling (sometimes even standing) and focusing the mind on an object, sound or feeling.

- ✓ **Mindfulness meditation:** Focuses on the here and now and uses an anchor of awareness to keep your mind from flitting off into ruminating, thinking or planning.

- ✓ **Awareness training:** Becoming more mindful by intentionally becoming aware of the present moment over and over again.

Awareness training (which is sometimes called focusing) is similar to mindfulness training: only the name is different.

Meditation comes in many different types and with many different names: transcendental meditation, visualisation and concentration, among many others. MBCT is a secular form using ancient meditative practices to put you in touch with what's happening in this moment. It's down-to-earth and pragmatic – an all-inclusive and productive way of working within a secular framework that's available to all (check out Chapter 1 for more about MBCT's development and history).

Believing that you can do it by yourself

Although you can find not having a teacher to guide you a bit daunting – and having a teacher is no bad thing – this book allows you to accomplish a great deal by yourself. You don't have to be harsh on yourself and act like a drill-instructor; MBCT is more about being your own mentor and friend, finding out how to trust yourself and holding a gentle discipline in mind.

No single perfect way exists of practising mindfulness. Just develop your personal approach (see the earlier section 'Creating a Personal Practice that Works') and remember that every moment can be a new start.

Being Actively Mindful: Theory Rooted in Practice

As I explain in this section, everything about the eight-week MBCT course is rooted in practice – you get to be active, not passively sitting and reading. Therefore, I suggest that you use this book in a particular way: read, leave the book, try something out and then return to the book for guidance.

Please consider reading through a particular exercise twice and then close your eyes and do a *speed practice run,* where in your mind you go through a five-bullet-point system of how to remember the meditation.

Here's an example: kindly read the breathing meditation in Chapter 6 twice. Then note down in your mindfulness diary five key points that can help you get through it the first time:

- ✔ Sit with dignity.
- ✔ Focus on feet being connected with the ground.
- ✔ Breath naturally.
- ✔ Observe the natural in- and out-breath – allowing the breath just to happen.
- ✔ Bring your mind back from wandering off and reconnect it to the breath.

When you finish the speed practice run, kindly read the instructions once more and see how much you remember.

Practising oriental disciplines

Buddhist, yogic and Taoist wisdom isn't mystical or old-fashioned: in many aspects, these philosophies contain down-to-earth tools for improving your life. The Buddha, for example, taught for half a century and in a nutshell his message is that 'life brings suffering and you can discover how to reduce it.'

In the West, what tends to happen to Eastern wisdom is that open-minded people see how practical and helpful many of the ideas are and incorporate them into their regular lifestyles, regardless of whether they're religious or non-religious. That's why you come across so few terms in this book that sound unfamiliar or foreign to you.

By beginning to integrate Eastern and Western psychology, you're already moving towards reducing suffering. So much suffering in the world is caused by the violence that people use to try to force their traditions onto one another, claiming that theirs is the only true way.

Nothing like this violence is going to happen in your MBCT voyage. I make it clear that no right or wrong way applies to MBCT, just your way of leading your life. In the end you're responsible for your actions and reactions, and mindfulness invites you to choose what sits comfortably with you and experiment with what looks promising or at least interesting.

Adapting old techniques

Several ancient meditative practices have been adapted and unravelled for modern-day use in MBCT. I guide you in simple, down-to-earth language. Furthermore, you don't have to torture yourself and sit on the floor in the lotus position; you can sit on a chair. If you do want to move to sitting on the floor, you can do so slowly and gradually.

In fact, only sit on the floor cross-legged if that feels comfortable. Alternatively, sit on a chair, up against a wall, kneel or stand.

In addition, the course includes a fair amount of cognitive behavioural therapy interventions, which have been used successfully for more than 50 years. (Chapter 1 describes this aspect of the MBCT course.)

Certain other practices (such as the 3-minute breathing space in Chapter 6) have been developed specifically for this course.

Joining body and mind

MBCT isn't a physical or a mental workout – it's about connecting body *and* mind.

The mind in itself isn't just your brain but also your emotional mind; your feelings. The Japanese and Chinese languages reflect this by having one single character (symbol) representing 'mind and heart'. Often thoughts and feelings affect how your body feels. Many times, the body gives clues as to what problem you're experiencing.

Perhaps you've ignored an inconvenient body sensation in the past and eventually your body had to knock so hard on your awareness door that you had to listen. Here are a few examples:

- ✔ **Feeling hungry:** Can lead to dizziness and feeling faint.

- ✔ **Feeling thirsty a lot:** Can point to diabetes.

- ✔ **Heart racing:** Can indicate anxiety or high blood pressure.

- ✔ **Knot in stomach:** Can mean you're afraid of something.

- ✔ **Light headache:** Can lead to a throbbing tension headache (can also be a sign of high blood pressure).

- ✔ **Lump in the throat:** You may be fearful of speaking your truth.

- ✔ **Stiff neck and shoulders:** Can lead to migraine or frozen shoulder.

- ✔ **Stomach feeling a little acidic:** May develop into an ulcer or gastroenteritis.

The more you bring awareness to physical sensations during the eight-week course, the more you can tell what may be going on emotionally or prevent a stronger, potentially more harmful, sensation from developing.

JARGON ALERT

Psychosomatic disorders

Body and mind are part of the whole; if one suffers, the other is affected too. You may have heard of psychosomatic disorders. The first part of this term (*psycho*) refers to the mind, the second (soma) to the body. A *psychosomatic disorder* is a disease which involves both mind and body.

Some physical diseases are thought to be made worse by mental factors such as stress and anxiety. Skin ailments such as psoriasis, for example, are very often heavily affected if not triggered by mental unease. Other psychosomatic connections are a little more subtle: somebody suffering from depression may not eat regularly or look after himself well, for

example. Other illnesses that are particularly prone to worsening as a result of mental factors such as stress and anxiety are eczema, stomach ulcers, high blood pressure and heart disease. It is thought that the physical part of the illness (the extent of a rash, the level of the blood pressure, and so on) can be affected by mental factors.

The term *psychosomatic disorder* is sometimes also used where mental factors cause physiological symptoms and no physical disease can be detected. For example, a chest pain may be caused by stress when no physical disease can be found.

Focusing on each individual task, and being present in the moment

Every day includes much more nonbeing than being . . . A great part of every day is not lived consciously.

—Virginia Woolf

Reading this insight Virginia Woolf had so many years ago is fascinating. Today people are probably even more mindless than during her lifetime. You live in a speedy society where everything has to be fast, has to be done quickly and efficiently.

In contrast, MBCT trains you in connecting with awareness and attention. When practising, please don't think ahead to the next task of the day. As best as you can, keep focused on the task at hand and be present and aware moment by moment. If your mind wanders off while you're going through an MBCT exercise, gently and kindly escort it back to the present moment.

This way you can enjoy the little miracles of life, like the miniature changes in your environment, in your own awareness and in your ability to skilfully stay sane in a frantic world.

Discovering the Advantages Awaiting You

You can gain a great many benefits from practising MBCT. You should never end-game, but realising what you're working towards is important to keep you motivated.

End-gaming in this context means when you're looking to the end result so much that you fail to make the most out of the journey you're currently undertaking and miss out on many a splendid thing. End-gaming is effectively the opposite of mindful living and being in the now!

Adding up the benefits

So many potential benefits are associated with MBCT that a whole book can be filled with them.

Here are some of the benefits to your mental and physical health you can get from adding a little dose of awareness to your life:

- Improves sleep
- Increases ability in coping with pain and loss
- Boosts your immune system
- Helps to decrease depression and prevent relapse
- Lessens anxiety
- Reduces compulsive behaviour (drinking, smoking, eating, fasting, shopping, gambling, and so on)
- Aids in the healing of, and being able to live better with, cancer
- Helps you cope with ageing
- Increases life satisfaction
- Increases acceptance of yourself
- Aids with dealing with anger
- Increases experience of calm and relaxation
- Increases energy levels and enthusiasm for living
- Increases self-confidence and self-acceptance
- Improves brain function (for example, memory, empathy, creativity)
- Increases attention, compassion and self-compassion
- Prevents you from losing the ability to access your memory
- Lifts mood

The benefits may also extend to you and your workplace. For example, you may find that you:

- Feel more empowered
- Remain more true to yourself/not sell out
- Overcome procrastination
- Cope better with shyness
- Show more kindness and patience
- Increase your resilience
- Can help you to overcome post-traumatic stress disorder
- Become a more mindful teacher
- Achieve more focus and attention
- Enhance creativity

✔ Achieve a more balanced mentality

✔ Increase your concentration levels

Your relationships benefit too. You may find that you:

✔ Have more acceptance of the idiosyncrasies of others

✔ Befriend yourself

✔ Forgive more readily

✔ Are better at caregiving

✔ Are better at parenting

✔ Really listen to and care for others

✔ Can amend relationships

✔ Are kinder

✔ Are more honest

✔ Have enhanced intimacy

✔ Can accept what is and what can't be changed

✔ Can let go of unhelpful arguments or demands

✔ Have better awareness of a problem

Tailoring the benefits to you

The MBCT course is a personal experience that you shape around you to deal with whatever you want to deal with. You may start with one particular aspect of your life and then realise, by enhancing your awareness, how the problem may also be part of the solution.

For example, you may be intending to use MBCT to improve your sleep. But you slowly become aware that your sleep isn't only affected by what you do and how much of it, but also by your environment. So, you may decide to de-clutter your bedroom and reduce your time on your mobile phone or computer before going to bed. Doing so gives you more space (physically, mentally and in relation to time).

Suddenly, many new doors open: not only do you have better, more restful sleep, but you also have more time for relationships, creativity and simply smelling the roses.

Living healthily

MBCT helps to improve your health generally. By practising meditation and mindful living, all your senses sharpen. You become much more aware of what you can do and what you should leave for another moment in time, when you need activity and when you need rest.

You increasingly feel which food really serves your body well, which may lead you to explore new avenues of cooking or experimenting with unknown ingredients. You may also notice what foods or drinks have the opposite effect and cause you discomfort or lack of energy. You may decide to reduce those in your diet, but only because you want to do so.

You become more aware of habits that are life-enhancing (walking in nature or eating healthy food) and those that are depleting (drinking too much alcohol, gambling, smoking – see Chapter 13). By doing so, you exercise compassion towards this one and precious life of yours. You know when a relationship is too demanding and you may have to put it on the back burner. Alternatively, you notice which friends are really nourishing and can be more present in your life (check out Chapter 16 which, although I aim at older people, contains useful advice for everyone on surrounding yourself with positive friends).

You're likely to become more adventurous – not in a dangerous way, but in a life-appreciating kind of way. You may start new hobbies, new explorations or even a new job.

Slowing right down

With life often moving at such a frenetic pace, MBCT can really help you to slow down. Not so that you have less time to do things; you just appreciate every moment so it doesn't feel like you're constantly moving forward without knowing what you're doing and why. You may well decide to let go of certain activities and decide to simply be more often.

Imagine that you relearn to listen to the birds, watch the clouds and feel the rain, just as you did when you were a toddler.

Helping yourself and others

MBCT helps create a better outlook on life for you, and thus also has a positive effect on those around you. It may well open your mind to more possibilities. You don't have to become a hippy or crusader (unless you want to!).

MBCT never puts an obligation on you to do anything, but you may find yourself wanting to help others and see that this activity brings rewards you can't get from just living for yourself.

Here are some examples that happened to people who engaged deeply with MBCT, and thus can happen for you as well:

- You become more aware of other people and their needs.
- You may surprise yourself by offering a seat to a person in public, someone you sense needs it more than you.
- You may become more aware of the planet, nature at large or individual countries or causes.
- You may start using reusable shopping bags.
- You may find yourself helping out in areas that you never have considered before (cooking or serving food in a soup kitchen, for example).
- You may also want to assist a charitable cause by donating time or money or both.
- You may simply be easier to live and be with.

Reading 'The Tortoise and the Hare'

Of course, you know this story. But real, significant awareness (a central point of MBCT) comes from seeing the familiar anew. So please read the story again, appropriately slowly, and then consider what responses it causes in you.

A hare once had the audacity to claim that he could run faster than anybody else. One day, the tortoise, who had grown tired of his boasting, said, 'Let's see your marvellous skill. I think you can be beaten.' The hare laughed so heartily that he got hiccups.

He challenged the tortoise to compete against him and was shocked when she accepted the challenge. The next morning the race began. The hare, showing off as usual, yawned as the humble tortoise started off slowly. The hare even took a short nap before he followed. When he woke, the tortoise was but a short distance in front, hardly one third of the race track. So the hare decided to have breakfast. After that he felt sleepy again. The tortoise had now covered half the course. So the hare fell fast asleep and was soon snoring contentedly. In the late afternoon the tortoise, who had persistently walked along, was almost at the finishing line. At this very minute, the hare woke from his second snooze. He saw the tortoise in the far distance and started racing. Soon his tongue was hanging out and he was panting for breath. But his last leap was too late. The tortoise had won. The hare was exhausted and felt humiliated; he flopped down and the tortoise was silently but kindly smiling at him.

The story certainly shows that one step at a time gets you where you want to go and that multi-tasking and then rushing to catch up certainly doesn't. I wonder what else you make of this tale: are you a tortoise or a hare, and how has that worked out for you in the past? Can you think of instances where slow but sure may have worked out better?

Introducing the Eight-Week Course

The chapters in Part II focus on what's normally an eight-week course for MBCT. However, you can go at whatever pace you choose – the eight weeks is just to help break down the elements into manageable chunks.

 I recommend that you focus on one chapter for a minimum of one week and that you practise the included exercises no less than six times each before moving on to the next chapter. Of course, you can absolutely take things more slowly if you prefer. After all, you have the rest of your life to practice.

I also encourage you to make notes and observations of your experiences regularly. This way you get a chance to observe how MBCT is affecting your experience of life.

Going over the core skills

You acquire a number of core skills over the course. The primary focus is on methodically becoming more aware, moment by moment, of physical sensations and of thoughts and feelings as mental events. This process creates a new relationship between you and your thoughts and feelings. You find out how to see them as aspects of experience that move through your awareness and may or may not be true at any one moment in time.

In short, you discover that thoughts aren't facts and that you aren't your thoughts.

Other key themes of MBCT include learning through experience (via the guided meditations and exercises) and the development of an accepting, open attitude in which you intentionally face problems, pain or negative thoughts.

 Increased mindfulness assists you in detecting patterns of negative thinking, feelings and body sensations, allowing you to address them at an earlier stage than if you ignore the warning signs.

Casting a look over the weeks to come

Here's a brief description of each of the eight weeks included in the course. A lot of research and experience has gone into devising this course and so I recommend that you follow the chapters in this order.

The first four weeks of the course demonstrate the practice of mindfulness meditation for all your senses, showing you how much thinking you're involved in when you aren't even doing anything:

- ✔ **Week 1, Chapter 4: Stepping out of autopilot mode.** This week introduces your mind and body to gentle, focused mindful activity in order to be mentally present. It includes an everyday mindfulness exercise and the body scan meditation, which may soon become an old favourite for you.

- ✔ **Week 2, Chapter 5: Overcoming obstacles and noticing living in your head.** This lesson helps you to create the right mental attitude for engaging with MBCT and managing potential barriers and stumbling blocks that invariably crop up. I introduce a great breathing meditation and the idea of keeping a pleasant events diary.

- ✔ **Week 3, Chapter 6: Developing physical awareness using mindful movement.** You meet such subjects as mindful movement and mindful walking, add the three-minute emergency breathing space meditation to your daily routine and explore creating an unpleasant events diary.

- ✔ **Week 4, Chapter 7: Allowing yourself to stay in the present while dealing with difficult thoughts and experiences.** The truth is that attachment and aversion cause stress and suffering. In this chapter I discuss stress, its triggers and resulting symptoms. You read more about unhelpful thinking as well as a sitting with thoughts meditation, which allows you to look at your thoughts as an objective observer.

Attachment is wanting to have something, not letting it go and needing reassurance that you can have it forever (or at least again and again): examples include a person, a car, your looks, youth, money, achievements, and so on.

Aversion refers to having an absolute disgust of something, a total intolerance, and investing a lot of effort into not having to do something or accept something or someone, such as being fat or looking old, being poor or losing your importance, or not getting the best results. Aversion can also connect to the inability to accept low or angry moods in yourself or others.

The second four weeks deepen what you discover, encouraging you to be observant of mood shifts and connecting you more deeply to everyday living in the moment. You're encouraged to be with what is, and only respond to it when doing so is the best option:

- ✔ **Week 5, Chapter 8: Allowing the difficult, as well as cultivating the right atmosphere for accepting adversity.** You experiment with acceptance rather than resistance in this chapter. If you experience pain, sadness or lack for something, for now just let it be: bring kindness and compassion to difficulties. Specific exercises include 'staying with discomforting thoughts' and 'being human'.

✔ **Week 6, Chapter 9: Dealing with and protecting yourself from negative thoughts and deepening your awareness that thoughts are not truths.** You aren't your thoughts and thoughts frequently get things wrong. I provide information on observing your own life narrative as just a story and not fact, and encourage you to experiment with the pebble meditation.

✔ **Week 7, Chapter 10: Being proactive in your own treatment and recovery and taking good care of yourself.** I discuss observing when your mood is fragile and planning nourishing and pleasurable activities to balance your mood and wellbeing (the three-minute breathing space is the first intervention when you feel that 'the weather is changing').

✔ **Week 8, Chapter 11: Assessing yourself and bringing everything together.** I lead you through deciding what you've discovered that's useful and you want to continue using, and whether you've noticed any changes in your perception of life. I also provide action plans for being mindful for the rest of your life.

Part II

Sailing Your Personal Ship – the Eight-Week MBCT Course

Day	Practice	Time	Body Sensations	Emotions	Thoughts
Monday	Body scan	7 a.m.	Difficult to sense legs	Curious, bored	This is hard
Monday	Shower	8 a.m.	Lovely tingling	Happy	I love my new shower gel

For some free bonus mindfulness-based cognitive therapy content, head online and take a look at www.dummies.com/extras/mindfulnessbased cognitivetherapyuk.

Part II

Sailing Your Personal Ship – The Eight-Week MBCT Course

In this part...

- Connect gently to your body and mind, and set out on an enlightening eight-week voyage of discovery into mindfulness.

- Create the right mental attitude for practicing mindfulness-based cognitive therapy and for developing mindful physical awareness.

- Find out how to stay in the present whilst dealing with and protecting yourself from negative thoughts and experiences.

- Discover how you can cultivate the kind of atmosphere you need for accepting adversity.

- Take the initiative and become proactive in your own treatment and recovery.

Chapter 4

Preparing for the Voyage – Week One: Practising Mindfulness and Stepping Out of Autopilot

In This Chapter

▶ Preparing for mindfulness practice

▶ Focusing your mind on the present

▶ Taking an awareness journey through your body

▶ Performing everyday activities mindfully

*I*n the first week of your mindfulness journey I invite you to prepare for what's ahead by developing the skill of experiencing each moment of your life as it unfolds or presents itself. The idea is to reconnect to *being* alive rather than constantly *doing* life (which sounds more like a punishment!).

This chapter talks you through preparing for mindfulness meditations and understanding how physical space is conducive to finding stillness within yourself. I help you unclutter your mind, take you on a gentle voyage through your body and show you how to experience everyday activities totally afresh. You become familiar with stepping out of autopilot (a condition I describe in Chapter 1) and viewing certain thoughts as unhelpful ruminations that arise involuntarily and aren't necessarily true.

All you need to bring to this activity is practice time and childlike curiosity. At this point, you don't need to feel any pressure to try to find solutions to the problem(s) that led to your interest in mindfulness-based cognitive therapy (MBCT). Right now, your aim is to simplify your focus on the actual experience you observe while meditating.

Preparing Yourself and Your Surroundings

Being present in the moment and your current experience sounds easy – and is by no means difficult – but it does require that you place yourself in suitably conducive surroundings and prepare your mind.

The present moment – the now – can be extraordinary in many ways, but you need to connect to it as fully as possible in order to sense it deeply. In the now, you can truly hear the birds, the wind or the humming of a plane in the distant sky. The more you can access this state of being, the more you're able not only to recognise the beauty of life but also to discover how to deal with the challenges it presents.

Awareness helps you to respond wisely to situations, as opposed to simply reacting to them automatically.

Creating your practice space

Designating a space at home that you can return to regularly for mindfulness practice is a very important starting point for creating an environment conducive to finding stillness within yourself. A whole spare room is great, but a quiet corner, for example in your bedroom, works perfectly well.

Ideally, try to choose a room where you don't work on a computer or watch TV, because you tend unconsciously to connect such spaces with being busy, active thinking or tasks. If your living space is limited, however, you can cover technical equipment with a cloth to create the quiet space your mind needs for coming into stillness.

When creating your surroundings, use your imagination and personal preference to design a peaceful area. You may want to have the following:

- A supporting chair (that is, one with a firm seat and straight back as opposed to one that whispers encouraging comments into your ear!) or perhaps a stool or cushion (for example, a *zafu* is a meditation cushion used in the Japanese Zen meditation tradition) to sit on, a shawl or blanket to keep snug, and a mat or rug to lie on
- A small table with a candle
- A photo of a favourite place of calm and tranquillity
- Fresh flowers and/or some shells or stones you may have collected on a walk

Please choose whatever items give you a sense of personal gladness. Place these items in and around your meditation space in order to signify it is a place of peace and stillness. These objects will hopefully help to keep you in this mindset whenever you enter the space.

By creating, reserving and using this special place over a period of time, it gently and automatically triggers a sense of awareness and peace when you go to it. After a while you'll be able to do your exercises anywhere you like, but at the beginning your meditation corner assists you in developing a regular mindfulness practice. Just like writers tend to have a particular writing place, people who meditate often select a special place for it as well.

Making yourself comfortable

Before you begin engaging with any of the mindfulness meditations in this book, I suggest that you allocate a specific time each day for practising awareness, and keep to it (having a special time helps just as reserving a special location does). I also recommend practising when you're neither too hungry nor too full, or too tired. As for clothing, wearing comfortable clothes such as leggings or loose trousers and a comfy T-shirt is best, as is ensuring that you keep warm.

If you feel very restless or have a to do list running through your mind, perhaps engage in some gentle exercise (walking, gentle yoga or Pilates stretches) or write the list down to get it out of your head before beginning.

Simply listen to Track Two, step by step, as well as you can (or follow the script in your mind). You may well discover that finding total silence is impossible, but whatever sounds occur in your environment try to put them into the background of your awareness; do not focus on them too strongly, rather like being aware of a few scattered clouds and yet seeing the surrounding blue sky.

Whether you choose to sit or lie down, the right posture is vital for maintaining focus during mindfulness exercises (you don't want to have to stop meditating because your back feels stiff, for example). If you're sitting on a chair, please:

1. **Place your feet flat on the floor, without crossing your legs.**

2. **Consider whether you want to wrap a shawl round your shoulders or cover yourself with a light blanket for warmth; if the chair feels a little high for you, position a cushion underneath your feet.**

3. **Try to sit upright and with dignity; by all means rest your lower back on the chair's back, but from the waist upwards see whether you can straighten your back so that it can support itself.**

4. **Sit comfortably so that your neck is straight and relaxed and your chin is ever so slightly tucked under it.**

5. **Rest your hands gently in your lap, with the palms pointing down or up as you prefer.**

If you're meditating on the floor, please:

1. **Lie down on a yoga mat or thick blanket or carpet, maybe placing a small cushion under your head.**

2. **Allow your legs to fall open, or make a triangle with them by placing your feet flat on the floor with your knees pointing towards the ceiling.**

3. **Rest your arms on the floor with the palms of your hands directed towards the ceiling.**

4. **Use the blanket or shawl to cover yourself if it helps keep you warm.**

The search for silence

A keen meditator decided to spend a week in silence away from all the worldly temptations and distractions. He packed a tent, a rolled-up mat, a sleeping bag and some basic provisions, and went up a mountain surrounded by the most beautiful woodland. By that evening he'd set up his tent, eaten a simple meal and meditated on being enveloped by the sounds of crickets, birds and the wind. He'd entered heaven.

His delicious sleep was, however, cruelly interrupted at dawn when he heard a commanding voice giving instructions on how to put up tents through a loud speaker. He emerged from his hiding place and was faced with a large group of teenagers and their guide who'd come for an adventure week in the forest. What could he do: move to another spot on another mountain top or remain where he was, accepting and working with the difficulties that life presented him?

Put yourself in his place. What do you think a mindful response would be, as opposed to an instinctive gut reaction? Bear in mind that even if he moves, can he ever guarantee to find peace at the second, third or fourth location?

As you may have observed yourself many times already, life is unpredictable. You can have aspirations, desires, make plans and think of everything, and still something unexpected just shows up. Do you remember, for example, when the Icelandic volcano Eyjafjallajökull spat out volcanic ash in 2010? The world experienced huge air traffic shut down: people missed weddings and funerals, could not come home from their travels and could not deliver their lectures. It lasted for a whole week but life continued, and when it finished everything fell back into place. Friends of mine were stuck in Korea on their way home from Australia and it was enormously interesting for them to get to know a country they had expected to just pass through.

So had the meditator decided to move to another location he may have been disturbed by other things like the weather, for example. By staying and working with the difficulty he would most likely learn a lot more about being mindful: acceptance, patience and insight into the fact that you can never predict what life will offer. Maybe he managed to meet some of the teenagers and tell them about meditation. Some might have thought him weird and others would perhaps have taken to it.

Uncluttering Your Mind

One purpose of developing mindfulness is to help you step out of the constant barrage of unwanted, unhelpful thoughts that seem to arise in your awareness day in and day out. People incessantly ruminate on the past – as in what they could've done better or why they didn't get what they wanted or hoped for – or worry about the future, imagining all the possible dangers and mishaps that may happen.

Mindfulness can help you let go of these automatic thoughts or at least make you aware of their existence and lack of substance. They certainly arise, but most of the time they're only partially, if at all, true. Although sometimes you can experience moments of stillness before another thought presents itself again, being able to see thoughts as simply formations of the mind that may not even be true is a big step towards gaining your emotional freedom.

Letting go of worries and concerns

Whatever concerns you may have at this moment can wait until you've completed your daily mindfulness practice; they'll still be there when you're finished. When practising mindfulness, you're being invited to engage with the idea of the impermanence of thoughts. The proverbial clouds in the sky are just like the thoughts in your mind; sometimes light and lofty, and at other times heavy-laden.

Being mindful simply means being aware of the nature of thoughts and the truth that they aren't facts.

Entering the now

Being truly present in this moment means fully inhabiting life as it presents itself to you right here, right now, and delving into the experience of living. I provide each mindfulness meditation in this book to help you practise being in the now more and more often, so that in the long run you can transfer your new ability into your everyday living.

You may feel at times that you've got so many things wrong in the past that surely you can't change. The beautiful message of mindfulness, however, says that every now is a new beginning. Again and again, you can start afresh and try things anew. The past is history, the future unknown and the now is a gift: a present of the present, if you like.

Exploring Your Physical Self Mindfully

All too often people tend to live in their heads, seeing the body as just a vehicle to travel in. But when you bring awareness to how inhabiting this physical structure feels, you can discover loads about yourself: perhaps you notice the many areas that are fine and which parts feel tender or sore, and so find out how to look after them better. The formal mindfulness exercise of scanning your body mentally, which I describe in this section, helps you to start uncluttering and slowing down your mind. As a result, you develop a much more intimate relationship with yourself and become more compassionate with your whole being.

You can carry out the body scan exercise, which takes around 40 minutes, laying down on a rug or a mat or sitting in your special chair (see the earlier section 'Making yourself comfortable'). Ensure that you're warm and not disturbed as far as possible (for example, turn off any nearby phone).

In this particular practice, I ask you to connect to your breathing initially and thereafter to travel through various areas of your body one at the time. Practising body scanning in this way gives you the opportunity to let any thoughts that arise during the exercise simply to pass by.

Creating a completely open mind that is focused on the now is rather difficult, so I recommend using each part of your body as an *anchor of attention* for your mind to keep it from fleeing off into ruminations, pondering, boredom, frustration and other states of mind that can get in the way of your mindfulness practice.

Understanding the importance of taking your time

Before I lead you through the various steps of the meditation in the next section, 'Engaging in the body scan practice', please bear in mind the following points about not rushing or cutting short the 40-minute process. Most people find that 15 or 20 minutes is easy, but this shorter period may not bring up all the underlying 'muck and fungus'. Doing it for 40 minutes, however, can positively help you comprehend your life and situation. And with time, more awareness can create a new way of embracing life, unconditionally, as it is.

Taking your time:

- ✔ Allows you to stop thinking intellectually and to focus your attention into your body.
- ✔ Stimulates feeling, sensing and hearing and reduces overactive thinking and ruminating.

- Shows you to re-enter the now again and again (your life is always happening now and every new area you attend to is a new beginning).

- Helps you to understand *mental exhaustion* (a state of tiredness and/or agitation that can affect the body and prevent you from focusing on the now) when you become aware of the busyness of your mind (which refuses to mind its own business!).

- Assists you in discovering how to avoid actively resisting, but accepting what is by repeatedly doing so.

- Reveals that no right or wrong way exists of doing this (or any other) practice, as you constantly just do it and observe. While I recommend useful ways to practise, the experience is entirely your own.

- Encourages you to stick with it when you experience discomfort, ride the sensation (that is, accept it for a while), and respond to it if it doesn't go away on its own – don't rush straight for the quick fix or the easy cure.

- Aids the journey for discovery; each body scan is like a laboratory session – what are you going to find out this time?

- Clarifies that this exercise is an invitation to wake up to life, although if you fall asleep, by all means allow your body to rest. It may just need to catch up with a little sleep. After practising for a while, you're likely to find more wakefulness each time you carry out your mindfulness practice.

If you need to be somewhere, using an alarm clock can help you finish the body scan in time.

Shortening the practice can make it more pleasant but less profound. If you seriously want to create/grow new ways of thinking and feeling I recommend, whenever possible, a minimum of 40 minutes. Even if your mind wanders off a thousand times, you're still practising mindfulness by noticing that fact and escorting the mind continually back to the task at hand.

Engaging in the body scan practice

In this section, and in Track Three, I provide a detailed guide to carrying out your body scan practice. Don't be put off by all the steps involved; just follow each one individually and forget about the time.

If your mind wanders off into thinking, just observe it doing so and then patiently and without judgement guide your focus back to your body. Even if you have to do this many, many times, you don't have to feel frustrated. Everyone's mind tends to wander, because the nature of the mind means that it tends to ruminate incessantly. So for now please accept this fact and congratulate yourself each time you notice that your mind is on the move. For more details, flip to the later section 'Becoming aware of your mind wandering'.

1. **Lie or sit down when you feel ready and gently cover yourself with a light blanket or similar to avoid feeling cold.** If you prefer, you may close your eyes or keep them in soft focus (half open, unfocused).

   Should you experience any discomfort while lying down, try placing your feet on the floor with your knees pointing upwards and placing a rolled-up towel or cushion under your lower back for support.

2. **Decide to bring your awareness slowly to your body, feeling the points of contact it makes with the floor, the rug, the mat or the chair.** Start with the intention of *falling awake* in order to sense your body in a new way. Perhaps you notice the pressure between your feet and legs on the rug or floor, and the sensation of your back touching the surface of the chair, bringing awareness also to your shoulders – checking mindfully whether they feel tense or loose. Also, notice the feeling of your hands resting in your lap or on the floor.

3. **Place one of your hands on your chest or stomach and notice how it rises on the in-breath and falls on the out-breath.** Don't feel as if you need to change your breathing deliberately (deepening or lengthening it) in any way. Please just allow your body to breathe itself (it knows exactly how!) and accept my invitation to experience each breath fully as it comes and goes.

4. **Observe whether each breath is different – longer or shorter, deeper or shallower – and after a while perhaps the pauses between each in- and out-breath.** See each breath as a new beginning. If your mind wanders off into planning, analysing or other forms of thought, gently become aware of this wandering and then patiently guide your focus back to your breathing. Even if you have to go through this process every few seconds, you've no need to get impatient or frustrated (though if you do feel these emotions, that's okay too).

   The nature of the mind is such that it tends to jump about like a monkey from branch to branch – everyone has plenty of automatic thoughts throughout every day. Not only are they present most of the time, lurking just beneath the surface of awareness, but before you start practising mindfulness you're probably not even aware of their existence. So for now just accept this fact and feel proud when you notice the wandering mind, for only a mindful observer can do that. Then bring your attention back to the anchor of breathing in and out, again and again.

5. **Put your hand gently back into its original position after a little while and please change your focus to your body as a whole.** In a moment I'm going to take you through a journey in which truly inhabiting your body – not just your brain – may help you get clues about your well-being, state of mood and health in a fresh and immediate way.

6. **Guide your awareness to your left foot when you feel ready to continue.** Start with the left big toe, then the left little toe, the toes in between and even the spaces between the toes. Feel them, sense them or simply know that they exist.

You don't need to move at all throughout the whole body scan. As best as you can, just switch on a torchlight from within, shining it onto the particular body part you're focusing on at this moment. Again, if necessary, notice your wandering mind, acknowledge where it has gone to and then patiently escort it back to the journey through your body. If you're following the audio track and have missed a few stages, just accept the situation and continue wherever your awareness picks up the guidance.

7. **Choose now to switch your focus to the rest of your left foot, the sole, the instep, the heel, the upper part, all the little bones, blood vessels and tendons, and then the left ankle, feeling these parts or just knowing that they're present.** Gently move your focus of attention upwards to your calf and shin, knee and kneecap, then focusing on your outer and inner thigh. Thus having scanned your whole left leg, I invite you to breathe in mindfully and mentally send the breath all the way down into your left leg and right down to your toes. On the out-breath, determine to release any tightness or discomfort from this area. Repeat this breathing in and out a few more times.

If you consider the idea of 'breathing into your leg' a little unusual, try picturing your blood carrying fresh oxygen into your leg on the in-breath.

8. **Consider how your left leg (through which you've journeyed) is feeling now versus the right one.** Are you aware of any differences in sensation, such as a tingling in one and not the other, heaviness versus lightness, and so on? Remember that no right or wrong way applies to doing this practice, and so whether a difference is or isn't apparent doesn't matter. Just gently bring your awareness to your experience and observe with interest what you find.

9. **Let go mentally of your left leg.** When you feel ready, carry out the awareness practice of Steps 6 to 8 on your right leg.

10. **Pause for a moment and allow your legs to recede into the background of your awareness after completing the passage, bringing your torso centre-stage.** Focus in turn on your sitting bones and buttocks, hips and reproductive areas, stomach and navel, chest and ribcage, collar bones and shoulders, upper, middle and lower back, and also your spine, vertebrae by vertebrae, being present in every moment.

11. **Now concentrate on some of your vital organs, starting with the heart and then lungs, liver, stomach and digestive tract, kidneys and urinary tract.** Of course you can add any other body part that seems relevant to you.

12. **Notice that you've scanned your whole torso, gently breathing into it and allowing any tension or discomfort to be released on the out-breath.** Please continue repeating this process a few more times.

13. **Turn your awareness to your left arm and hand, starting with the fingertips and then the thumb, pointer finger, middle finger, ring finger**

and little finger. Then shift your focus to the palm of your left hand and the back and knuckles, moving up to the left wrist, forearm and upper arm.

14. **Breathe into your left arm and hand on the next in-breath, releasing any tension or discomfort on the out-breath.** After repeating this action, breathing in and out a couple more times, move to the right arm and hand and repeat the practice.

15. **Shift your awareness now to your neck and head area, starting with your neck and throat, cheeks and chin, mouth, lips, teeth, tongue and gums.** Continue with your ears and earlobes, nose and nostrils, and eyes, including your sockets, lashes, lids, brows and eyeballs. Then move your awareness to your forehead, temples, and back and crown of your head.

16. **Imagine now, if possible, a big blowhole in the crown of your head.** Breathe in deeply through this opening, sending clear and refreshing energy to every cell of your body, releasing any tension or discomfort on the out-breath. Repeat this activity a few more times and then return for a while to observing your breathing.

17. **Start stretching gently, wriggling your toes and fingers, opening your eyes and orienting yourself (on the audio track a bell rings three times at the end of the body scan).** After a couple of minutes or so, if you're lying on the floor, turn to your left side, and then very slowly sit and stand.

Although bringing awareness to each body part creates a way into mindfulness, you may at times experience discomfort or even pain in certain areas. If you are currently experiencing pain or discomfort that is not relieved or is exacerbated by this exercise, consult your GP or health practitioner as to the safest way to engage in the exercise.

After the practice, noting down any experiences you remember is extremely useful (check out the later section 'Recording your reactions and responses'). Good, neutral or uncomfortable – any experiences are okay from the perspective of mindfulness practice. Seeing how each body scan practice varies from the others can be interesting, too. Each *now* really is a new beginning.

I suggest that you carry out this formal mindfulness exercise at least six times per week for the first two weeks, giving yourself sufficient time to create a new positive habit.

Becoming aware of your mind wandering

Sooner or later you notice that your mind is no longer focusing on the body scan but is engaged in making to do lists, worrying about tasks that need to be done, daydreaming, and so on. This is the nature of the mind; it seems to need to keep busy all the time. Perhaps this tendency is due to humans having to scan to survive in earlier times – your brain's control centre is incessantly checking whether an immediate threat to your survival is present. This ability helped humans survive as a species, but now people feel on the go all the time.

Your mind wandering isn't your fault; it's what everyone's mind does. So treat yourself kindly, and without judgement invite your attention back to the body scan, even if you have to do this every three seconds.

I suggest that you don't try to resist actively, because in general whatever you try to resist continues to persist. Instead, choose to treat the natural behaviour of your mind as a fact, just like breathing is a fact. As soon as you notice that your mind has wandered, start again. In the initial phases of the body scan, you can follow the guidance on the audio track and just continue wherever you find yourself when you notice the mind has strayed; no need to catch up with aspects you may have missed. Gently observe where your mind has gone to and then release whatever thought you come across so that it moves into the background of your awareness, and then continue with the body scan.

Engaging in this releasing behaviour is hugely beneficial. Think of it like you're tending to a little child or animal that doesn't know any different, bringing an attitude of kindness to the whole experience.

Slowing Down and Living Your Life Mindfully

Too many people live their lives automatically and habitually, doing the same thing over and over without examining whether this is good for them or making them happy. Slowing down to smell the roses (or in this case to become more mindful) helps you to reappraise your life and see where you can improve things.

Ask yourself what other daily habits you can experiment with and bring awareness to, and read through this section for some more ideas.

Performing everyday activities mindfully

In this section I suggest a few daily tasks that you can try and carry out mindfully but informally (that is, not as part of a formal meditation session), immersing yourself totally in the experience. Please feel free to follow your own intuition and creativity as well.

As always, whenever you notice the mind starting up its planning and list-making, make a note of this tendency before gently and kindly returning to the experience you're choosing to bring mindfulness to. The lists can wait until you choose to attend to them. Slowly but surely you may notice that you can start each morning by waking up and getting up mindfully and seeing throughout the day whether you can dip into a mindful moment here and there.

Experiment with performing the following activities in a mindful way:

- **Treating yourself to a shower:** Feel the water on your skin, its temperature and sensation. Smell the soap or body wash and really notice it. Bring your awareness to the wonderful gift of having running hot water available at the turn of a tap.

- **Brushing your teeth:** Notice how your hand holds your toothbrush and applies the toothpaste. Observe the action of brushing itself. What does it feel like having clean, smooth teeth at the end?

- **Getting dressed:** Notice how many actions and moves are necessary just to put on one sock.

- **Travelling to work (or anywhere):** Be mindful of how you get into your car or onto your bike; mindfully follow all the actions necessary to get from A to B.

- **Going shopping:** How do you know whether you need a basket or a trolley? Take a breath and choose mindfully what you need or what you want.

- **Waiting in a queue:** At the checkout, train station or bus stop, observe your environment or attend mindfully to your breathing.

- **Speaking to others:** Deeply listen and mindfully reply; notice that certain words can hurt and impatience can make others feel less happy to talk to you or accept your opinion.

- **Choosing what to read or watch on TV:** In this area of your life you may be able to reduce the amount of time you spend on these activities in order to create space for mindfulness practices; however, you can watch or listen to programmes that nourish rather than deplete you.

Eating with awareness: Raisin exercise

This meditation endeavours to show you how any ordinary daily activity can become a mindful experience. With practice you soon realise that living mindfully doesn't just happen in your special meditation place, but can be incorporated and fused with anything you care to experience day by day.

Put a few raisins on a little plate and take a seat anywhere you feel comfortable. Now try the following:

1. **Look at these raisins as if you've never seen raisins before.** Perhaps observe your initial reaction. Do you feel curious or a little self-conscious, or are you becoming aware of feeling any other emotion?

2. **Decide to focus deeply on these little objects.** Do they all look the same or do they vary in size, shape or colour?

3. **Select and pick up a raisin, feeling its weight and texture.** Can you squeeze it: does it change shape when you do?

4. **Feel its surface structure between your thumb and forefinger.** Are you aware of smoothness or roughness? Now touching your lips with the raisin, how does the sensation on the surface of your lips vary from the surface sensation on your finger? Is it the same, different? Anything else you notice?

5. **Move on when you feel ready to explore the raisin's smell.** Do you become aware of any particular aroma?

6. **Bring the raisin close to your ear and squeeze and rub it.** Can you hear a sound? If you do, what emotion do you notice in this very moment?

7. **Pick up this raisin or another one with the intention of putting it in your mouth.** While doing so, observe how your body knows exactly when to open your mouth and move the raisin towards the opening; see what your tongue does and how eventually the raisin ends up inside your mouth. The intricate process is quite incredible! Can you notice a taste before you start chewing? Do you notice saliva building up?

8. **Take the first bite.** How does the flavour explode in your mouth? What flavour(s) do you notice and what emotions do you become aware of?

9. **Chew this one raisin slowly until its original shape completely changes and you feel ready to swallow.** Again, I encourage you to observe precisely how the body swallows food. Do you notice how the pulp lands in your stomach?

10. **Assess your feelings now.** Do you feel like eating another raisin mindfully or was one enough? What thoughts, sensations and emotions are present when you decide to stop? You may be curious to check in with your breathing. Has it slowed down? Are you feeling somewhat still, curious, giggly, playful and childlike (not childish)?

This exercise is a way to be truly in the moment; it may even help you find your *raison d'être* (groan!). Feel free to be adventurous and try any everyday activity in a similar way. And remember to note down any experiences you have (see the later section 'Recording your reactions and responses').

Good, neutral or uncomfortable – all reactions are valid. Appraising each and every day how mindfulness exercises affect your experience of life can be fascinating.

Of course, you can perform mindful eating with any item of food, as an experiment or when you're having a meal (though best not to smell the host's food too obviously at a dinner party!). You can even just attempt it with the first few bites. Or maybe try to drink your favourite cup of something (for example, tea, coffee, juice) mindfully. Feel the shape of the cup, the texture of the outside: is it smooth or rough? Notice the temperature and how your lips prepare to receive the first sip. Do you notice the liquid running through your throat into your stomach?

The point is to take a lot of time and swap an automatic daily habit with doing the whole thing differently. It may take a little longer initially, but you never know – you may find that a potentially mundane and rushed action becomes even more exciting than tasting valuable wine or champagne.

From a health perspective, slowing down provides a clear advantage and means that you need less food to feel full. In fact, certain enzymes are present only in your mouth and eating slowly and repeatedly chewing helps you to digest food more easily. So slowing down can help your whole digestive system!

Practise informal mindfulness activities such as the ones in this section at least six times per week, or however frequently you need to create a new beneficial habit.

Making time for regular practice

I'm sure that you know the expression, 'I need to find time to do this'. But the truth is that each day contains only 24 hours – you can't create any more time for your mindfulness practice than that. So your efforts are helped initially by keeping a daily action diary to see how you spend your time. Then ask yourself what you can do less of and what you can cut out altogether. Begin, at least, to observe how you make time for your mindfulness practice this week, and start getting ideas of how you might be able to do so more easily next week.

Try not to see mindfulness as another duty to be performed. Think about how children live, truly in the moment, really enjoying this ice cream or that game. See whether you can remember, somewhere in the depth of your awareness, what not worrying about time feels like, or how well you did something, just being yourself, not needing anyone's approval.

Recording your reactions and responses

In the first few months of practising mindfulness, but at least for eight weeks or so, noting down each formal and informal exercise is very helpful: such as what time you did it, and what came up emotionally or what you were aware of while you engaged in it.

Keep a diary of what you experience (the things you enjoy and the things you have trouble with), what you want to try again, and general thoughts and discoveries. Be curious and keep an open mind and attitude.

You can create your own personal mindfulness notebook (be creative!) or use Table 4-1 as an example.

Table 4-1 Sample Diary Layout for Recording Your Reactions

Day	Practice	Time	Body Sensations	Emotions	Thoughts
Monday	Body scan	7 a.m.	Difficult to sense legs	Curious, bored	This is hard
Monday	Shower	8 a.m.	Lovely tingling	Happy	I love my new shower gel

Reviewing Your Accomplishments This Week

As a central part of the MBCT course, and to assist you in building week-on-week progress, I ask that you appraise and reflect honestly on what you've been doing each week. As part of your reflection for week one:

✔ How is your private, calming meditation space working out for you and are you managing to meditate comfortably (as I discuss in 'Preparing Yourself and Your Surroundings', earlier in this chapter)?

✔ How are you faring with the formal mindfulness exercise (in the 'Engaging in the body scan practice' section) and your informal everyday practice (in 'Eating with awareness: Raisin exercise')?

✔ Did you manage to practise each exercise six times in the week?

Don't worry if you need longer to adapt to a more mindful way of being. You have the rest of your life to experience and explore mindfulness.

Chapter 5

Plotting the Course – Week Two: Cultivating the Right Attitude

*I*n week two of this programme on mindfulness-based cognitive therapy (MBCT), the main objective is to enhance your awareness and ability to experience the present moment (which I describe in Chapter 4). I lead you towards engaging in deeper, regular mindfulness practice while demonstrating how not to be judgemental about your unfolding mindfulness experience. Creating the right mental attitude is crucial and to help I introduce you to a brief sound meditation and a longer sitting practice.

Everyone comes up against certain obstacles to practising mindfulness and I talk you through dealing with common barriers to staying motivated as well as issues that can arise during your practice, such as negative emotions or a constantly wandering mind. To this end, letting go of your internal self-critic and not worrying about particular outcomes is vitally important. To assist, I provide a story for you to read and invite you to observe your initial and subsequent, possibly alternative, reactions.

In general, kindly bring an attitude of gentle curiosity or even playfulness to this whole chapter, instead of seeing it as another chore on the proverbial 'to do list'.

Getting Your Bearings on the Course

Constantly assessing where you are and what you've already achieved is an essential step in making progress over the whole eight-week programme (if following the course in order is your approach), so that you can build on each week's exercises and develop and deepen your practice. Here are the mindfulness exercises or interventions to bear in mind from week one (they're all in Chapter 4) and how they can help to set you up for the material in this chapter.

A mindful *intervention* is a formal practice that teaches you the art of non-doing (that is, *being* rather than *doing*):

- ✔ The body scan, which guides you through your whole body, and which you may want to practise six times a week.

- ✔ Mindful breathing, which focuses on the simple breath of life and reminds you to observe it and not change anything at all. I suggest you practise this six times a week, as part of the body scan or separately if you prefer.

- ✔ The raisin exercise, which serves as an example of everyday, informal mindfulness.

To these meditations, in week two you add the sound and breath exercises (see the next section, 'Going Deeper into Self-Awareness'), which act as two anchors of awareness, helping you to reduce thinking brain activity and hook into the sensory experience of life. For more on building your regular routine, flip to 'Engaging in your mindful routine' later in this chapter.

As for all the exercises in this book, please bring a childlike attitude, letting go of interpretation and just sitting and *being* with them. These exercises of being rather than doing only require two things: your willingness to create space for them (letting go of other activities to make room for a time frame in which to practise) and the willingness to try, start again when necessary and then try some more.

Going Deeper into Self-Awareness

The intention of week two is to help move you towards becoming more mindful during the day whenever you remember the mindfulness concept. I provide some opportunities to deepen your experience and practise the skill of awareness.

Many people experience more awareness just by becoming familiar with being in the now, as opposed to the constant activity of doing, planning, reacting to things in a habitual way, and so on. In Chapter 4, I introduce the concept of living with awareness in the moment versus living automatically on autopilot. To detect any change that may already be taking place in your life after your week one practice, please ask yourself the following questions:

✔ Have you noticed any changes in yourself? Maybe just beginning a meal with a mindful spoonful of food or using the words mindful, aware or now in your daily speech more often?

✔ Can you think of any other observations related to MBCT? Recalling them may be interesting, so you may want to note them down in your mindfulness diary (flip to Chapter 4 for creating this essential aid to your practice).

Make the effort not to be cynical or dismissive at this stage. If you feel that mentioning mindfulness in conversation or performing small tasks mindfully is pretentious or unimportant, let such feelings go. And don't worry about making progress or not using enough of what you've discovered in your day-to-day existence: this journey is *your* journey and whatever route you travel and whatever pace you take is fine.

Listening mindfully: A ten-minute sound meditation

In everyday life, you may often be exposed to sounds you dislike (perhaps a motorbike passing by your meditation room) or sometimes choose to listen to sounds you like (such as the sounds of nature or music that pleases you). In this practice, which you can also listen to in Track Four, I invite you to use sound as your anchor of awareness.

Of course, at the outset you have no idea what kind of sound will present itself, so please accept whatever comes your way and try as best as you can to listen to the distance and closeness, the pitch and vibration, the length and brevity of sound. Try not to judge sound as pleasant or unpleasant but just as something that passes through your awareness.

Should you experience tinnitus, you may still be able to practise with sound. Try to allow the humming or buzzing inside you to be one of the sound patterns that arise during your practice. Many people say by not specially focusing on tinnitus they managed to reduce its effect on them; it kind of moved into the background and was just one of many sounds. You may indeed change your relationship to this problem. By reducing your resistance, acceptance may arise.

Please go to your special meditation place, switch off any phones and sit down comfortably. Perhaps initially set an alarm clock or timer to ten minutes. Bear in mind throughout that the anchor of attention for this practice is the awareness of sound. For a reminder of how to prepare a place (and yourself) for the meditation exercises, and to read an explanation of anchor of attention, flip to Chapter 4. When you feel ready:

1. **Bring your awareness to the surface that your feet are resting on and what it feels like.**

   Perhaps observe the temperature of your feet and the surrounding air, the roughness or smoothness of the floor, cushion or carpet you've placed your feet on; even bring awareness to the sensation of the socks or slippers you may be wearing. In the same way, scan through your whole body and notice the areas that are in contact with the floor or the chair, or notice your hands resting in your lap or on your legs.

2. **Close your eyes or maintain a relaxed focus on an object such as a candle, gradually bringing your awareness to any sounds you can hear.**

   These sounds may be inside the room and from outside. Here are a few examples to get you started: your stomach rumbling, the floor creaking, footsteps outside, cars, planes, motorbikes, voices, animals moving or communicating, the wind, the rain, and so on. Don't worry about labelling or naming these sounds consciously, but just allow them to arise in your awareness and pass through it. Don't cling on to pleasant sounds, judge unpleasant ones or interpret unfamiliar sounds; just accept any sound for what it is, receiving each sound with interest and curiosity.

   Imagine being a child hearing all these patterns of sound for the first time. Simply listen to them with curiosity but without judgement, so that you feel the vibration of the sounds and respond to them emotionally rather than evaluating or intellectually understanding them.

   As in all mindfulness meditations, every so often you're going to find yourself back in thinking mode: planning, wondering, daydreaming or just thinking that you really liked one sound and disliked another. As soon as you become aware of having involuntarily switched focus, observe where your mind has wandered off to and, without judgement, begin to escort it back to listening to sounds. Don't worry about how often you need to return it; just gently remind yourself that the nature of the mind is to jump from tree to tree like a squirrel. (For more details, flip to the later section 'Observing the Wandering Mind' after you complete this meditation.)

3. **Try to focus on the distance or closeness of a sound, its pitch, strength, length, its coming and going, and whether or not it repeats itself.**

   Sooner or later you may become aware of the spaces between the sounds – in other words, the sound of silence – and you may even notice that your hearing appears more acute, more focused.

   Enjoy this feeling, and remember it for future meditative exercises; the ability to discover silence is a useful one indeed.

4. **Notice the sound of the timer or alarm after ten minutes, returning your focus gently to the sensations in your body and the points of contact with the surface you're sitting on.**

    Connect to the floor, with your feet firmly planted and your body feeling grounded, and slowly open your eyes.

Write down any interesting or unusual aspects of the experience in your diary. Doing so is useful and when you reread it in the future, it helps to bring home two points of mindfulness:

- ✔ The reality of *impermanence* – that everything changes all the time. You will hear different sounds and have different reactions to the same sounds each time you engage in this exercise – you might say that change is the only constant truth.

- ✔ The fact that every time you do this exercise you're developing the muscle of *mindful awareness*; noticing the wandering mind in itself enriches awareness. Thus no right or wrong way exists for doing this exercise and you're always getting something out of it.

Bring an innocent attitude of curiosity and acceptance to all the mindfulness exercises in this book. Let go of interpretation and just 'be', instead of feeling that you have to do anything. All you need is the willingness to create space for the exercises (by letting go of other activities to make time) and the persistence to try repeatedly again and again.

Engaging in your mindful routine

Establishing a daily mindfulness routine is vital so that you can apply the insights you gain when life gets rough. The brain tends to become less organised when under stress, and so having a skill that's second nature comes in handy in times of trouble. The brain can create thinking routes that with time and practice become automatic, just like driving a car.

Perhaps start your day soon after getting up with at least a brief mindfulness meditation, because the more you condition yourself to regular practice, the easier it becomes. After a period of time, you may even come to feel as if something's missing when you haven't done it. Don't see practising mindful techniques as yet another necessary task in your day-to-day existence, but instead as something that you always do because you know how much calmer, thoughtful and receptive you are having done it. You tend to feel much more alive afterwards!

I provide the following helpful tips and guidelines to assist you in establishing your daily routine:

✔ Don't worry about progress – mindfulness and mindful living will occur sooner or later.

✔ Set aside 10–15 minutes for mindfulness in the morning before you start your day.

✔ Consider using a part of your lunch break for everyday mindfulness: for example, listening to sounds, eating mindfully, or talking kindly and mindfully to a co-worker.

✔ Engage in a formal mindfulness meditation in your quiet room every day, at a time designated by yourself as your time for practise (such as the body scan exercise from Chapter 4, the listening one from the preceding section or the breath-awareness one in the later 'Regulating the breath: Mindful breathing exercise' section) before doing more work or sitting in front of the TV.

Eventually your practice becomes a rewarding routine and a time simply to be yourself.

To help establish your routine, kindly write down in your diary the activities you dropped or reduced in order to have time for your mindful explorations. Doing so is particularly helpful because writing things down can create even more ideas. Writing by hand is usually best, because you engage a number of right-brain skills – such as vision, touch and maybe even smell (such as of the paper or pen) – and so help reveal more subconscious insights.

As a guide to your routine during the second week of this book's eight-week course, your home practice looks something like this:

✔ Practise the body scan exercise (from Chapter 4) six times per week.

✔ Engage in a second practice, such as sitting with sound or the breath, for 10 to 15 minutes each day. (Check out the earlier 'Listening mindfully: A ten-minute sound meditation' and the later 'Regulating the breath: Mindful breathing exercise' for more details.)

✔ Fill in the pleasant-event diary (from the later section 'Taking note of thoughts throughout the day') for six days a week.

✔ Choose one mindful everyday activity per day (I provide a few ideas in Chapter 4), perhaps varying it from one you did the previous week.

Retaining your awareness

The following exercise is here to show you the power of thoughts and imagination. Allow yourself to go with the instructions and see what thoughts, emotions and sensations arise. You may discover what your usual tendencies and reactions to such a situation are. In fact, you may even learn more by running it by a friend and seeing what her or his responses are. You will find that minds interpret things in a unique way and that being more self-aware can show up the thinking and reaction patterns that can drive you into negative emotions.

If no friend is at hand you could just try a second, more objective response yourself and see how your emotions and sensations follow suit. Remember, thoughts are not facts!

1. **Imagine yourself as the central figure in a story in which you enter a gathering of people at a party.** What are your thoughts, feelings and body sensations at this moment? Perhaps check out briefly what you're wearing, how many people you can see in the room, whether it contains a buffet table and a bar area where people are queuing for drinks.

2. **See yourself recognising someone in the far left corner of the room, someone that you know, whoever comes into your mind first. Go with your initial impulse.** Who is the person; is it somebody you know well, are they male or female? Observe who first comes into your mind – don't make a judgement, just make a mental note of it and think about it later.

3. **Decide to approach the person and find yourself doing just that.** When you're almost there, the person suddenly walks towards the buffet table. What are your thoughts, feelings and sensations now? You follow the person; what are you thinking as you cross the room? The person is filling a plate with various food items, but again moves away as you get near. What are your thoughts and feelings now? How does your body feel, has your mood changed?

Please note down everything you observed about your own reactions. Many different thoughts and emotions can come up in such a situation, for example:

✔ You may feel rejected and upset.

✔ You may feel annoyed or even angry.

✔ You may wonder why the person was avoiding you and what you'd done wrong to deserve such treatment.

✔ You may just think that the person didn't want a conversation and was simply starving.

✔ You may even think that the person forgot to put in their contact lenses.

Depending on what explanation you find reasonable or true, observe how it affects your emotions and even physical sensations in a different way.

You can never know the full truth of the situation. Perhaps the person just looked like the person you knew, was having an off-day, or thought you'd done or not done something, which in fact has nothing to do with you. Thousands of possibilities exist. Therefore, all you can do in such a situation is to simply be yourself and not judge things that you cannot possibly be certain of.

Responding wisely, as opposed to reacting automatically, depends on how mindful you can be in such moments; in this case, keeping the intention not to harm yourself or the other person who, possibly unintentionally, hurt you.

One thing, however, is absolutely true: *thoughts aren't facts*! For more on this issue, check out Chapters 9 and 14.

Dealing with Barriers to Practising Mindful Exercises

Coming up with reasons why you can't, won't or even that you aren't allowed to do your mindfulness practice is relatively easy (and very human!). In this section, I take a look at a few different obstacles you can face when trying to establish your new mindfulness routine and stay motivated:

- **Lack of time:** You can have difficulty making and consistently maintaining a period of time for mindfulness, which may one day be an intrinsic part of your existence. To help, think about something that you already do every day without fail, for example, brushing your teeth. I doubt you question doing it every day, because it becomes a habit. In the same vein, I encourage you to include mindfulness into your probably frantic lifestyle.

- **Lack of trust:** Perhaps you don't trust yourself to continue to practise mindfulness, or to do it right in the first place. But don't overthink the process – simply do it, staying always in the moment. Or perhaps you don't trust in the exercises themselves, or even in this book (I'm not offended, honest!). The key is to try to be open, putting your scepticism to one side. These exercises can help you and become part of your life if you let them. At least give them a good try before rejecting them.

- **Lack of belief in the message of mindfulness:** You may have trouble getting over the notion that mindfulness (and thus MBCT) is just a fad. However, people carry out mindfulness contemplation all over the world; they may apply it within different traditions and employ different terms, but ultimately their practice uses the same basic principles. Would the message of mindfulness have survived this long (2,500 years and counting) and still have a profound influence in so many cultures if it was completely useless?

- **Lack of motivation:** This can be a problem when you're really busy, but then again that's likely to be when you need mindfulness the most! Brushing your teeth isn't the kind of activity you perform only when you start to experience pain; you don't need a visit to the dentist and treatment before feeling the motivation to start brushing again. It's something you do consciously in order to avoid and cope with any potential discomfort you may have in the future. Check out the later section 'Suggesting changes to maintain motivation' for more tips.

✔ **Commitments to work, family and friends:** Being committed to things that require energy and motivation, such as developing skills and relationships, is great but why not add to these experiences something that can indeed enhance your appreciation of them. You may feel at first that practicing mindfulness puts restrictions on the amount of time you spend with loved ones, or affects the emotional connection you share with them. However, mindful practices are designed to work in harmony with all aspects of your life, and part of your journey is to discover this harmony and bring it into being. Indeed, you inevitably find that the support of your loved ones can be an important part of your mindfulness practice.

Please take a seat, write down any obstacles in your mindfulness diary now, and then ask yourself this question and search deeply for the answer: 'Would I continue to look for ways of avoiding this exercise if my life really depended on it?' After all, research shows that stress and anxiety can have an adverse effect on your well-being and indeed your very lifespan. So, if you treat mindful exercises in the same way as regular cardiovascular exercise (that is, as something necessary to reduce harmful components in the body, only in this case stress rather than excess fat), perhaps this mindset can lend you further motivation.

Also, as a constant reminder, please write down the reasons why you decided to buy this book and discover MBCT. Were you close to getting depressed or burnt-out? Did you feel that life was no longer fun? Did you find yourself arguing with people you love, having no inspiration for your work, waking up with headaches or indigestion, or constantly catching colds? You probably hoped to improve your quality of life by reducing these harmful situations through practising mindfulness, so remind yourself of this fact from time to time.

To help further persuade yourself to commit to regular mindfulness practice, I invite you to try the following exercise:

1. **Imagine what you'd say to your best friend who had just been diagnosed with *burn-out* (that is, being off work or socially reclusive due to a nervous breakdown or high stress levels)?** How would you 'sell' mindfulness to her, based on what you've discovered so far? Think about the words you'd use, how you'd describe the effect it has had on you and how you think that it may help your friend.

2. **Make a note of what you come up with in your mindfulness diary.** Add to these notes as your experience increases.

3. **Look back on these notes whenever you feel unmotivated.** Doing so can help you remember what mindfulness does for you and the reasons you seek to practise it.

Suggesting changes to maintain motivation

Here are some of the most common problems people have shared with me when first establishing a mindfulness routine, along with how I responded:

✔ **'I often fall asleep when I do some of the meditations (such as the body scan from Chapter 4) – does this practice still count and does it have any benefits?'**

Of course it counts; you probably have (like 40 per cent of the adult population in the Western world) some sleep deficit. When I first started, I fell asleep every day for a whole month. You still experience aspects of the meditation even when not fully awake. Slowly but surely, train yourself to stay with the meditation. Perhaps experiment with different postures: sitting on a chair, sitting against a wall or even standing to experience *falling awake*. You can also try different times of the day.

A mat on the floor may be more helpful than your bed, because your body probably associates the bed with sleep.

✔ **'I experience aches and pains during the body scan meditation that I never noticed before.'**

Good point: you're intending to get to know the territory you inhabit a little better, so a few minor discomforts coming to light when you focus on them is only natural. You may just need to change position, or this experience can be an early warning sign for something that, if treated immediately, won't cause you major troubles. For example, a sore throat may be an early sign of a cold coming on, but if you take some vitamin C and slow down, your immune system can take care of it.

Fresh orange juice is the best source of vitamin C. If you choose to ingest it in the form of vitamin supplements, never exceed the recommended dose.

Never continue to perform an exercise in the same way if it causes you physical pain. None of these practices are in any way designed as physical muscle workouts, and thus any pain you experience may be a sign of an inappropriate posture or positioning of your body. Don't consider mindfulness as a test of endurance – preferably you want to feel at ease and pain-free throughout, so adjust your practices in order to nullify any pain. Pain isn't the same as a little discomfort, however. The latter eases after a while, but if it gets worse and becomes an ordeal the practice is no longer mindful and compassionate.

✔ **'I get bored after a few minutes.'**

Noticing that you're bored is a good sign. Research reveals that the brain is unable to multi-task and so if you know that you're bored, you're no longer doing the exercise. As soon as you notice boredom, agitation because of the to-do list in your mind, judgement about the sounds you hear or disturbing noises from outside your room, you can be sure that you're no longer fully engaged. Refocus your mind in the next now moment, and continue with the meditation.

Let go of any expectations or desires about what the mindfulness meditation can do for you, and certainly don't think that you're so flawed it can't work for you. (Check out the nearby sidebar 'Two cracking good ideas for maintaining your confidence' to lay that misconception to rest.) View your practice as a planted seed: the more you poke around and interfere, the less it can develop. Giving it the right conditions – peace and quiet, regular and frequent practice – is sufficient. Allow yourself to be surprised by the outcome. When you stop resisting unpleasant feelings, you can find that they drift away by themselves. When you stop trying to make something happen, a whole new world of unexpected experiences may become accessible.

Two cracking good ideas for maintaining your confidence

Never feel that you're somehow not good enough to practise mindfulness. In fact, your flaws often hold the key to improving your life. For example, in his song 'Anthem', Leonard Cohen writes: 'There is a crack in everything / That's how the light gets in'. Think about this beautiful message: an imperfection is in everything, and through these imperfections real beauty and worth can be appreciated. If you apply this thought to yourself, soon you realise that your cracks – your own foibles, flaws, faults, idiosyncrasies – are the stuff that make you human and the individual that you are. Not only that, but the people who love and care about you do so not in spite of but possibly *because* of these cracks. If they can love you, cracks and all, what's to stop you from loving yourself in the same way? So, every time you identify a crack in yourself, remember this line and invite in the light.

Here's a story to give you another angle from which to look at your flaws. An old lady leaves her cottage every morning and walks quite a distance to a pond to fetch water. She carries two pots, but one has a small crack and by the time she gets home a third of the water is missing from it. Her clever grandchild observes this fact and one day asks: 'Grandma, why don't you get another new pot? You walk so far and yet always lose a lot of water from the old cracked pot. I feel sorry for you.' The old lady takes her grandchild by the hand and says: 'Let me show you something.' She points to right side of the path, for she always carries the cracked pot with her left hand and so on the way home the cracked pot is on the right side of the path. She asks: 'Can you see a difference between the left and right side of the path?' The child gets excited and says: 'Yes, lots of flowers are growing on the right side and barely any on the left.' The old lady pats the child's head. 'Well done. The cracked pot is feeding the flowers on the right side and now we can enjoy their beauty.'

Maybe you can look at your own cracks with compassion and see what gifts they bring to the world inadvertently. My mother, for example, was never good at saving money, but her children and grandchildren always received many gifts from her.

A great idea is to write down a few helpful phrases or words of wisdom on sticky notes and dot them around your home where you come into contact with them on a daily basis, such as on the bathroom mirror, on the edge of your computer, on the fridge, or even on the front door so you see them when you go off to work. Here are a few suggestions, but please feel encouraged to find words and phrases that work for you – keep looking back over your mindfulness diary to find what inspired you:

- Just be.
- You are who you are.
- This too shall pass.
- Live now.

Having confidence in your practice

Practising MBCT is very much something that you develop to suit your own needs. Don't look for a right way to follow or a wrong way to avoid; in fact, the only wrong way is to be striving constantly for something that's correct and yet not feeling connected to it. Each practice is like an experiment in a laboratory and so every session varies. And as with an experiment, you're unlikely to see results immediately. I encourage you to be patient. To mix metaphors, like learning to play the violin, at first all you hear are screeches – kindly work through these screeches and let mindfulness unfold moment by moment.

Whether you enjoy an individual practice or not, be kind and give yourself the gift of doing something purely for your mental well-being during the course of a busy day.

Maintaining a productive attitude

To help you nourish the motivation you need to engage deeply in mindfulness practices, make a point of not underestimating the courage involved in discovering MBCT and making such a bold, positive step towards improvement in your life. The process is never going to be as easy as you perhaps think it should be. Sure, this book eases you into the process as fluidly as possible, but you still need a huge amount of willpower and self-belief to start and then maintain a new way of life.

Remind yourself from time to time what you want to improve about your outlook on the world, but don't focus on the negatives you're trying to escape (for example, 'I want to stop being so scared of commitment' or 'I don't want to be so angry at everyone'). Instead, focus on the positive notions that help give you a reason to continue (for example, 'I want to find contentment in my life' or 'I'd like to have a positive influence on myself and on others').

If at all possible, bring a playful attitude to this whole adventure. You're trying to find out how to live in the moment, letting go of past fears and regrets and connecting to being alive right now. That sounds like an exciting adventure to me!

 Reflect on and explore the life of an adventurer you admire: Shackleton, Livingstone, Columbus, and so on. Clearly they had obstacles to overcome, but their journeys were inspirational. Think about these obstacles, while focusing on the positives that arose by the way the individual overcame them.

Staying focused and committed

In this day and age, steering clear of anything except quick fix solutions is all too easy. Hungry? Get a takeaway. Lonely? Start chatting online or turn on the TV. The path you follow in this book, however, is a longer one of moment-to-moment awareness, of *being with* whatever comes up, of discovering how to respond wisely and not react automatically or too quickly. You may need a while to get your head round this approach and something more than vague interest to continue practising long term.

 Take encouragement from skills that you've taken up and developed in the past – no doubt improvement took time and effort. Think also about something that you've learned or studied just for self-fulfilment – at times it was no doubt difficult, but worth it in the end. The truth is that most worthwhile achievements require effort.

Coping with Setbacks, Pain and Emotions During Your Practice

I don't want to mislead you into believing that as long as you carry out your, say, 45 minutes a day of mindfulness practice, everything is going to proceed perfectly; in addition, striving too hard for goals usually causes the opposite result. I know from experience that, with practice, positive changes do occur, but I also know that these changes often arise unexpectedly, or at a time or in a way that you never anticipated.

When you're really open to the present moment and fully experience it, you can observe tremendous joy, but also pain, discomfort and frustration. Accepting this reality in advance is useful, because you can then prepare for it. Change is happening all the time and isn't necessarily good or bad in itself, but just a fact. When your practice is going well, certainly enjoy the moment and make the most if it, but don't kid yourself that all your problems are gone forever, because that way lies disappointment. But every time you feel that a mindfulness exercise wasn't good or deep enough, remember that you're not in a competition and that change means that the next practice may be totally different. You're not passive, however, and in this section I help you deal with certain setbacks that can arise during your practice and meditations.

I encourage you to act like a good friend towards yourself. When choosing to practise mindfulness, you're discovering a new way of being and existing, and potentially changing the rest of your life. You're experimenting with the whole idea of being human, which is bound to be a tough challenge at times as well as incredibly rewarding. Give yourself credit for taking on this task!

Trusting your own judgement

You are, and indeed have to be, the best judge of your own emotions. While performing exercises within your mindful routine, allow yourself to feel whatever you feel, but also be prepared to let these feelings go and continue with what you're doing rather than feeling the need to pause and reflect for too long.

Practising mindfulness isn't goal-oriented, so if an exercise doesn't get the desired outcome it doesn't matter; you're not meant to be striving for any particular outcome. Of course, most people want happiness and joy and often these mood states are welcome by-products of mindful living. On the other hand, the more aware you are, the more you also notice the small changes in mood – the ups and downs – and discover that you can trust yourself to deal with the different experiences of being alive, instead of having an artificial life experience.

When you attend to emotions that hurt, the best recipe isn't to want to change them but to find out how to understand and accept them. The less you resist, the less the pain persists. Letting go of striving for particular results may seem like an alien concept at first, but with time mindfulness may lead you to exactly this conclusion: let it be, let it be, let it be, let it be.

Accepting difficult emotions

The more aware you are, the more you feel pain or strong sensations that exist. Simply acknowledging discomfort during your practice, without immediately fixing it, is a new way to relate to it. If you can accept what is, without questioning why and how, the sooner you can pass it by.

Emotions and the brain

Often people avoid *experiencing* their bodies because they carry messages of suffering on a deep, subconcious level. In essence, the human brain comprises two hemispheres: left (that controls cognition and logic) and right (in charge of senses and emotions). At an early age, you mainly process emotions through a felt experience, while only from the age of ten (when most people begin secondary school) do you begin to transfer motor, sensory and cognitive information between the brain hemispheres. You may experience certain emotional moments as a child and not remember them clearly the way they really happened, meaning that they can surface unexpectedly during your practice. You then not only experience the emotional moments again, but are able to put them into context. This is not something to be afraid of, merely something to have in your awareness as a possible element of your practice and your journey into mindful living. See dealing with such subconscious emotional responses (that is, making them conscious) as an opportunity for growth and for healing.

Of course, stating this fact is easier than understanding and integrating it into your daily life. In this regard, mindfulness is a new way for you to experiment with life's challenges. Therefore, when you start re-engaging deeply with yourself, the possibility exists that you may unlock emotions stored in the brain from early experiences. Usually when this happens, you come to understand yourself better the more often you visit the painful site. For the scientific aspects of this process, read the nearby sidebar 'Emotions and the brain'.

If you become aware of an overwhelming memory of a traumatic incident during or after any mindfulness meditation I advise you to seek help from a qualified psychotherapist in order to gain additional support.

Knowing your physical limits

Physical discomforts can occur during your practice, for example as a result of poor posture. Please don't try to be a martyr. If you reach your limit and feel pain or discomfort that doesn't shift, simply change position or perhaps seek the advice of your GP. You may want to adjust only slightly or change from sitting to standing, or from sitting cross-legged on the floor to sitting with stretched-out legs and your back against a wall. Your only objective is to complete the whole practice, not to create pain.

Observing the Wandering Mind

Everybody who practises mindfulness meditation can tell you that the mind wanders and adopts thoughts of its own. Believe me, you get to know your mind intimately when you sit with it! If you follow the exercise and advice in this section, you'll soon know what I mean.

Think of your thoughts as streams or clouds of thinking – as ephemeral and not hard facts. So when your mind wanders, kindly observe where it goes to and then gently escort it back to your chosen anchor of awareness (something I describe in Chapter 4).

Regulating the breath: Mindful breathing exercise

Breath is your daily ally. Breath is with you all the time, even though you are often barely aware of it. Breathing is a gift which you may take for granted. People with bad colds or even worse, asthma, know how special it is to breathe freely. If you watch a baby its whole body seems to breathe.

Natural deep breathing can be soothing and calming, so the next practice endeavours to help you bring awareness to your breath. You're not trying to change and force it, but simply to allow it to unfold naturally while you pay attention to it. Notice how each breath has its own life span – some are longer and deeper, others are shorter. Please watch and change nothing, allowing your body to breathe naturally.

This exercise (which you can also listen to in Track Five) is similar in many respects to the early parts of the body scan meditation from Chapter 4, but features more focus on the relationship between the breath and the body. It takes 15 to 20 minutes. Prepare yourself in the usual way, by wearing comfortable clothes, keeping warm and sitting down in your meditation corner. When you're ready, please:

1. **Place yourself in a comfortable yet dignified posture, with your spine erect and self-supporting, chin slightly down. Allow your shoulders to rest in a comfortable, neutral position (neither falling forward, nor thrust backwards) so as not to inhibit your breathing in any way.** You may choose to experiment with sitting on a chair or on a rug and cushion on the floor, kneeling on the cushion or sitting with crossed legs. If

you're kneeling, please make sure that you put a soft towel underneath each shin; if you cross your legs, support your knees with small rolled-up towels or cushions, so that you sit on a tripod, so to speak.

2. **Close your eyes gently.** By all means, keep them in soft focus (half-closed) if you prefer.

3. **Bring your awareness to certain body sensations by focusing your attention on the touch or contact your body makes with the floor and whatever you're sitting on.** Spend a few minutes exploring these sensations.

4. **Turn your attention to your abdomen.** Feel it rising/expanding gently on the in-breath and falling/deflating on the out-breath.

5. **Focus on your breathing, being with each in-breath for its full duration and with each out-breath for its full duration, as if you're riding on the waves of your own breathing.** Sooner or later, you may also notice a little pause after each in-breath and after each out-breath. You may also become aware of the unique nature of each breath. Sometimes you breathe longer and deeper, which may signify a state of calmness, and at other times you may breathe shorter and shallower. No need to ponder on these differences; simply accept that each breath is a unique moment and just allow your body to breathe.

If your mind wanders off, as it probably will, gently and without criticism notice where it has wandered to and then gently bring your attention back to your abdomen and the feeling of the breath coming in and out. Even if this wandering happens a thousand times, gently and without judgement bring your mind back to the breath every time, no matter what it becomes preoccupied with. Becoming aware that your mind has wandered and bringing it back to the breath is just as important as remaining aware of the breath.

6. **Let go of the anchor of awareness (your breath) after about 15 minutes or so, and slowly focus on those parts of the body that are in touch with the surface you're sitting on.** Deeply ground yourself and feel rooted in your seat before gently opening your eyes.

Controlling your breathing in any way isn't necessary, because your body knows exactly how to breathe by itself. The only difference is that you've decided to experience each breath deeply. This attitude to your breathing allows you to savour the moment of being alive.

Write down anything you notice during or following this exercise in your mindfulness diary – only when you've finished the exercise, of course!

Exploring automatic thoughts and the connected feelings

Negative automatic thoughts (NATs) are thoughts that lurk just beneath the level of your awareness and can significantly affect your mood. By definition, these thoughts occur automatically and you aren't consciously aware of them. You need to become more aware of NATs, however, so that you can respond to them wisely (check out Chapter 7 for much more on this subject).

One example is when you wake up in the morning, look out of the window and suddenly feel down. A NAT may ramble along the lines 'oh no, another grey, rainy day', but this thought is so superficial that you aren't really aware of it. You are, however, aware of the emotional change that occurs soon after looking out of the window.

You can also experience a PAT (not the Postman, but a *positive automatic thought*). For example, when you find yourself running outside because snow is falling, and you absolutely mustn't miss it.

Please be mindful when NATs and PATs draw you away from your selected practice time. If your mindful exercises are regularly affected in this way and your practice never becomes a priority, the mindfulness seed may never grow.

Daily mindfulness practice helps you become more and more aware of your particular NATs, which then makes it much easier for you not to react to them but just let them pass by – or indeed, respond in a helpful way. Over time, you get to know your old friends, these mood downers, and simply say 'hi' and 'bye' to them.

Taking note of thoughts throughout the day

One way of bringing automatic thoughts into your conscious awareness is to write them down and note what effects they have on your body sensations, moods and other thoughts and actions. In this way you discover not only how to ignore them, but also how to work with them and use the gained insights for the future.

I invite you to complete a pleasant event diary for a week. Begin by writing down a pleasant event as soon as possible after the experience. Table 5-1 shows a layout you may want to use, along with a sample entry.

Table 5-1   Pleasant Events Diary Layout and Sample Entry

Day	The Experience	Were You Aware of the Pleasant Event?	How Did Your Body Feel?	What Moods, Feelings and Thoughts Came Up?	What Thoughts Do You Have Now While Writing?
Monday	I heard the sound of an ice-cream van passing by.	Yes, I was aware of some joyful vibration in my chest and a sense of giggles.	My body felt light and active.	I had an upbeat mood and the thought crossed my mind to buy a huge amount of ice-cream, which I did. I feel happy that I allowed myself to get a little mad and eat two whole por- tions of ice-cream.	I felt like a big kid; I enjoyed regressing a little.

Although the word pleasant may imply that this exercise is going to be all joy and laughter, please really take time on each column and see for yourself what discovering automatic thoughts can unveil.

You may, for example, wonder how a positive automatic thought (of the sort I describe in the preceding section) can ever have negative consequences. Well, take a look to the last column of Table 5-1: 'I felt like a big kid; I enjoyed regressing a little.' Instead of this positive reinforcement, imagine that you write: 'I hate myself and my fat tummy, and why can I never eat just enough and always overindulge.' By embracing this critical self-evaluation, you manage to turn the positive joy about the ice cream into a negative battle with guilt. The idea is not to simply dismiss all negative thoughts but to see all thoughts as having equal value – you should be able to enjoy eating some ice-cream, but also be aware that you shouldn't overindulge yourself. Finding the middle path that allows you to live your life without making excuses, ignoring the facts or beating yourself up about things is one of the key aspects of practicing mindfulness.

For a more subtle example, consider the following alternative to the entry in Table 5-1:

> *I heard the sound of an ice-cream van passing by. Yes, I was aware of some joyful vibration in my chest and a sense of giggles. My body felt light and active, I had an upbeat mood and the thought crossed my mind that as a child I always got an ice-cream from my mum when one of these vans passed by. But now I'm so much older, my mum is no longer with us and I would feel silly to go outside and buy one for myself. Thoughts now: I feel sad that this part of my life will never return and I'd much rather be a child than an adult.*

This example demonstrates how a positive event can trigger NATs and negative emotions, depending on how your mind orients itself. So writing down at least one pleasant thought each day and seeing how they unfold over a week is one way of becoming more familiar with the nature of your mind.

Reviewing Your Accomplishments This Week

Please consider the following questions to help assess how you're getting on with the practices in this chapter:

- ✔ What are your experiences of practising the sound meditation in the earlier 'Listening mindfully: A ten-minute sound meditation' section?

- ✔ Are you managing to maintain your motivation and a regular routine of mindfulness practice?

- ✔ Have you encountered any of the common problems that I describe in the earlier sections 'Dealing with Barriers to Practising Mindful Exercises' and 'Coping with Setbacks, Pain and Emotions During Your Practice'?

- ✔ When you realise that your mind is wandering during meditation, are you trying any of the techniques I suggest in the earlier section 'Observing the Wandering Mind'? If so, think about how well they're working.

Chapter 6

Setting Sail – Week Three: Developing Physical Awareness

Connecting deeply to the sensations in your body is a central (and essential) part of practising MBCT. As a young child you made this connection naturally, sharing any pain or discomfort with your parents or the adults looking after you. A bump on the head, a tummy ache, a grazed knee – you listened and responded by seeking compassion from another person without feeling guilty about doing so. And yet as an adult this connection between pain and seeking compassion seems to be lost. When you become aware of pain or discomfort now, you're likely to take a painkiller or grin and bear it until you get home, where a little gin and tonic is waiting for you. MBCT teaches you how to find compassion within yourself, so that you can look after yourself whilst experiencing pain or discomfort without resorting to quick fixes. MBCT also helps you to realise that nothing is wrong with seeking help and compassion from other people.

In this chapter you (re)discover your physical sensations, including using your senses to the full to notice and experience deeply the world around you. As part of this, I provide a brief but effective meditation to use in stressful situations. Also, I invite you to a session of formal mindful moving exercises to discover how your body feels and, less formally, how to move mindfully throughout the course of a whole day.

All I ask is that you bring a playful and curious attitude to this week's sessions, because they reconnect you to areas of your body that – except when they're hurting badly – you may have forgotten all about.

Getting Your Bearings on the Course

You may now have been practising mindfulness for three weeks, and so I ask that you take stock of where you are. No doubt you're getting to know what helps or hinders you: perhaps meditating first thing in the morning is your thing, while everybody is asleep, or just before your evening meal. Personalising your practice in such ways is fine and particularly important for the more physical exercises in this chapter; some people are fine with stretching in the morning whereas others are simply more physically ready later in the day.

If you don't live alone, try putting a notice on the door of your meditation room and asking kindly: 'Please don't disturb, I'm meditating.' Surprisingly, this often works. Also, as your mindfulness muscles start to grow and you notice more and more little details and hone this growth, I invite you to note it down in your mindfulness diary (see Chapter 4).

Whatever time of day works for you, I request that you practise this chapter's mindful movements (within your personal comfort range) for a minimum of ten minutes or longer every other day. In addition to that, your home practice at week three looks something like this:

- ✔ Carry out Chapter 4's body scan six times per week.

- ✔ Engage in a second practice, such as sitting with sound (from Chapter 5) or the breath (Chapter 4) (or a combination), for 10 to 15 minutes, ideally six times a week. Record your reactions in your diary if you find doing so helpful.

- ✔ Practise using the meditation for stressful moments (that I describe later in 'Finding the breathing space: An emergency meditation') from time to time so that this meditation is ready for use at a moment's notice.

- ✔ Choose one mindful everyday activity per day, varying them from what you did the previous week. (Chapters 4 and 5, and the later section 'Getting physically in touch with daily tasks', contain plenty of ideas.)

- ✔ Fill out an unpleasant-event diary for six days this week (of the sort I describe later in the section 'Making a Note of Unpleasant Events').

Results don't just happen; you have to make them happen by creating the right time and right space for meditation, ideally six times a week. Of course, you may consider practising more often if it feels right for you. (For all the necessary info on creating a peaceful, conducive environment for your practice and getting physically comfortable, flip to Chapter 4.)

Applying Mindfulness to Your Body's Senses

This section gives you the opportunity to develop the skill of seeing, feeling and listening more acutely and bringing awareness to all your physical senses. The body scan exercise from Chapter 4 gives you a flavour of this experience (and remains a regular part of your practice), but now you set sail for the territory of deeper sensing and feeling. Observation is the key to this section, using your body's senses to the full.

If you're strapped for time, I suggest writing down a list of activities you like but can easily give up for practising mindful meditation. The emphasis is on the word 'easily'.

Seeing mindfully: Making a short mind-movie

If you've ever fancied yourself as a film director, this brief viewing exercise is your chance to create a mini movie (on a really low budget!). You might watch TV often, or frequently notice billboards and other ads around you. Your visual sense is probably the most active one on a daily basis. But in this exercise I ask you to look at a microcosm of life. The longer you observe the little picture frame you've chosen, the more you'll notice and the more you'll really see what is there.

Please choose an outlook that you want to explore closely, such as through a window frame or door. I ask you to look at only that one view with awareness and curiosity. For example, you may look through a window frame at the view outside, watching only what comes into view without moving your eyes to search for something else. Let the moment dictate what you see and what forms your personal slice-of-life film.

You can choose to sit or stand. If standing, please opt for a relaxed posture, letting your shoulders hang loosely and bending your knees gently.

For the next ten minutes or so, see the world go by and really look with attention. Even if nothing much happens, you may start to notice minuscule details that otherwise you'd never have spotted: the branches on a tree, perhaps – an odd one that looks like a gnarled arm, or one that has no leaves. Ah, a sparrow is flying in and placing herself on the barren branch. Beyond the tree on the opposite side of the street is another window with some lovely flowers in the window boxes – yellow, purple and blue.

Allow this little movie to unfold and let yourself be surprised by how much you can see even when you're just looking through one window for ten minutes. I once chose a blank white wall and within ten minutes it became an abstract work of art, with tiny dabs, lines, dots and dimples!

Often a special, unexpected object may appear on your personal cinema screen. Instead of just thinking 'that's nice', see this event as an opportunity to practise mindfulness. For example, perhaps a classic car parks in the street. You can spend several minutes looking at its shape, colour, markings, striking accessories, and so on.

Getting physically in touch with daily tasks

As I discuss in Chapters 4 and 5, choosing a mindful everyday activity and experiencing it anew is a valuable part of your mindfulness practice. Ideally you can do one each day and they work particularly effectively with physical sensations. How about washing the dishes? Here's a lovely story told by the famous mindfulness teacher Thich Nhat Hanh. When he was a novice at the monastery in Vietnam, he had to wash around 90 breakfast bowls every day. They contained the residues of rice porridge, rather sticky stuff. As tools he had only cold water, rice husks and his bare hands. Often the washing up caused a lot of pain, maybe even cracked skin, by the time the job was completed, and yet he was able to experience the task as a whole in a pleasurable and exciting way when he thought about feeling the texture and shape of the objects he was washing up. All this required was a mindset of gentle curiosity and exploration, and with this the notion of washing up as a chore was gone.

You have many advantages over him, however, and can choose a wonderful, preferably organic, deliciously smelling washing-up liquid. When you next go shopping, spend a little time and choose one where the smell really tickles your nostrils. You can also carefully choose the sponge or cloth you intend to use, gloves or none. Then find the right temperature and you're ready to go. See whether you can really stay focused on each piece you wash up and use your sense of smell and touch for a washing-up feast!

Practise heightening your physical senses while carrying out any little everyday activity, because they can all help you to just be: stroking the cat, smelling herbs and spices in the kitchen, listening to the rain or wind, or the creaking steps in your home.

Finding the breathing space: An emergency meditation

One of the flaws of the human brain is that you can forget many a useful exercise when the going gets tough. In essence, naturally occurring stress-inducing hormones and chemicals affect areas of your memory so that you may not be able to remember the details of the mindfulness exercises designed to help you in these very situations. Therefore, practising this section's breathing space meditation at least three times a day is important, so that it becomes second nature for when you need it in a real-life situation. It can be useful to escape a foul mood or panicky feelings and help calm you before a stressful event, such as a presentation or an interview.

The breathing space provides a way to step out of autopilot mode and reconnect with reality: what is, right here, right now. Also, it helps you embrace the fact that every moment eventually passes, but that you should stay with this moment rather than avoid it and get lost in a state of anxiety and fear.

You can carry out this brief meditation anywhere, standing, sitting, kneeling, jogging, lying down . . . you name it. This short practise takes a maximum of three minutes to engage in, making it an effective tool in case of emergencies.

1. **Imagining the shape of an hourglass:** See how it starts wide, becomes narrow and eventually widens out again. In the same way, you begin this exercise with a broad awareness, focus into a narrow awareness, and then broaden out again, as you'll see in the next three steps.

2. **Growing awareness of what is:** Bring yourself into the present moment. Gently close your eyes and ask yourself:

   • What thoughts are going through my mind right now?

   • What feelings are present right now?

   • What sensations am I aware of in my body right now?

   Acknowledge everything, even unwanted thoughts and feelings.

3. **Focusing in:** Redirect your full awareness to the sensation of breathing; focus on each in- and out-breath as they come and go. Your breath is your anchor, helping you to stay in touch with the now. Breathe about ten mindful breaths.

4. **Expanding awareness:** Expand your sense of awareness to your entire self and integrate awareness of your body as a whole: consider the circumference of your body and sense the inhalation and exhalation from every pore of your body. Feel your feet firmly grounded on the floor.

Allowing awareness of sight, sound, breath and body

This 25-minute sitting meditation (a variation of which you can also listen to in Track Six) is a fusion of individual practices that I describe in Chapters 4 and 5. You start with the awareness of sight and sound, move to anchoring your awareness in the breath and finally focus on your body as a whole, even bringing awareness to discomfort or intense sensations in certain areas. Flip to Chapter 4 for how to make yourself comfortable and check your posture to ensure your safety and ease (particularly as the exercises become longer over the eight-week course).

1. **Sit in a comfortable posture with your spine erect and let your shoulders drop.** Close your eyes if doing so feels comfortable.

   As with all the sitting exercises, your aim is to adopt an erect and dignified posture, with your head, neck and back aligned vertically. This position is the physical equivalent of the inner attitudes of self-reliance, self-acceptance, patience and alertness that you're trying to cultivate.

2. **Bring your awareness to the sensations in your body.** Focus your attention on the sensations of touch and contact your body makes with the floor and whatever you're sitting on and spend a little while exploring these sensations, just as you do with Chapter 4's body scan.

3. **Focus your attention on your stomach, feeling it rise gently on the in-breath and fall on the out-breath.** Keep the focus on your breathing, being with each in-breath for its full duration and with each out-breath for its full duration. If you're sitting, this will feel more like your stomach is moving away from and towards your spine.

4. **Notice when your mind wanders off into thinking, pondering and worrying.** Softly note what took your attention away and then gently escort your focus back to your stomach and the feeling of the breath coming in and out. Repeat this process however many times it happens, no matter what the mind becomes preoccupied with. Congratulate yourself for noticing these wanderings because it means that you're being mindful.

5. **Focus on your breath and the sensation of your body touching the surface you're sitting on.** Expand your body awareness even further, noticing all the areas that are involved when breathing and even picturing all the cells of your body breathing in and out. This exercise is an invitation for you to explore the sensations in the body and the awareness of breathing. Slowly but surely you become your own guide and follow what intuitively helps your mind and body to settle.

From time to time some sensations in your body may appear intense or even uncomfortable, which naturally causes your attention to switch to this discomfort. By all means explore the discomfort – is its intensity continuous, does it come and go like waves? Then, breathe into it to see what unfolds. But if you start thinking too much about it and creating a story around the discomfort, I advise changing position and returning to the breath as your anchor of awareness.

As your mindfulness 'muscle' starts to grow with increased practice, you'll probably start to notice more and more little details. In order to sharpen and refine this growth, I invite you to note these observations in your mindfulness diary.

Engaging Your Body in Mindful Movement

Your body needs, yearns for and relishes movement and, even if it's not well in one or a few areas, doing simple movements shows you that probably a lot more is right than wrong with you. The point of movement is to provide a direct way to connect with your body, because that's where emotions often get stored – under the surface and without your awareness. For example, you may have suppressed feelings of anger which can explode without warning, affecting you and those around you; mindful movement can help you to get in touch with and release this anger.

The formal exercises in this section intend to show you that almost anybody can move their body mindfully. I take you through a few treasures of mini movements, and if you develop an appetite for more, check out *Yoga For Dummies* by Georg Feuerstein and Larry Payne (Wiley) to take this journey further.

Your body loves to move and will thank you for it!

Only engage in movements with which you feel comfortable. You can take these exercises really slowly and do several of them standing or sitting.

Discovering movement exercises

Many people see physical exercise as a chore, but it needn't be. The following exercises are here to show you how miraculous your body is, even if not everything is working perfectly. These exercises also show you how, with minimum effort, you can re-enter a sense of experiencing your body, noticing the subtle changes before and after each practice. Maybe you could bring an attitude of curiosity to these exercises, and see for yourself what this experience brings up.

All the formal exercises start with the standing Mountain Pose position of the following section.

Standing strong: Mountain Pose

This exercise strengthens your legs, improves posture and may help you feel like a mountain, both physically strong and mentally able to cope with events. When you feel ready, try the following:

1. **Position yourself with your feet hip-width apart.** By this statement, I mean that while standing your feet are within the frame of the pelvis (I'm not referring to the outer hip measurements you may use for buying trousers), arms by your side, palms facing in, gently touching your thighs.

2. **Take a few breaths in order to help you become aware of your breathing.** When you're exhaling, contract the pelvic floor muscles and lift them up until you feel a squeeze at the base of your buttocks, a physical sensation as if your sitting bones are coming closer, then release this squeeze as you inhale. This action supports the spine from below. Continue to breathe evenly in this way, drawing the abdominal muscles to your spine and at the same time lengthening the spine upward.

3. **Stand tall, with your spine erect and head lifted.** Breathe deeply and widely into your lungs, with each in-breath creating a sense of space in your whole chest area. With the exhalation, roll the shoulders up, back and down, releasing any tension that may be in your upper back.

4. **Lift your entire spine with each in-breath.** With each out-breath, gently draw your navel to the spine, feeling the support you're giving your lower back.

5. **Shift your weight first into the right leg, noticing what an empty left leg feels like, and then into the left leg.** Really notice the focus you need in order to do that.

Strengthening and energising arms and wrists

Adopt the opening stance of the preceding section and then proceed as follows:

1. **Move your arms forwards and up until they're parallel to the floor.** Keep standing in the Mountain Pose and feel the weight of your arms while mindfully breathing in and out.

2. **Start gently rotating your wrists in one direction for five times, followed by the opposite direction for five times.** Gently feel any changes and

sensations in your arms and wrists and entire body. Can you feel warmth, tingling, the muscles working to keep the weight of your arms suspended?

3. **Allow your arms to return slowly to the original position.** Breathe and stand in the Mountain Pose, noticing any changes in your entire body. Has your breathing accelerated? Are you aware of any changes in temperature? Does your body (or just your arms) feel more alive?

Relaxing your shoulders: Chicken Wings

This exercise releases tension in your shoulders and helps to increase flexibility in your shoulder joints. When ready:

1. **Stand in the Mountain Pose (from the earlier section 'Standing strong: Mountain Pose') and gently bend your arms at the elbows, placing your palms and fingers onto your shoulders.**

2. **Breathe in and, with every out-breath, rotate your folded-up hands (chicken wings) backwards.**

3. **Repeat five to ten times.**

Loosening your neck

Please place yourself into the opening Mountain Pose:

1. **Position your chin parallel to the floor and breathe in.** On the out-breath, gently turn (but don't tilt) your head towards the right shoulder, keeping your chin always parallel to the floor.

2. **Reach the point where the stretch comes to a natural end.** The breath takes you to the endpoint, which after a few rounds may extend naturally and without force. Then breathe in again and move your head towards the starting point in the middle, and on the out-breath move it towards the left shoulder.

3. **Repeat these gentle moves and stretches.** I suggest three to five times in each direction.

4. **Finish with your head in the middle and drop back into the Mountain Pose.** Really reach into your body and sense as best as you can any subtle changes you may become aware of: temperature, tingling, energy changes, and so on.

Massaging yourself: Qi Gong self-massage

This exercise is designed for energising and waking up your body:

1. **Take up the Mountain Pose, barely changing anything apart from bending your knees a little more.** Try as best as you can to stay loose and relaxed.

2. **Lift your left arm and start tapping your left hand and arm gently with your right hand.** Starting at your fingers, slowly move up your arm, tapping gently all the way up and around, taking time to do this action mindfully and not leaving out any area. Even tap gently under your arm pits to stimulate the glands and the shoulders as far as you can reach. Gently reverse the exercise on the opposite side of your body. Complete this process with both arms and hands.

3. **Continue tapping lightly the crown of your head.** I suggest using the tips of your fingers and both hands simultaneously, as if rain drops were falling on your head. Then gently massage the face, again with the tips of your fingers: forehead, temples, around the eyes, nose and sinus areas, lips and around the lips, chin and throat. Now pull your earlobes gently and massage between forefinger and thumb with a bit more vigour. Then continue tapping with both hands your chest area, stomach area, hips and buttocks. Thereafter, continue tapping the right leg and finish off with the left, so that you've gone round your body in a full circle.

4. **Gently rotate your upper body from left to right and vice versa, with arms dangling at your sides. Allow the momentum of your rotation to carry your arms in a swinging motion. Do this a few times before returning into stillness and the Mountain Pose.** I invite you to feel deeply into your body and sense anything you may become aware of. Notice your breathing, your skin, the temperature sensations and anything else that occurs.

Stretching yourself

Your body loves to move, so why not give it space for letting go and energising itself. If you're feeling adventurous and up to it, I include some stretching exercises in this section that you can add to your mindful movement practice. You can do these exercises at home and don't need to join a gym or buy special equipment.

Stretching helps you to lengthen and relax your muscles and is best done after engaging in a few warm-up practices. In the context of meditation, stretching is another way to get to know and appreciate your muscles and to notice if any tense areas need particular care.

The main purpose of all mindful movement practices is to reconnect with your body and to get to know it so well that you can recognise when any signals indicate mood change, tiredness and tension.

You can do all movements in this section, apart from the Cat Stretch, sitting down, and so carry them out even if you've limited mobility. But always take note of any pain because this pain is your body's way of letting you know when to stop. Only do exercises that feel comfortable and don't do any that induce fear.

Releasing tension in your back, spine, shoulders and neck: Cat stretches

Any cat owner can tell you that cats are expert stretchers! These stretches are designed to help your body achieve a limberness and free sense of movement like that of the cat.

1. **Begin on your hands and knees.** Form a box position with the frame of your body by placing your wrists directly under your shoulders and knees straight under your hips.

   If your wrists are vulnerable, roll up the edge of a mat or a towel and place your wrists on it. To protect your knees, place a small cushion or folded towel under them.

2. **Stretch in order to lengthen the entire spine from the top of your head to the tailbone.** When inhaling, feel your stomach moving away from the spine and with the exhalation draw the stomach muscles and navel up towards your spine.

3. **Repeat three more times and with each exhalation draw your navel more towards the spine.** Doing so creates the abdominal pressure you need to protect the lower back.

Another position, called the Angry Cat, is great for increasing the mobility of your spine.

If you've a lower back problem and/or neck issues, start with a small movement and slowly increase the range of movement.

The Angry Cat starts from the position in Step 1 of the Cat Stretch above on your hands and knees:

1. **Draw your navel up towards the spine, tucking the tailbone under, at the same time moving your chin to the chest.** You're now rounding the spine vertebra by vertebra into a C-shape as you bring your pubic bone and forehead closer, just like you've dropped yourself over a big beach ball.

2. **Begin to reverse the movement in Step 1 while exhaling.** As you release your stomach slowly and in a controlled way towards the floor, elongate your spine into a neutral position. Still inhaling, continue the move, lifting your chest and breastbone forward and up, and look up. Keep your arms strong and shoulder blades back and down, as if you're pocketing them in your back trousers.

3. **Repeat these actions six times (or whatever feels comfortable for you).** Keep your navel pressed towards the spine throughout the entire movement to protect your lower back. Don't bend your arms and keep your shoulder blades in the middle of your back as you round it into the C-shape and let them slide down in the reverse C-shape.

Pulling faces: Lion Pose

This exercise helps you feel powerful and in control. It's a great stretch for the tongue, many muscles in the face, throat muscles and tension in the chest, but you can use it to let go of tension throughout your body because relaxing the facial muscles has a positive effect all over. You may even giggle or laugh, which is the best antidote to anger and stress. When you feel ready:

1. **Begin on a chair or kneeling on the floor with a cushion between your legs.** Draw your navel towards the spine (which helps to support the lower back) and at the same time lengthen the spine vertebra by vertebra, straightening your body upwards.

2. **Inhale and allow the chest to expand, and on the exhalation roll the shoulders back and down (supporting the chest to stay open).** Draw the top of your head upwards towards the ceiling, with your palms resting on your thighs, facing down, elbows bent.

3. **Slide your palms towards the knees, gently hinging forward from your hips.** Keep your arms straight and stop this movement when your palms cup the knees.

4. **Press your palms against your knees and spread your fingers wide.** Inhale deeply through your nose, and exhale while opening your mouth wide without bringing tension to the jaw, stretching the tip of your tongue towards the chin as if you want to touch it, raising your eyebrows, and either rolling your eyes back and looking to the point between your eyebrows or looking towards the tip of your nose. Breathe out through the mouth with the sound 'ha' – similar to the roar of a lion – and then relax the facial muscles.

5. **Repeat the movement sequence twice more.** Then return to your starting position.

Avoid bending your arms when you're 'roaring'. Keep your shoulder blades down in the mid-back, and avoid tension in your jaw.

Activating your pelvic floor and back muscles: Palms Press

A stronger pelvic floor supports your bladder and intestines and may even help you to avoid becoming incontinent later on in life. When you feel ready:

1. **Sit on a box or a chair.** Place your feet parallel on the floor, with hips and knees at a 90-degree angle and your palms resting on your thighs, pointing towards the knees.

2. **Inhale, and when you're exhaling draw the navel to your spine, at the same time pressing your palms down onto your thighs.** This movement activates your pelvic floor muscles and supports you in lengthening the spine towards the ceiling.

3. **Repeat three to six times.** Then relax.

Keep your shoulders relaxed and in the mid-back. Avoid hunching them up and apply equal pressure on your palms.

Going for a stroll: Walking exercises

An everyday activity, and yet also a chance to move mindfully, is going for a mindful walk. In a *mindful walk,* you intend getting from A to B as with any walk but you decide to do every part of it mindfully and not use the time for planning or ruminating on anything that's occupying your mind. Your intention is to be fully present as soon as you make the first step and focus on everything you sense when your feet move onto a variety of surfaces. Furthermore, visually you take in any object that presents itself, however fleetingly, while also listening deeply to the sounds around you and perhaps the air that touches your face: is it moist, dry, warm or cold? You complete this practice when you arrive at point B.

Mindful walking means simply walking *and* knowing that you're walking.

A more formal alternative to a mindful walk is the following walking meditation in which, contrary to the previous walk, you're not trying to get anywhere. *Walking meditation* involves deliberately attending to the action of walking itself, and bringing your awareness to the sensations in your feet while you walk slowly across a room and back or from one end of your garden to the other:

1. **Find a stretch for walking forwards and back that's safe (you may want to try it with bare feet as long as you're indoors and know the walking territory).** All you need is about ten steps in each direction. You may feel more at ease if you choose a space where nobody else can see you.

2. **Start standing naturally and begin by shifting all your weight into your left leg while lifting the heel of the right foot.** The whole process may feel a little wobbly at the beginning but try your best to now shift the right, lifted foot forwards and gently place it down so that you complete a single step.

3. **Feel your body and notice where the weight has shifted to.** Feel the sensations in both feet; the right one that's mainly carrying you now and the left's emptier feel.

4. **Repeat the same motion with the left foot.** Notice that while you place the right foot down, the heel of the left foot starts peeling itself off from the floor.

5. **Shift your left foot forwards and place it down as well.** Again, the right foot has been waiting for this action and starts peeling its heel off as the left foot prints its stamp on the ground.

Alleviating physical discomfort

Many people become interested in mindfulness because they suffer from chronic or re-occurring pain, even during such everyday activities as walking. Mindfulness isn't a panacea or magic wand to take all your pain away, but discovering how to see your pain experience as just one of many can help you to stop adding to it, because you learn not to make things worse by tensing up. You may even become curious about the pain experience itself, by looking at it and observing its nature: is it really constant; are there different sensations to it; are there little pauses?

Over time, you may start to live your life rather than living around the pain. Check out Chapter 15 for much more on living with pain and what MBCT can do to help.

When the mind wanders away from your feet, and undoubtedly it does from time to time, just stop for a moment and reconnect to the purpose of this exercise.

You may notice that the notion of simply walking isn't as simple as it sounds. Whenever you slow down and do an activity as if for the first time, it seems to be much more complex and cumbersome. In fact, seeing toddlers learning to walk gives you an inkling of how difficult it is. They end up with a lot of bruises and frustrated efforts before they can do it properly. How wonderful that they don't give up easily!

The slower you walk, the more aware you become of the intrinsic details of walking: the lifting, shifting and placing, the weight moving from right to left, left to right, and so on. Walking meditation can bring home to you what a fantastic invention the human body really is and how wonderfully body and mind work together.

You need not look around your surroundings, just fix your eyes in front of you and don't look at your feet. The intention is to observe how your mind and body unite and deliver a step. Just feel how this action unfolds, that's all. Being with each step is enough, moment by moment.

You can practise mindful walking at a more natural pace too. After some practice, you can even try it when moving quickly. Perhaps experiment with mindful rushing!

You may at times observe the critical part of your mind rearing up, getting impatient with this whole practice, accusing you of wasting your time. At this point, you need to remind yourself that you're exercising your muscle of mindfulness, just like somebody training for a marathon who not only works out by running but also does stretches and muscle-strengthening exercises.

Observing Mindfulness in Daily Movement

All day long you move around and change position, from lying to sitting to standing, sitting, standing, sitting, standing and so on until you end up lying down again. Any of those movements can act like a ringing bell of mindfulness – an opportunity for you to practise informal mindfulness and become more truly aware while you shift and move your body each and every day.

 Try to observe deeply every experience you have – bearing in mind that every experience has two sides to it. For example, think about the possible benefits of observing boredom, anger or a bad body position. All these observations tell you something about your mind, your present state of emotion or what you perhaps need to change.

Getting up in the morning

When you first wake up, before you move, bring awareness to your breathing. You may even notice how your body connects to the bed you're sleeping in. Thereafter, sit up mindfully and stand up with awareness.

Proceed to walk with awareness to the bathroom, kitchen or wherever and really feel your feet lifting, shifting and placing. Observe how your body knows where to go, how to open doors, unscrew the toothpaste tube and so on. Everything in your life can become a mindfulness practice ground.

Preparing a mindful breakfast

People tend to be a lot more mindful about cooking when they're preparing a meal for friends. Now apply the same attitude of compassion and kindness when preparing your own breakfast.

When you prepare your cereal, really notice how you bend down or stretch up to fetch the bowl, how you perhaps choose which type you're having today, how you fetch it and transfer the right amount (not too little or too much: mindful eating starts here) into the bowl. Do you add milk or yoghurt or both? Notice how you fill the kettle with water and when it has boiled, prepare your favourite beverage.

Really take time over your breakfast, enjoying each spoonful of food and sip of drink. So much was involved in preparing it, now mindfully consume this labour of love and remember that eating a meal mindfully is just as viable a practice as sitting and focusing on your breath.

Helping yourself relax

Although mindfulness isn't primarily relaxation training, people often feel more relaxed when living a mindful existence:

✔ You stop constantly comparing yourself to others.

✔ You stop rushing.

✔ You respond mindfully instead of reacting automatically to any given situation.

✔ You give time to yourself just to be, and don't constantly have to do something.

✔ You're a participant in your own life, as opposed to just noticing that it happened while you were planning or ruminating on something else.

Exercising mindfully throughout the day

Ideally you need to do any mindful exercise you engage in (formal or informal) with complete attention. Mindless actions can lead to injury. I managed to break my big toe when doing a yoga headstand because I was showing off (to a new admirer) and didn't focus on mindfully coming down onto my whole foot. My weight landed on my big toe!

Be mindful when vacuuming, walking down the stairs and picking up heavy objects. Many household accidents can be avoided if people add a pinch of mindfulness to their moving activities. Ask yourself which movements you do every day – such as taking out the rubbish, bending, lifting, shopping and so on – and how you can be really in the moment while performing these activities.

Retiring for the night

Many people suffer from sleep deprivation or disorder. One principle problem is that they engage in many stimulating activities prior to going to bed. Research shows that your nervous system benefits from two hours of rest from TV, computers, mobiles and so on before you retire. How about using some of this time to create a little mindful ritual before going to bed?

✔ **Have a mindful bathroom routine:** Be truly present when brushing your teeth, having a relaxing bath, taking off make-up, putting on face cream (or whatever applies to you).

✔ **Put on your night clothes mindfully:** Close each button with awareness.

✔ **Lie down, appreciate your bed, maybe listen to calming music or read mindful poetry:** In your mind, let go of all your duties that can wait until tomorrow morning.

Making a Note of Unpleasant Events

In Chapter 5, I encourage you to maintain a diary of pleasant events for one week. No doubt this makes sense, because reminding yourself of your blessings and holding on to them is great way to motivate yourself and maintain your practice. But you may be surprised to discover that itemising *un*pleasant events is equally important.

Keeping an unpleasant events diary helps you not to simply shrug off the little or big discomforts and fears that happen throughout each day. They exist and often people suppress them and then wonder why they have an off day. The diary can assist you in uncovering what may have caused your low or angry mood. It may, however, also help you to see that little irritations are best let go of or are simply part of the human experience.

Complete your unpleasant event diary (one entry per day) along the lines of the illustration in Table 6-1. It offers you the chance to gain greater awareness of the thoughts, feelings and body sensations that occur in one unpleasant event each day. Observe and fill it in as soon as you can after the event and in detail, for example, use the actual words or metaphors and sensations that occur:

- ✔ What unpleasant events really affect you?
- ✔ What do you most *not* want to work through?
- ✔ When do you move into autopilot and what causes this to happen?

Table 6-1   Unpleasant Events Diary Layout and Sample Entry

Day	The Experience?	Were You Aware of the Unpleasant Event?	How Did Your Body Feel?	What Moods, Feelings and Thoughts Came Up?	What Thoughts Do You Have Now While Writing?
Monday	I heard the sound of an ambulance outside my home.	Yes, I was aware of an internal shiver.	My body felt off kilter and tense.	I had a worried mood and the thought crossed my mind that it may mean that my lovely neighbour needed to go to hospital. I felt tense in my chest and unable to move.	I still don't know what happened outside. I'm feeling more tense and more worried. Tomorrow I'll try to find out what happened and whether my neighbour is okay.

Reviewing Your Accomplishments This Week

To help you get the most from this chapter's meditations and practice, please reflect on these questions:

- ✔ How is your sensory meditation progressing (check out the earlier 'Applying Mindfulness to Your Body's Senses' section)?

- ✔ How are you getting on with the mindful movement exercises (from 'Engaging Your Body in Mindful Movement' earlier in this chapter)?

- ✔ Are you managing to vary your everyday mindfulness practices (see the earlier 'Observing Mindfulness in Daily Movement' section)?

- ✔ Did you complete your unpleasant event diary that I suggest in the preceding section, and if yes, has doing so altered your perception of difficult occurrences and situations?

Chapter 7

Weathering the Storm – Week Four: Dealing with Difficulties

In This Chapter

▶ Understanding stress

▶ Accepting the reality of negative thoughts

▶ Facing your anxieties

▶ Handling difficult thoughts

*I*n some ways stress is a modern plague, adversely affecting the lives of millions of people. If you're one of them, the first step to alleviating your symptoms is to comprehend the nature of the problem. Therefore, I introduce you to the world of stress, guiding you towards an understanding of the triggers and symptoms with which stress is often associated. Some of these symptoms resemble certain diseases – you may even have had a physician or someone at an A&E department check them out without being able to find an explanation for your discomfort.

Armed with this understanding, your mindfulness practice can then assist you in coping with and perhaps relieving these symptoms and the resulting anxiety. To this end, I provide several practical meditation exercises that use MBCT to tackle your negative, anxiety-inducing thoughts and deal with difficult and stressful worries.

Getting Your Bearings on the Course

Knowing where you are at each stage of the MBCT course is important. As those of you following the course step by step (which isn't compulsory, of course) are approaching the halfway point of the eight-week programme, I suggest asking yourself how it has served you, how you can make better use of it and to what areas you may want to pay more attention. Keep in mind your original trigger for buying this book – what did you want to change? – so that you don't forget why you made this resolution for the future.

Take the time to remind yourself what you're discovering, and assess what you need to do to get the most from the rest of the course:

✔ Re-familiarise yourself with the formal practices that I describe in Chapters 4, 5 and 6.

✔ Ensure that your ideal meditation spot is making your meditation as private, enjoyable and comfortable as possible (check out Chapter 4).

✔ Be sure to carve out enough time for your mindfulness practice and make good use of your mindfulness diary (see Chapter 4), noting down after each exercise what issues and thoughts arise for you, what surprises you and what you definitely don't want to forget.

✔ See whether you can discern any patterns by asking the following questions to help focus your practice on your own requirements:

- Do particular exercises always seem to help you in some way whereas others seem like a chore? Why do you think this is?

- Have you managed to do one everyday activity (of the sort I introduce you to in Chapter 4) in a mindful manner on a regular basis? If not, stop reading now for just five minutes and try the following exercise before continuing:

1. Before you commence, feel into your body, sensing any feelings of stress or anxiety you have at this very moment. Now go and make yourself a cup of tea or coffee to enjoy whilst you read.

2. Listen to the sound of the water boiling in the kettle.

3. Observe and feel how your hands open the jar containing the tea or coffee, smelling the tea or coffee as you put it into the cup.

4. Notice how your hand grips the kettle and pours the hot water into the cup, watching the rising steam and smelling the aroma.

5. Carry the cup back to the place where you're reading, and notice how you sit down and make yourself comfortable.

6. Observe every action you perform in order to get the cup to your mouth before smelling it and taking that first glorious sip. With each sip, allow yourself a deep, satisfied sigh.

7. Feel into yourself again. Try to sense whether or not you still feel the same amount of stress or anxiety as before. Maybe you still feel anxious, but also feel slightly more grounded or able to relax now that you have a cup of a comforting, hot drink in your hands. Don't try to judge how effective this exercise has been at this point; merely observe, make a note in your diary, then continue reading.

- Have you or your friends and family noticed any mood or behaviour changes in you?

- • Are you finding that you make little use of your mindfulness diary? If so, ask yourself why and consider whether writing in it more often would be useful.

✔ Be proud of your achievements up to now!

Exploring and Explaining Stress

[F]or there is neither good nor bad, but thinking makes it so.

—William Shakespeare

Man is not disturbed by things but by how he views them!

—Epictectus

You experience stress when you can no longer meet the demands placed on you, perhaps because you can't tackle the large number of challenges involved or you think that you lack the necessary skills to meet and accomplish what's required. This overload causes your body to release certain chemicals, which in the short term may help you function better, but in the long term are very destructive for your body and mind.

As the quotes that open this section imply, a lot of stress is triggered by *perceived* threats, such as 'being found out as not good enough' for a job or relationship. Thus, any negative mental patterns create a warlike state inside you. Other factors also feed into the stress response, such as environmental triggers (such as air pollution) and genetic predisposition.

Some researchers talk about 'good' and 'bad' stress, but I prefer to make a clear distinction between the following:

✔ **Pressure** indicates a demand but also your ability to meet it.

✔ **Stress** indicates an overwhelming demand that you feel unable to meet and that, in my opinion, is never good for you.

Grasping the nature of stress

The fact that the human body can swiftly respond to threat is fantastic and partly why people have survived. Humans may not be equipped with protective body armour, like a hard skin or a shell, or with razor-sharp claws or teeth, but they do have highly evolved brains that can prevent them from getting killed by making life-saving decisions in a split second. On the other hand, Mother Nature doesn't seem to care much whether humans feel at peace or not! Whereas zebras, for example, run for their lives when lions attack, but after one is captured and is being devoured, the others immediately forget and start grazing again.

Because humans don't seem to be able to differentiate well between real danger and perceived danger, many people find themselves on high alert and in a state of agitation most of the time, which doesn't create a calm and settled life. So they survive, but suffer. Great, isn't it! If you're curious about what havoc ongoing stress chemicals can cause in your brain and body, read the sidebar 'Stress causes real physical problems'.

Stress causes real physical problems

Humans have two nervous systems:

- The *parasympathetic nervous system* (PNS) is what people ideally want to operate in as often as possible; it is the one in which they feel relaxed, at peace and in equilibrium.

- The *sympathetic nervous system* (SNS) is the one used when people feel under threat. The SNS is switched on for survival and enables you to be swift, effective and purposeful. Breathing becomes rapid, and your lungs take in more oxygen. Blood flow increases, strengthening the muscles, lungs and brain to deal with short-term added demands. You can run faster or hit harder. This system focuses on areas that may get wounded in a fight, sending the immune-boosting troops to the body's front lines where injury or infection is most likely to occur, such as the skin and the lymph nodes.

Often, however, the SNS gets switched on many times each day, even though no danger is present, and remains switched on if you feel stressed a lot of the time, adversely affecting your heart, lungs and blood circulation. When the body prepares to defend injury, other areas are left unprotected and so long-term stress can be responsible for respiratory and other infections.

These are physical problems that long-term SNS activation can cause, perpetuate or exacerbate:

- Gastrointestinal problems, frequent urination and diarrhoea

- Lupus, multiple sclerosis, thyroid dysfunction, chronic fatigue syndrome and frequent infections of the respiratory tract, the skin and the digestive system

- Depression, suicidal thoughts and burn-out (see the later section 'Hearing the good news')

- Lack of energy and motivation, sleep disorders, appetite disruption, obesity/diabetes, psoriasis, fibromyalgia, chronic pain, high blood pressure and infertility

- Increased fear/negativity, becoming stuck in old, fearful ways of thinking, impaired memory and an inability to concentrate and make decisions

In short, long-term stress causes damage to almost all regions of your body and mind.

Hearing the good news

The good news is that the MBCT practices that I describe can alleviate the symptoms of chronic stress and allow your brain and body to heal and return to vitality. Grasping just how your body and mind systems strongly connect under pressure (the human survival system) is key to accepting how you can use mindfulness interventions to avoid and treat stress symptoms. Mindfulness tools enable you to accept more readily what life brings and to deal with the challenges in the best way possible.

You have to allow for and acknowledge stress before you can start to think about how to respond to it wisely. Here are two serious potential results of stress if you leave it untreated:

- ✔ **Burn-out** is caused by a real or perceived overload of responsibilities and is considered the most debilitating consequence of long-term stress. It's a complete breakdown of psychological responses and abilities and can often be accompanied by physiological diseases (see the sidebar 'Stress causes real physical problems' for details).

- ✔ **Rust-out** is caused by a lack of direction or purpose in your work and/ or life. The psychological and physiological reactions are similar to the effects of burn-out. The trigger, however, is often connected to feeling strongly unvalued, or staying in a job only out of fear rather than finding another opportunity.

In general, you react to experiences in one of three ways:

- ✔ **Indifference:** Switching off from the present moment and going somewhere else in your head (daydreaming, remembering a holiday, planning exciting trips for the future, and so on). Nothing is wrong intrinsically with switching off, but it doesn't help the problem go away. For example, that difficult conversation or telephone call still needs to be done and becomes harder the longer you postpone it.

- ✔ **Attachment:** Wanting to hold on to the current experience or desiring experiences that you aren't having right now. Enjoying yourself is absolutely fine, but feeling that every similar future experience must be just as fantastic or even better isn't so great. For example, every future meal may not be just as delicious as the current one and every time you kiss your beloved can't realistically be as intense and breathtaking as the first time.

- ✔ **Aversion:** Wanting to get rid of experiences that you're having right now or avoid experiences that may be coming along that you don't want. For example, standing in a long airport queue before flying may be uncomfortable, but do you really want to give up travelling altogether just because queuing is involved? You may then have to stop going on any public transport, shrinking your life experience and even leading to *agoraphobia* (fear of large or public spaces).

Instead, see having to queue anywhere as an excellent opportunity to practise mindful breathing (which I explain in Chapter 5).

Each of these three ways of reacting can cause problems, particularly the tendency to react to unpleasant feelings with aversion. The starting point to tackling these reactions is to become more aware of your experience so that you can respond mindfully rather than react automatically.

Avoiding aspects of life you find difficult usually worsens them when they come round again. Instead, remind yourself that everything changes on an ongoing basis and so everything passes in time. For more on the connection between negative thinking and body sensations and emotions, read about keeping an unpleasant events diary in Chapter 6.

Dealing with Unhelpful Thoughts

I introduce you to unhelpful negative automatic thoughts (NATs) that can lead to destructive emotions in Chapter 5. You may have picked them up in childhood by copying a parent or being repeatedly told something and believing it to be true. NATs that lead to ruminations are a major trigger for chronic stress and anxiety. Ignoring them allows them to fester so you need to bring NATs into your conscious awareness; only then can you let them go for good, change them or just let them be but not act on them.

To help you identify stress-causing NATs that you may be harbouring, the following list itemises a few common ones. Many are uncompromising all-or-nothing statements that offer no grey area. Consider taking time to peruse the thoughts and if you spot one that you recognise in your own thinking, ask yourself whether it can really be true and whether you've ever seen any of your friends or family being as bad as you think you are:

- ✔ No one understands me or my suffering.
- ✔ I wish I wasn't so pathetic.
- ✔ My life's going nowhere.
- ✔ Nothing feels fun anymore.
- ✔ I'm so bored with everything.
- ✔ What's wrong with me?
- ✔ I wish I were somewhere else.
- ✔ I wish I could just vanish.

- ✔ I can't sort out my life.
- ✔ I'm totally worthless.
- ✔ I'm a failure.
- ✔ I'll never make it.
- ✔ I feel so hopeless.
- ✔ I've had enough.
- ✔ I don't think I can do this anymore.
- ✔ It's just not worth carrying on.

If you find yourself regularly experiencing extremely dark thoughts, along the lines of the last five in this list, please see your GP – urgently. If he prescribes medication, please accept it. Only when you've been able to gain professional help to alleviate these thoughts should you continue learning and practicing MBCT on your own.

Being with negative thoughts

I hope that seeing the negative statements in the preceding section gives you an insight into negative thinking. If you engage in even some of these thinking patterns, you're sure to perceive your life as one huge challenge and as a result feel anxious and stressed. But at least knowing that everyone shares such negative thoughts is also a little comforting.

The more mindful you become of your NATs, the less likely you are to hold on to them. So, in your diary, kindly write down any NATs from the list in the preceding section that apply to you and add others that you catch yourself thinking. You can also try the following meditation, where you look at your thoughts and let them pass by:

1. **Kindly sit down in your preferred meditation place and give yourself 15 to 20 minutes.**

2. **Wrap a shawl around you and sit in a dignified, upright posture.**

3. **Bring your awareness to your breathing. Allow your body to breathe naturally, neither deliberately lengthening nor deepening your breaths. Just observe each breath as it enters your body, travels through it and leaves through your nostrils (or mouth if that feels more comfortable).**

4. **Feel your body's connection points to the chair and floor and see whether this helps you to settle more and more.**

5. **Keep observing your natural breathing. Breath in each in-breath for its whole duration and each out-breath for its whole duration.**

6. **After a while, when you feel ready, allow your thoughts to freely arise: maybe see them as clouds in the sky or leaves in a river.**

   One moment your thoughts are here and then they are gone. The invitation here is to look at and relate to your thoughts as an external observer, without judging them or believing their content, as best as you can. Whether your thoughts are true or not is not important. For now, all you're trying to engage in is observing these thoughts and then letting them pass on.

   Should some of your thoughts be difficult or fear-provoking, kindly remember that thoughts are not facts. Thoughts occur, but they are not permanent or necessarily true.

7. **Eventually close the thought-window and return for a few more minutes to observing the in- and out-breath.**

   If giving your NATs up completely appears too difficult, perhaps try to modify and soften them, in order to open spaces in your mind where new ways of thinking can grow. For example, instead of saying, 'I can't sort out my life', tentatively state, 'It's difficult, but I'm attempting to sort out my life step by step. Practising the exercises in this book is step one.'

The power of compassion

Here's a true story about Sue, who was suffering from a degenerative muscle disease. Moving was becoming more and more difficult for her and the ongoing chronic pain had made her a bitter woman. One day she arranged an appointment to see a Buddhist monk and healer, with high hopes of getting back to being mobile and free of pain. She told the monk her sad story and he listened attentively. When she finished he didn't pray, chant or put his healing hands on her. He just said, 'If you want to be well again, make sure that you help somebody who's suffering every day.' Well, Sue was beside herself with anger and resentment and left in a huff.

On her way home, she went shopping in her electric wheelchair. At the checkout, supporting a basket of purchases on her lap, she became aware of a highly strung customer behind her. This woman was constantly on her mobile phone trying to rearrange appointments, tutting a lot and muttering that she always ended up in the slowest queue. Soon Sue noticed that people were staring at this frantic creature and the pale cashier was getting anxious about serving her. Sue doesn't know what compelled her to turn round and offer to let the woman go ahead of her in the queue; but she did and the woman's energy changed completely. She accepted Sue's offer, saying that Sue had saved her life, was the kindest person she'd ever come across in her life and so on. Everyone in the store was gob-smacked, not least the cashier, and after the woman paid and left people started applauding and cheering Sue until she lefte. On the way home Sue noticed that she felt less pain and a kind of joy; she remembered the monk's words and smiled.

Sue kept up the good deeds, her symptoms reduced week by week and she was repeatedly touched by the difference a kind deed can make. The monk had seen how Sue had spun a web of sadness and self-pity around herself. He knew that she needed to get out of her much-reduced life that revolved only around her sickness and start living again, engaging with others to see that, as well as suffering, gladness also exists in the world.

An essential aspect of mindfulness is compassion for yourself and others. Resting with your negative thoughts during mindfulness exercises helps you to see that nobody is perfect and that you're not as bad as you may think. The more you feed this kind of awareness, the less likely you are to be a harsh critic of yourself. The result is a natural, gentle 'letting go' of negative thinking and a slow broadening of your perception.

Creating more helpful thoughts

A little dose of awareness and compassion engages your mind in developing a more helpful mental outlook. Over time you become an expert on which thoughts sustain you positively and which ones disrupt and sadden you, helping you to reduce the amount of stress and anxiety these thoughts cause.

Please consider taking some time to examine your favourite nasty NATs. Mindfully and with compassion look at the opposite side of each one. For example, if in relation to a situation your thought is 'I'll never make it', instead tell yourself 'I often do make it' and think of evidence to support this positive thought. Similarly, you can flip 'I'm a failure' into 'I often manage things; for example, 'I'm doing well with my mindfulness practice'.

Addressing Your Anxiety Demons

This section is about approaching anxiety or anxiety-provoking tasks – finding out how to identify and rest with the associated thoughts rather than challenging them or reacting with aversion (check out the earlier 'Hearing the good news' section for more on reactions). I encourage you, initially as an experiment, to accept anxious thoughts for what they are: figments of your imagination and very rarely facts. The mindful approach to thinking is to allow thoughts to arise, acknowledge that they're there, and see what happens when you stop resisting them, and simply observe them – just like choosing to hear and interpret the ticking of a clock or the dripping of a tap as a welcome, repetitive, soothing sound to help you drift off to sleep, instead of as a pain in the neck.

Speak to a number of people who experienced a challenging event together – for example, escaping from a hotel when the fire alarm rang in the middle of the night. Ask what they remember most about the challenging event and in all likelihood you'll get a whole bunch of different answers. Each individual has a different perception, awareness, memory, and so on. In the same way, thoughts are no indication for truth or reality. Negative thoughts have the tendency to stick like Velcro to your memory pad. Furthermore, some people like to embellish the truth. Their escape from the hotel might well sound like escaping from a towering inferno even if the whole thing was just caused by somebody smoking a cigarette near a fire detector.

Please select an activity that you've been intending to do forever but that you avoided because you were scared of it. This could perhaps be something like trying to learn to swim. In this example, you could see whether you might be able to walk into a pool until the water reaches your neck, and then gently allow your feet to let go of the ground just for a few seconds. Remember the ground is always there. Do it again and again until you might swim for a minute in the direction of the shallow water. If not the first time, then maybe the second or third time round you might find the strength to do it. Your main objective here is to give yourself a chance to apply a new method to an old pattern you've been stuck with. I invite you to do something different because changing your behaviour is easier than changing an old negative thought. By changing an old fear that holds on to old thinking and feeling patterns, you may arrive at a sense of achievement and break free from the clutches of anxiety. This in turn will positively impact on your thoughts and feelings.

Here are a couple of other ideas to stimulate your imagination and to break a habit that is no longer serving you:

- **Eating spaghetti with chopsticks:** This may sound like a weird suggestion, but from my own experience of living in China, eating with chopsticks really does change the taste of food. The air flow intensifies the taste. Just as red wine tastes better when exposed to air, spaghetti is similarly improved.

  I suggest you do this exercise on your own, so as not to feel self-conscious or embarrassed; you may make a mess!

- **Drinking juice or water with a straw:** The straw touches your lips and they contain some of the most sensitive skin of your whole body. Just like children sucking on a dummy or their thumb, adults smoking cigarettes and people biting their lips when nervous, sucking and stimulating the lip skin creates a soothing effect. For self-soothing, a straw seems the least harmful option.

Attending to an anchor of awareness – or two

The main purpose of much mindfulness meditation is to keep your attention on your anchor of awareness – your breath, a view or a sound – but no rule says that you have to stay with just one anchor for a whole practice. In this ten-minute meditation exercise I request that you experiment with finding a visual viewing point, focusing on it for a while and then switching to the awareness of a sound:

1. **Select an object to focus on.** Maybe select something that at first sight would not be overwhelmingly beautiful. Make it something small or neutral that only gets your attention because you choose to focus on it. See what you become aware of when you focus, such as the intricate little details you would ordinarily miss.

2. **After some minutes, choose to switch your attention to listening to a sound, any sound.** You need not listen out for anything in particular, or judge the sound. Simply hear the sounds coming from inside or outside of the place where you're practising.

3. **After some further minutes, return to viewing the object.** Notice whether, now you've switched to viewing again, there are any changes in your perception and whether your mood or body sensations are different in any way.

4. **Experiment and see whether switching enables you to stay away from thinking, worrying and planning.** This may help you to be just a little more deeply engaged with your senses. The more you focus on your senses, the easier you may find it to let go of constant thinking.

The more you disengage from your worrying mind and focus on what is in front of you, the less you feed your mind with thoughts that create higher levels of anxiety.

Using mindfulness with unpleasant tasks

In Chapters 4, 5 and 6 I encourage you to transfer the skills you discover in mindfulness meditation to everyday activities, such as brushing your teeth or washing up. If you did so, I think that I'm safe in assuming that you mainly chose things that you have to do anyway, or things that you like doing. Mindfulness, however, can help you break free from old beliefs about disliking, as well as liking, certain activities. By approaching them mindfully, you may discover that a task you thought you hated can actually be pleasurable, or at least neutral. For example, if washing the dishes has always been an annoying chore for you, you may find that by engaging in it in a new, mindful way, it becomes a less irritating and even therapeutic activity.

As part of combating the anxiety of unpleasant jobs, I now ask you to consider applying this same attitude to something you usually avoid doing (or don't do at all) because you so strongly dislike it: for example, driving or travelling to work in the rush-hour, changing dirty nappies (urgh!), cleaning the toilet or the oven, ironing shirts, phoning somebody you'd rather not talk to, doing your tax returns and so on. This practice helps you to overcome any anxiety that is fed by procrastinating from jobs that you need to do. (Rest assured, you're not alone – nobody on this planet only has joyful actions to perform!)

Tackling two problems, step by step

One of my clients, who suffered from social anxiety, wanted to do some home practice that would tackle two problems at the same time. She made a contract with herself that went something like this: 'I will invite my neighbour for a cup of tea. If I fail to do this, I have to clean my toilet every day for a whole week.'

My client did fail to invite her neighbour over and thus started her penalty. She felt very anxious the first time round, but noticed that every day she cleaned her toilet, the task felt less unpleasant. She mindfully focused on taking one step at a time and by the end of the week was no longer anxious and rather liked the fact that she had overcome one of her anxieties. This left her with only one problem, and – guess what – on day six she had already put an invite for cake and tea in her neighbour's letter box.

When you realise that anxiety is often based on an erroneous thought, you can undo the unhelpful behavior, step by step.

Bring the lightness of touch of your mindfulness practice to these challenging activities and see whether it changes your experience at all. If you think that such activities can't be transformed, read the sidebar 'Accepting the itch' and then see whether you can respond to anything cumbersome and unpleasant in your life differently, with more ease and less pressure. Try doing so a few times and observe how adopting a matter-of-fact attitude can really reduce difficult feelings. Maybe allow a little humour to enter your awareness and be open to the idea of doing something in a new way.

Coping with Troublesome Thoughts

In this section you start to gently address some of the difficult stressful issues that may have caused you to turn towards MBCT in the first place, particularly discovering how to cope with stress-producing thoughts. I encourage you to move forwards one step at a time into these sometimes longer and perhaps more challenging meditations. For this reason, I suggest that you're familiar with at least some of the meditations and exercises in Chapters 4 to 6, which act like a warm-up. In Chapter 4 I introduce you to finding your practice space and how to make yourself comfortable, and in Chapter 6 you look at the basics of sitting. Here, you use these skills for the start of your meditation, but after settling comfortably and focusing on your breathing, you slowly expand the practice and actually invite thoughts to arise in your awareness.

Whereas in many of the meditations in Chapters 4 and 6 I encourage you to let go of thoughts, in this section I ask you to look straight at them, because what you resist persists. I ask you to let go of resistance and to feel the fear if it arises. The purpose of actually being with thoughts and neither letting them go nor struggling with them is to objectively (as much as possible) look at the nature of your thoughts without needing to fear them or follow them. By actually staying with your thoughts you may come to understand that thoughts are not facts, that you're more in control than you may have previously believed and that your fear response was much greater than perhaps was reasonable or necessary.

In general, thoughts have a tendency to take over. Ideally, you want your thoughts to be like obedient passengers in your bus of life, but sadly they are rarely that well behaved. They get up from their seats, rush around the bus and try to take over the driver's seat from you! No wonder they make you stressed. But you're not going to let this happen any longer. To help, I introduce you to a meditation that gives you the power to look at your thoughts, get close to them, feel their power and intensity, but not act on them immediately, secure in the knowledge that like an unpleasant sound, they will pass. However uncomfortable they may be, you discover how to notice such thoughts, give them a name and put them in their place so that you remain in the driver's seat.

Tracing your stressful thought patterns

One of the reasons why I suggest that you've practised mindfulness for a couple of weeks before acting on this section is that you need to have become consciously aware of your most common obstructive thoughts. The observations in your mindfulness diary (which I describe keeping in Chapter 4) are invaluable here, allowing you to look at which thoughts cause you to feel down, stressed, anxious or unworthy.

Accepting the itch

A woman attended one of my courses suffering from severe eczema. She had to go through a cumbersome daily routine of putting ointment on her whole body. She decided to bring mindfulness to this activity. After some days, she says she started noticing more feelings of kindness and gratitude towards the fact that she was alive and that she'd been given a remedy to help improve her life whenever she applied the cream. She began to see that it kept her skin from cracking, itching and burning. She also noticed that she worried less about the time the process took and stopped putting herself under pressure to get it over with. The chore slowly changed to a comforting experience that was no longer an annoying burden.

Review your diary and see which thoughts or entries gave you the idea that a certain exercise wasn't working for you or that all this mindfulness stuff is a waste of time. Observe which thoughts lead to which negative feelings, and if possible how these connect to form a chain that holds you down, tying you to the experience of suffering. If you find negative entries, read them and then kindly go back to the experiences you had in those entries, perhaps engaging in the same activities again but from a more mindful perspective. This way, you're able to change your focus when you look at entries that refer to negative experiences and you're able to identify how, through mindfulness practice, you're able to have a different timbre of experience – a neutral one or even a pleasant one.

Looking at the overall tapestry of your experience gives you a real insight into how your mind works, the changeability of experiences and the newness of each moment (even throughout the same practice).

Sitting with difficult thoughts

The meditation in this section (and in Track Seven) is one in which you invite thoughts to arise. This approach is decidedly different from allowing thoughts to rumble on, draw you into some kind of story and so develop significance because you remain in control. Instead, here you look at your thoughts as if you're an external observer, seeing them for what they are: events of the mind, and not necessarily true, false or important in any way.

Kindly start this practice with thoughts that may be a nuisance but that don't totally unbalance you. You start with the easy thoughts first and work your way towards more challenging ones. If you notice shortness of breath, heart palpitations or sweating, kindly bring your awareness back to just listening to sounds or feeling connected to the ground. Work gently and with compassion. If an issue arises out of the blue – an issue that you'd buried for a while – I recommend seeking therapeutic help.

To achieve a detached position, I suggest a few meditation frameworks that allow you to observe the thoughts without needing to act or react:

✔ **You're watching your thoughts as clouds in the sky.** They're there one moment and then slowly passing through your awareness.

✔ **You're standing on a bridge across a river.** Watch leaves representing your thoughts floating beneath you and away.

✔ **You're looking at your thoughts written on individual balloons you're holding.** Read each one and then let it go and float away. Repeat with the next balloon, and so on.

✔ **You're watching a presentation in which each slide represents a thought.** When you've taken it in, click on to the next slide.

✔ **You're in a theatre.** Actors representing your thoughts come for an audition; listen to each briefly, thank them and move on to the next.

✔ **You're in a sushi bar.** On the conveyor belt, you observe the little plates passing. Each plate has a thought written on it; let it pass by even if it returns after a while.

✔ **You're standing at a train station watching a long train go by.** Each carriage has one of your thoughts written on it.

If you prefer, create your own metaphor for acknowledging your thoughts but not getting involved with them. When you have a framework in mind, kindly proceed as follows:

1. **Begin your meditation as usual.** Sit in your meditation corner, having decided how long you'll spend meditating and having set an alarm clock for helping you to finish on time.

2. **Gently close your eyes, if this feels ok for you. Now start focusing on a sense of your body as a whole. Bring awareness to the space you're taking up and the connection points that you can feel between your body and the ground or chair you're sitting on.**

   With time you may notice your mind settling and focusing more and more on your chosen anchor of attention, such as sound or body awareness. You may even focus on the skin, the largest organ of your body, and how it feels, whether it is cool or warm and whether the differences in temperature are the same on both sides of your body.

3. **Allow thoughts to arise in your awareness.** Thoughts may arise or they may not; please let yourself just be with or without thoughts moment by moment. Whenever a thought appears, use your preselected metaphor. Give the thought space, look at it and then let it go without needing to understand it fully or change anything. For now, you're simply bringing awareness to the patterns of thoughts that may appear in this particular practice.

4. **Invite difficult or stressful thoughts to arise in the safety and security of this meditation.** I'm not suggesting that you deal with thoughts of a traumatic nature here. Maybe you could look at an argument with a friend that needs resolving, for example. Just observe how both of you acted.

5. **End the meditation after 30 minutes.** Your alarm clock will help you to keep to this time. Before you stop, ground yourself properly once more and let go of any content of the meditation before you open your eyes. Have the intention not to continue ruminating on a thought any longer but to simply let it be for now. You can always decide to return to the thought in your next meditation.

Strengthening your position by finding new perspectives

You may be aware of certain repetitive thoughts that have been there for as long as you can remember. More often than not they circle around you not being good enough, pretty enough, clever enough, and so on. These thoughts may appear like old friends because they've seemingly always been there. However, they are more likely old foes who stop you from being the person you really want to be. Maybe your parents planted them into your subconscious; not necessarily because they were bad people, but because they didn't know that they were harming you.

Here I will share with you one of my childhood foes, which both of my parents fed into. I had been a very skinny little girl until I was around nine. Eventually my parent's constant endeavour to make me look normal was successful and I put on weight. The problem was that I didn't stop doing so and suddenly I was deemed to be fat. Not only was this frequently mentioned but my Christmas gifts usually consisted of anti-cellulite treatment creams and slimming tablets. I totally lost touch with feeling good in my body. I do know, however, that nobody meant to harm me, and that in reality I am fine, or at least fine-ish!

The more you can create an open-minded awareness and come to see your thoughts as nothing but mental events, the easier you find not buying into them wholeheartedly. Finding a new perspective is good for all thoughts, because there's no proof that those thoughts necessarily represent reality. All they do represent is reality as you see it right now. Also notice how just briefly connecting with these thoughts may affect your mood state.

I invite you now to sit for a while and scan through ancient thoughts that have burdened you forever. Choose one that you think you can handle and experiment with this meditation (in which I use my issue with weight as an example. Kindly replace this with your own issue when you meditate):

1. **Sit in a dignified posture, close your eyes and put one hand in the centre of your chest.** This may give you a sense of security and of being compassionate with yourself.

2. **Deliberately bring your unhelpful, ancient thought to mind.** For example, 'I am too fat, I am not pretty and I will never be happy and find real love.'

3. **Reply with your compassionate self.** 'That Dad bought you this potion and Mum told you how much prettier she looked than you means nothing. If they think it is true, it's only their opinion. If you look at their life, they have not exactly been happy.'

4. **Think a helpful thought.** 'You're ok as you are. You have a few friends who like you. You may be a little curvaceous but you're not fat. It is

simply not true. But even if it were, this wouldn't mean that you won't find happiness and love.'

5. **Now just sit with the beneficial thoughts.** For example, friendship, happiness, love and acceptance. Repeat a few helpful thoughts in your mind for a while.

6. **Slowly let all thoughts move into the background of your awareness and just focus on your breathing. Allow a smile to arise in your face. Feel the smile.**

So when you next catch yourself rambling aimlessly down the worry lane, experiment with turning it around and finding a new perspective. When retirement is looming, for example, and perhaps you worry whether you'll have enough money, imagine the opposite: freedom, and time to enjoy your hobbies. If you like the outcome of this experiment (that is, feeling lighter and more joyful), make a conscious decision to let the neuro pathway of worrying dry up (by not feeding it with more negative thoughts) and instead focus on positive possibilities and adventures.

A *neuro pathway* is a type of thinking pattern. Changing a neuro pathway means building a new way of thinking, one that deepens with time and overrides unhelpful methods of thinking.

A 'gather-yourself' meditation

Facing up to and dealing with troublesome thoughts can be difficult. Here's a beautiful meditation by the well-known meditation teacher Christopher Titmuss to help gather yourself and return you to positive thinking. It has a light and lovely touch. Maybe read it a few times and then just allow the words to guide you in your next sitting practice:

Let us be still for a few moments,

without moving even our little finger

so that a hush descends upon us.

There would be no place to go,

nor to come from,

for we would have arrived in this extraordinary moment;

there would be a stillness and silence,

that would fill all of our senses,

where all things would find their rest.

Everything would then be together in a deep connection,

putting an end to 'us and them', this against that;

we would not move in these brief moments,

for that would disturb this palpable presence;

there would be nothing to be said or done,

for life would embrace us in this wondrous meeting,

and take us into its arms as a loving friend.

Reviewing Your Accomplishments This Week

If you're following the eight-week course in order, you're now at the end of your fourth session of MBCT. Well done! You've explored most of the new information and techniques, and in week five (see Chapter 8) you can enter a period of refining and deepening your new skills. Please don't underestimate how far you've come; be proud of yourself and allow yourself to enjoy a mindful celebration.

Take a look at these questions as a way to appraise your experience of this chapter's material and conduct a halfway review of the programme:

- ✔ How are you finding the process of handling your difficult stress- and anxiety-inducing thoughts (using the techniques and meditations that I introduce in this chapter)?

- ✔ What do you feel that you're discovering through this week's practice and the first half of the course? You may find it useful to skim leisurely through weeks one to four as a reminder.

- ✔ What do you need to do over the next four weeks to get the most out of the rest of the course?

Always note down in your mindfulness diary what you discover and what insights you gain. I recommend that you practise daily, but mindfulness is more about being than doing.

Chapter 8

Navigating Troubled Waters –
Week Five: Relinquishing
Attachments

- -

In This Chapter

▶ Dealing with difficult thoughts

▶ Coming to terms with past experiences

▶ Letting go of attachments

- -

*A*ll people face difficult periods from time to time and have events in their past that they need to deal with. The common (and quite understandable response) is often to turn away from and reject the resulting painful thoughts, memories and experiences. But resistance and denial require an enormous amount of effort and in fact such non-acceptance usually creates a whole lot more discomfort than it alleviates.

As an alternative approach, in this chapter I lead you towards cultivating the right atmosphere for accepting and handling adversity. I show you ways in which you can allow yourself to accept difficult thoughts – letting them just be – and only respond to them when doing so seems helpful. I also encourage you to let go of *mental attachments* (in other words, your habitual thoughts about how life should be, what you deserve and your own expectations of yourself and other people) and develop a radically different relationship with your unwanted life experiences.

Initially, accepting something that hurts or burdens you can be a difficult prospect to engage in. I want to assure you that this chapter isn't about becoming resigned to your problems, but involves expanding a limited or constricted view about the problems confronting you. Kind and compassionate awareness allows you to consider getting really close to your pain and, by embracing it, perhaps cause it to change or even disappear altogether.

Getting Your Bearings on the Course

If you're following the eight-week mindfulness-based cognitive therapy (MBCT) course, this chapter forms week five and begins the second half of the programme, which helps you implement mindfulness more into your daily life. You not only practise new meditations, but also become even more aware of which thinking patterns and behaviours cause you suffering so that you can decide to engage in them less and less often.

To get the most from this chapter, you may want to ensure that you're up to speed with the following aspects of mindfulness:

- ✔ Your private meditation space, which I discuss setting up in Chapter 4, is proving suitable for your continuing, regular practice.

- ✔ You know how your brain develops neuro pathways (see Chapter 7).

- ✔ You're aware of the importance of the breath-monitoring exercises (check out Chapters 4 to 6).

- ✔ You understand that negative automatic thoughts (NATs) cause problems that you can challenge by being mindful (see Chapter 7).

Mindfulness is more about real-life application than meditating formally every so often. It's about knowing that you have available the possibility of inviting kindness and compassion into every area of your life.

Allowing the Presence of Painful Thoughts, Emotions and Memories

As part of helping to change your relationship to your past experiences, I want to get back to basics with a couple of definitions. You may think that you know what the words *pain* and *suffering* mean, and you may even sometimes think that they indicate the same thing, but I use them to mean two quite different aspects of life:

- ✔ **Pain** is what you experience directly in your body or mind when life deals you difficult challenges: for example, physical pain from an accident or mental pain from a relationship break-up.

- ✔ **Suffering** is created secondarily when you refuse to deal with or accept such negative incidents: for example, pretending that an accident hasn't happened by taking painkillers without trying to find out what damage really occurred, or pretending that you couldn't care less that your partner left you. Each denial that you're in pain feeds into your secondary suffering.

These definitions help to reveal that suffering is an aspect of a difficult life experience that you can hugely reduce by allowing it to exist, at least initially, and then responding to it wisely.

In this section, you discover how to bring this wisdom to bear so that you can sit with the uncomfortable and cope with the unpleasant. Bear this quote in mind:

> *The overall tenor of mindfulness practice is gentle, appreciative and nurturing. Another way to think of it would be heartfulness.*

> —Jon Kabat-Zinn

Jon Kabat-Zinn points out that while people find it difficult to treat themselves and others in a heartful way, it is exactly what you're endeavouring towards through mindful living. Learning about forgiveness and the alleviation of suffering is part of this endeavour.

Staying with discomforting thoughts

You focus on your breath in meditations in Chapters 4 (such as the body scan), 5 (sitting with sounds) and 6 (sensing physical pain). Now I invite you to carry out a similar exercise, but this time look out for anything you may label as 'uncomfortable'. The idea is for you to move between awareness of the world around you (seeing, hearing, smelling) and awareness of the sensations that this world elicits within you (the effect it has on your body and breath). If you need reminding of my tips for scheduling and conducting your practice time and space, see Chapter 4.

 In this exercise, instead of focusing on the general, you now focus on the specific, learning how to use the breathing space to deal with an individual problem or grievance and so mindfully achieving closure and/or progress. When you feel ready, please:

1. **Select a discomfort or problem you want to deal with.** I recommend that you start with a small irritation rather than a major issue – for example, a little discomfort or disappointment, such as nagging thoughts and feelings about a promise a friend has made but forgotten about. Any larger or more overwhelming problem should be approached with the help of a therapist to protect and guide you.

   Your aim here is either to kindly remind your friend to fulfil her promise or to let go of any resentment and do whatever your friend promised yourself.

2. **Visualise how your friend completes the task she agreed to handle, or see yourself, without too much effort, getting it done.** Closing your eyes may help you to visualise this. Whenever you notice that your

awareness is being pulled away from your focus, either by critical or non-related thoughts arising or by discomfort anywhere in your body, briefly focus on those distractions.

Maybe if you're experiencing negative thoughts, feelings or sensations, you'll experience a non-accepting response. If, on the other hand, you experience something pleasant, you may want to hold on to it and might develop attachment. Both of these mind-states – the pushing away and the attaching – are the opposite of acceptance. Don't judge yourself, for this is the human condition. Most untrained minds end up grasping or rejecting, which is where mindfulness practice comes in. It teaches your mind to see what actually is going on moment by moment and sometimes that is all there is to do.

3. **Kindly and deliberately bring your awareness back to your intended visualisation.** The breath provides a useful vehicle for doing this. Bring friendly awareness to the part of the body in discomfort by breathing into it on the in-breath, and breathing out from it on the out-breath, letting go of any discomfort as much as possible. You can observe and then let go of critical thoughts as if you had a bunch of balloons that you let go up into the sky.

4. **When your attention moves to the bodily sensations and you locate what's pulling at your attention you could simply say to yourself: 'It's okay. Whatever it is, it's okay. Let me feel it.'**

5. **Stay with your awareness of these bodily sensations and/or thoughts and how you relate to them; breathing with them, accepting them, letting them be. Repeat the same words as in Step 4 when necessary.** Use each out-breath to soften and open to the sensations you become aware of. For each difficult thought or emotion, say, 'It's okay.'

The important insight to gain from this meditation is to become more aware of what is most dominant in your experience right now. So, if you're constantly lured back to specific thinking patterns, feeling patterns or body sensations, the invitation for you is to bring a gentle and curious awareness to this experience. The easiest method to be with any experience is first of all to simply accept it as it is, just allowing it to be there, rather than trying to change it or fight it.

I'm not encouraging you to try to resolve anything by being with these uncomfortable emotions, but instead ask only that you act like a detective, simply investigating the nature of the discomfort. By turning towards rather than pushing against these thoughts, you may begin to notice a change in your perception.

In the nearby sidebar 'The Guesthouse' I discuss a poem by the 12th century mystic and Sufi poet Rumi. It talks about the human condition and puts an unexpected slant on it.

'The Guesthouse'

In the following poem Rumi compares being human to a guesthouse. The 'guests' are thoughts, pain, illness, loss, and so on that seem to arrive on an ongoing basis and vary from pleasant to despicable. They're uninvited, often even unexpected. As the host, you're supposed to welcome them all and accept them as they are, even though some of the visitors may throw you off balance and maybe even bring you destructive intensity.

The invitation is to be open and accepting, for even when a visit causes life as you've known it to crumble, a new perspective and new beginning may arise that would never have arisen without the upheaval. Intentionally accepting someone's malice, for example, is proactive – rather than automatic – you see it for what it is and it can no longer hijack you!

Without doubt what Rumi asks you to do is a huge challenge. One thing is for sure though, whatever negative thoughts or emotions rear up in you they're definitely not you, just an aspect of your experience at this moment of being human. The poem provides an invaluable invitation to let go of labelling yourself, and just see the unpleasant visitor as something temporary that will, sooner or later, be no more.

This being human is a guesthouse

Every morning a new arrival.

A joy, a depression, a meanness,

some momentary awareness comes

as an unexpected visitor.

Welcome and entertain them all!

Even if they're a crowd of sorrows,

who violently sweep your house

empty of its furniture.

Still, treat each guest honourably.

He may be clearing you out

for some new delight.

The dark thought, the shame, the malice.

Meet them at the door laughing,

and invite them in.

Be grateful for whoever comes,

because each has been sent

as a guide from beyond.

Translated by Coleman Barks

Developing the coping breathing space exercise

In Chapter 6, I describe an emergency breathing space exercise that works as an excellent intervention when you feel that life is overwhelming. However, when you're in a highly stressful situation, such as having an argument with a co-worker, for example, that exercise may not be enough to enable you to deal with the situation in the most mindful and effective way possible. In such a situation, you can use the following version of the breathing space meditation to cope with the discomfort.

By practicing this version of the breathing space meditation three times daily, you can really get to know it by heart for the eventuality of having to use it as an intervention.

1. **Direct your awareness and bring attentiveness to the stressful situation as it presents itself in this moment.** Observe with curiosity any inner experiences. Notice thoughts, feelings and body sensations. They are what they are.

2. **As best as you can, describe in thoughts and words how this experience feels.** For example, 'I am feeling hot anger arising from my chest, into my face. My face feels red and twisted. I sense that I would like to shout out some swear words.' See what you experience when you actually name everything (in your mind) as it unfolds.

3. **Carefully redirect your focus and attention to the action of breathing.** As if you are dissecting this physiological aspect of life, really get in touch with each tiny step that leads to a full breath.

   • You may want to use a phrase to help you stay focused on the breath: for example, 'breathing in' and 'breathing out'.

   • Notice the little pauses after each in- and out-breath.

   • The breath can function as an anchor to bring you into the present and to help you enter a sense of stillness in a short while.

4. **Expand your awareness around your whole body.** Take special care to direct your breath towards any discomfort, strain or resistance you experience, breathing in to the difficult sensations. On the out-breath you gently soften and remember that this sensation will pass.

   As best you can, take away your expanded awareness to where the stressful situation awaits. You have, however, now taken more control of the situation. Maybe your argument can now become a focused conversation where you and your co-worker agree to disagree.

When dealing with such situations, see yourself standing strong, surrounded by a protective see-through bubble. Your bubble is undetectable and protective. You know it exists but whoever is attacking you feels only the sensation of the attack bouncing back and not getting through to you. This helps you to step out of automatic pilot when dealing with difficulties, and to reconnect with the present moment and your own inner wisdom. Practise it so often that you know it by heart without having to think of it.

Tackling Troubling Past Experiences

Maintaining your general focus on the present moment when practising mindfulness is always of paramount importance, particularly when you're handling difficult memories and emotions connected to past events. Yet when they reside deeply in your whole being, often old patterns or traumas can become unlocked. If an old pain rears its ugly head for you, the best approach is to pull out the root of the problem. I liken it to having a reappearing mouth ulcer and only ever putting cream on it. Although it calms down for a while, sooner rather than later it returns.

Mindful awareness is the key to helping you accept painful past events and to choosing a helpful response (as opposed to an immediate reaction that can be flawed by your wrong interpretations of perceived facts). Perhaps you can think of past incidents where you reacted straight away only to find out that the facts were rather different to your assumptions.

Bringing painful experiences to mind

After you've been meditating mindfully for a period of time, and when you feel strong enough, you can make the effort to remember deliberately the pain of a challenging past experience (such as an argument with someone close). Here's an exercise that helps you to do so and feel safe.

Don't push yourself too far, too fast at this early stage of your practice and make the experience you use in this exercise one that is extremely painful or traumatic (for example, a memory of sexual abuse). Situations like this would require the presence of an experienced counsellor or MBCT instructor in order to provide you with additional support.

1. **Visualise a place or room from your childhood where you always felt safe.** Really see it, sense the smells, the feel of furniture or landmarks. Keep breathing mindfully until your mind feels really settled.

2. **Picture yourself in the difficult situation or past event.** For example, in the school playground where you were bullied, or coming home to a cold house and finding nobody to greet you or cook for you.

3. **See this suffering child and bring compassion to the situation.** Put your hand over your middle chest (or wherever you feel your emotional heart resides).

4. **Allow your adult self or another compassionate person you know or have read about to appear.** Let this adult take care of you and say to yourself 'all will be well at last' (for more, check out the later section 'Noticing strong attachments to the past').

5. **Stay with this sense of vulnerability.** Remind yourself that it's supported by your personified compassion.

For techniques on dealing with strong emotions connected to difficult experiences, flip to the later section 'Coping with strong emotions'.

After several such retreats into your past, you may be able to leave that event or experience behind for good.

Letting go of fear (and your lunch!)

Chris was a sturdy young man who came to an eight-week mindfulness course in order to let go of his phobia of being sick in public (*emetophobia*). He was working as a cook on scuba-diving boats and enjoyed being among the divers, cooking for them and hearing their stories, and on his days off even joining them for a dive. Whenever the sea got rough, however, he was seasick. He'd developed emetophobia as a child when his dad smoked in the car when picking him up or taking him to school. Seemingly not the most empathic of people, his father always smoked when Chris was in the car, causing him to often feel nauseous, with his father telling him to be sick out of the open door of the parked car (in front of passers by).

Chris was left with this extreme fear of being sick in public and it resurfaced every time he felt nauseous onboard ship. After completing the mindfulness course, he boarded his next job and sure enough the heavens opened and Chris quickly felt unwell. He focused on his breath and alternated with the body scan, but alas his sense of sickness got worse by the minute. Suddenly he just knew what to do. He braced himself and allowed his stomach to relieve itself. Thankfully he had enough time to go to an appropriate place to do so.

Ever since, he has simply allowed it to happen, just giving in to sickness when it occurs. No more fear, no more holding back, no more 'what if people see me'. The best thing is that the nausea now occurs less and less often, even when the going gets rough.

Chris's story is a typical example of how being mindful can help you to embrace the difficult; even though it didn't change the outcome directly, the amount of suffering Chris endures now is significantly reduced. Being less anxious about the possibility of feeling sick also means that he produces less adrenaline, which in itself may have added to the sense of feeling unwell.

Seeing your past as the midnight movie

If you try to bring up painful memories (such as by engaging in the practice in the preceding section) you may discover just how hard it can be. The reason is that you probably spent a lot of time trying to suppress them, and undoing perhaps years of such effort requires time. But remember the well-known saying again: 'what you resist persists!'

Unless you deal with the memories so that your brain can store them away as completed 'files' ('this was nasty, it happened and now it's over'), they often continue to affect you and your outlook on life. They need to be confronted, which requires a lot of bravery on your part.

 Here's a method that makes dealing with painful recollections easier – watching the experience on an imaginary television screen. Kindly consider the following:

1. **Ground yourself by feeling deeply connected to the earth and keep breathing calmly.**

2. See yourself putting on a DVD of the painful memory, sitting down and then observing the drama.

3. Feel the fear, the hurt and the loneliness, but also understand that it truly happened and that you're here to prove you survived it.

4. Watch the film several times in your mind and then add compassion and awareness to the story you see on the screen.

5. Write the story down in a letter after your meditation, telling the tale and voicing the disappointment towards those who caused your suffering.

6. Burn the letter (safely, perhaps in an iron bucket outdoors) when you feel the process is complete, and also visualise the DVD breaking into tiny little pieces that are carried away by the wind.

Letting go of past events is vitally important. Even so, you may find that you always have a tender spot, like a mental scar, that you have to adjust to living with. Everybody has such scars; again, it's part and parcel of being human.

Pre-empting future events

Like all human beings, your past experiences condition how you see the future. A highly human response is to pre-empt future events by basing them on your experiences in the past – *prejudice* in this sense is a survival tool for lots of creatures. Human beings, however, can learn and understand much more deeply than other species, and so you have the option and ability to acknowledge this tendency to prejudice and choose to keep your mind open.

Ask yourself what kind of things you avoid because you assume you know how things are going to pan out. Could you be wrong? Is more than one outcome possible? How can you find out how to leave yourself open to new possibilities?

As so often with mindfulness, the answer is being in the ever-newness of the present moment. Change can and does occur, and you need to persuade yourself to try something anew that caused you pain in the past. So if you tend to abstain from engaging in certain experiences because they may cause another disappointment, free yourself from these shackled beliefs by starting afresh moment by moment. If you do, at least you stand a chance of having a new experience. Try something once and see what unfolds because every moment is a new possibility! Otherwise, you may slip back into a life that's merely an existence rather than an adventure.

I remember hating tomatoes as a child, mainly because my mother did too. When I was 19 years old, I went on a holiday to Greece and ordered a typical Greek salad. It contained these huge slices of tomatoes and they smelled heavenly. I took a chance and a bite and was in heaven. I never looked back.

Perhaps you too remember disliking something in the past that you now love or used to shy away from doing something that today you feel a strong pull to engage in.

Consider engaging in an activity that causes you only mild anxiety or worry and involve ten other people in the project (this is called a *behavioural experiment*). The project can be discovering a new skill, or revisiting an old one that teachers or parents told you that you were no good at. Just do it mindfully, without a specific outcome in mind, moment by moment, whether your project is singing in public on a street corner (joined by your co-researchers), going to a painting or language class, or trying to learn to swim. Be the best you can, in the moment, letting your arising thoughts of the past just flow past, like birds in the sky.

Think about how you experience this experiment and then ask all your co-researchers about their 'story'. You probably find that a whole bunch of different tales come to light. Although you were together experiencing the exact same moment, your personal interpretations and expectations create a number of different accounts. Of course, make sure that you write it all down in your mindfulness diary (which I describe in Chapter 4) so that you don't forget or later focus just on the negative.

Coping with strong emotions

Past experiences often bring up very strong emotions that can be difficult to deal with. Whatever emotions you identify with yourself when you think of past events, here's a list of techniques that you may want to try for letting go/dealing with them:

- **Ride the difficult emotion as if surfing on a big wave:** It reaches a peak and then slowly ebbs away; use mindful breathing and observe it with interest and curiosity.

- **Allow yourself to fully feel the emotion but not act on it:** Go right into sensing and describing it; for example, 'this anger feels hot, looks bright orange, makes my body temperature go up, causes my breathing to speed up'. Take a scientist's curious perspective, observing the difficult event and staying with it as best as you can.

- **Look behind the emotion:** Ask, what's the source of it? Are you copying your mother's hysteria, are you trying to be the opposite of your brother? What feeds this emotion? What if you turn off the tap?

- **Search for the opposite of the emotion:** What's the other side of this coin? Is fear behind your rearing anger, which often looks more impressive than shaking and crying?

- **Sit with it:** See what happens if you just breathe and be with the difficult emotion.

My left-foot scan

Dr NN Singh, a creative writer and researcher in the field of mindfulness and mental health, developed a mindfulness-based self-discipline plan for a young man with learning difficulties. The man had been frequently aggressive, breaking and throwing things, even a television, which almost led to him being ejected from his sheltered housing accommodation. He was trained to practise a simple mindfulness intervention. Whenever he felt so angry that he wanted to smash, hit or throw something, he was taught to move his attention from the angry thought to the sole of one foot. After repeating the foot scan several times a week, for a number of weeks, he was able to remain free from reacting violently in situations that would in the past have triggered a physical explosion. He was able to keep this new behaviour up for more than six months, which was the minimum period required before he was no longer perceived as a threat to the community he was living with. He succeeded in remaining in the accommodation without relapsing into his angry behaviour.

Resisting the urge to fight or run away

Just as most animals share the instinctive fight-or-flight response to physical threats, you can respond similarly to memories of traumatic past experiences. When things get too rough, you may want to escape and run back to your place of stubborn ignorance.

But in your meditation practice, try your best to stay present rather than regress. You're to be congratulated for having reached this point of dealing with your past, and turning away now would be a shame.

Return to a mindful, observant, non-judgemental place whenever you feel yourself getting too emotionally heightened. Breathe gently and steadily, and ground yourself by feeling your feet deeply rooted on the surface they're resting or standing on.

The objective of this practice is to move away from the thinking mind, which is ruminating around 'attack' and 'fear' thoughts. When you feel ready, kindly close your eyes or maintain a soft focus (half-closed):

1. **Bring your awareness to your left foot.** You're not looking at your foot but gently bringing awareness to it. Really feel your foot and slowly guide yourself through the terrain of your foot gently and with kind attention. You can use words like this: 'I'm becoming aware of my left foot, my big toe, my little toe and all the toes in between, even the spaces between the toes, feeling them, sensing them or just knowing that they're present. Now I'm bringing awareness to the tips of my toes and to my toe nails, to the heel of my foot, the instep and the front part and now the whole sole of my foot.'

2. **Continue bringing attentiveness to your foot as a whole.** Include all the little bones, tendons, blood vessels and finally even the skin covering your foot.

3. **Spend a couple of minutes on your foot in this mindful way.** Doing so directs your conscious thinking away from the beliefs that had been feeding your anger. This meditation may be enough, or you can calm your mind further by carrying out a sound meditation (from Chapter 5) or going for a mindful stroll (check out Chapter 6).

Maintaining a gentle approach

Discovering how to deal with difficult experiences is an important skill. But don't torture yourself – trying to work out how you may have done things differently before you knew how to be mindful isn't helpful. Now that you're integrating this new way of living, you can be ready to do everything with more awareness and consequently with less harm towards others. The past is history and the future yet unknown – the present is the gift!

If you feel the need to make amends, do so with gentle awareness and compassion, letting go of guilt and all the while being conscious of how unaware you were before. Gently let go of old unhelpful habits and be compassionate towards yourself as much as towards other people.

Consider trying the following meditation of strength and gentleness and feel for yourself how it affects your wellbeing:

1. **Picture the most beautiful mountain you know or can imagine.** Notice its overall shape, the tall peak, the base rooted in the rock of the earth's crust, the slanting sides. Note how massive the mountain is, how unmoving, how beautiful.

2. **See whether you can bring the mountain into your own body.** Your head becomes the lofty peak, your shoulders and arms the sides of the mountain, your buttocks and legs the solid base rooted to your cushion on the floor or to your chair.

3. **Become the breathing mountain, unwavering in your stillness, completely what you are.** Beyond words and thought, you're a centred, rooted, unmoving presence.

4. **As the light changes, as night follows day and day night, the mountain just sits, simply being itself.** It remains still as the seasons flow into one another and as the weather changes moment by moment. Storms may come, but still the mountain sits.

5. **Imagine the mountain in spring time.** See the blue sky, with scattered clouds and the warm rays of the sun shining down. Imagine nature in

spring: soft green leaves, multi-coloured buds, birds and the first sign of insects scattering through nature, earth and air. The mountain remains – still and abiding.

6. **Imagine a rich summer's night.** Full moon; the sounds of crickets, frogs, toads and an owl; rich fragrance of roses and other blooms lies heavily in the air; a gentle breeze touches the bushes; leaves in the trees and the grass. The mountain remains – still and abiding.

7. **Create a rainy autumn day in your mind, if you want to.** Heavy clouds, opening heavens, multi-coloured leaves scattered around; imagine the soundscape; hear the strong gusts of wind. The mountain remains – still and abiding.

8. **Visualise the mountain in winter.** Snowflakes are slowly covering the empty trees and also the slopes of the mountain – still, calmness, white serenity.

9. **See the change in all the seasons.** Among all this change, the mountain abides, stillness within.

You may want to ask yourself how to translate the story of the mountain into your own life. You may of course have your own ideas and please feel free to add or reject images and aspects of this meditation. Your mountain may have a rounded, soft peak. You may want to see it morning, lunchtime and night. Be creative and feel free.

For me, the message is this: whatever life presents, with its beauty and challenges, deep inside people can remain calm and grounded. Of course, remaining so requires practice and continuity.

> *Serenity is not freedom from the storm but peace within the storm. What lies behind us and what lies before us are tiny matters, compared to what lies within us.*
>
> —Ralph Waldo Emerson

Beginning a new relationship with your experiences

Mindfulness isn't telling you to forget about your past experiences altogether, which would be impossible. You do however want to find novel ways of living or dealing with difficulties in the now. I encourage you to change the way you treat your experiences by changing the relationship you have with them. You become aware of them as thoughts or sensations and start to experience life around them, rather than having them controlling every moment of your life.

Here are a number of possibilities, to which you can add your own personal ones that you want to turn around. (*Remember:* all the while, ground yourself and be aware of your breathing and of using mindful speech – that is, using only those words that are essential for clarifying what you want to convey, not being overly abrupt or rude but also not skirting around the issue. See Chapter 11 for more about communicating mindfully.)

✔ When you're invited to a big gathering or party, which you'd have avoided in the past, try a new approach. Tell the host that you may pop in for a short while. Really mean it. Give yourself the opportunity to create a new option in your list of behaviours. Remember, if you really don't like it, you can still leave after a short stay.

✔ When annoying telephone sales calls come through, you may want to try and say something compassionate to the person who's on the receiving end. 'I'm sorry, I really don't like this type of call. I'm also sorry you have to do this job. I send you kind thoughts.' And after saying goodbye, hang up. Yours may be the only friendly response the person who phoned you heard all day.

✔ When somebody makes a mistake at work, draw it to their attention but all the while remember that everyone makes mistakes. Think of a kind way to point it out and finish the conversation with praise if at all possible. Use mindful language.

Now write down a list of behaviours and experiences you'd like to change. Perhaps one a week is doable.

Using storytelling to understand suffering

Storytelling is a good way of seeing how your past experiences can be useful in understanding how you attach to or reject opportunities. Without adding mindful consideration to the experience, you may unwittingly undo the joy of an experience.

After reading the story that follows about the blue balloon, kindly sit down for a meditation. See the story unfold in your inner eye. Notice the main characters and see what they could have done differently in order to find out how to be less superficial, more caring and less attached.

After doing this meditation, return to mindful breathing and see whether one of your own stories arises in your memory. If so, what's it trying to tell you and why does it remind you of the blue balloon story? Would you do anything differently by adding a small dose of awareness if you experience a similar situation again?

'I want to have a blue balloon! A blue balloon is what I want!' 'Here you go Rose!' Someone had explained to her that the balloon contained certain gases, lighter than air and because of this it floats. 'I want to let it go,' she simply said.

'Don't you want to give it to the poor little girl over there?' 'No, I want to let it go!' She lets it go, watching it rise into the blue sky. 'Don't you regret not giving it to the poor little girl over there?' 'Yes, I'd have rather given it to the poor little girl!' 'Here you are, give her this blue balloon!' 'No, I want to let this one go as well . . . see it fly up into the blue sky!' She simply lets it go. Then she's given a third blue balloon. She goes to the poor little girl of her own accord, gives her the balloon and says: 'Now let it go!' 'No', says the poor little girl looking excitedly at the balloon.

In her room back home it flew up to the ceiling where it remained for three days; it then changed colour, became darker, smaller and finally dropped dead to the floor like a little black sack. The poor little girl thought to herself: 'I should have let it go outside in the garden, up into the blue sky, I could have watched it fly away, watched it and watched it. . .'

The rich little girl was given loads more balloons and even 30 balloons all at once. She let 20 fly up into the sky and gave the remaining 10 to poor children. And from this moment onwards she was never interested in balloons anymore. 'Those silly balloons. . .' she tended to say.

So Aunt Ida suggested that she was really advanced for her age.

The poor little girl however dreamed: 'I should have let it go, rise up into the blue sky, I would have watched it and watched it. . .'.

Peter Altenberg, 1910. Translation by Patrizia Collard

This story can be interpreted in a number of ways. Are you focusing on the poor girl, feeling sorry for her and her narrow grasping view that ends in disappointment, or are you more interested in the phenomenon of affluence as portrayed by the rich little girl? Perhaps letting something go is much easier when you're experiencing life in abundance? What can you discover from the two children who are painted at the extreme end of the behaviour spectrum? Any idea where you'd place yourself? Are poor people necessarily holding back and the rich definitely generous? Most importantly, what can you take away as an insight for yourself from this story?

Unchaining Yourself from Attachments

In this context an *attachment* is anything that has you so strongly in its grip that you can't be without it even for a few hours, and which leads to suffering when it's absent from your life. Attachments, which can include holding onto good, pleasurable things, can lead to huge amounts of suffering if you must have them and can't be without them. An attachment can be the proverbial first cup of tea in the morning, having your dinner at a precise time every day or needing to watch the TV news every evening. Of course, attachments can also be memories of traumatic part events, toxic relationships or current addictions.

The idea isn't that you shouldn't allow yourself to like or love things or other people, but that you don't try to hold onto and possess those things and instead add a certain amount of spaciousness and flow. This involves not holding on to something to the point where it is crushed or suffocated, and accepting that things must be allowed to change; that life is constantly flowing. All good things end sometime, even if they return again later. So fully enjoy what is, being mindful not to hold on so tightly and perhaps squashing the good thing in the process.

This advice even refers to your meditation practice itself. When you've been meditating for a while, you may well have experienced some lovely or even perfect meditations: stillness resided within you and you had no care in the world. But you can't rely on meditation being so perfect and may miss it when a meditation goes differently. Each meditation is unique and each moment in it is unique, so continue to practise moment by moment dealing with whatever comes up.

People are often unable to let go of attachments and negative thoughts because of self-imposed labels (which have often been previously imposed upon them by others). But how can you expect to overcome an addiction if you never allow yourself to let it go? You aren't a 'fluic' if you have a cold! The same logic applies to all other aspects of your life. No attachment defines you as a whole and thus your whole human experience. Please try to remember this fact because it requires a certain discipline.

Watch out when you label yourself in these ways, even if it only happens in an inner dialogue.

Helping others to help yourself

One of my favourite poems by Mary Oliver finishes with these lines: 'determined to do the only thing you could do – determined to save the only life you could save'.

Maybe you're ready to start freeing yourself from unhelpful attachments by looking outside yourself and directing mindful everyday actions into areas that concern other people. Can you (or rather *do* you) want to care a little more for others who are barely present in your consciousness? The stranger on the tube who forgets his umbrella or her tissues; the old lady struggling with her shopping. Ask yourself who's in need of help right in front of your nose? If you ever wanted people to be a bit more open, a bit more sensitive to your needs, perhaps it starts with you.

Noticing strong attachments to the past

Observing what strong attachments you may consciously have to past experiences is important because they can chain you to that past. Perhaps you were bullied at school, abused in some way by trusted people, or experienced a great loss or upheaval in your life? If so, ask yourself gently how you cope (or fail to cope) with these memories and examine the ways in which they affect you today. Be specific about the details and the emotions you experience in a detached, non-judgemental way. You can experiment with letting go by revisiting the actual event during a meditation and processing it by picturing a compassionate person standing by you.

Perhaps see yourself with a strong martial-arts master walking through your old school playground and all your former bullies looking down in shame and feeling sorry for what they did to you. Or maybe imagine being back at home and telling your neglectful parents how sad you feel about their actions, but that you're trying to be compassionate because surely they didn't know any better.

Although your aim is always to find your own personal path to a healthier lifestyle through MBCT, occasionally challenges may arise where you possibly feel that you require extra assistance. If the root problem is so big that you sense you can't deal with it alone, please seek advice from a mental health professional, whom you might find through your GP or by searching the Internet for an accredited psychotherapist local to you. Many now offer psychotherapy, coaching or counselling together with mindfulness applications. Never be too proud to ask for help.

Co-existing with aversion

When you've a strong attachment to something and you don't get it, you can react with aversion. *Aversion* is an experience that you find hugely upsetting and that creates a sense of disgust and repulsion. It seems to originate in the instinct to survive by avoiding contracting a disease or procreating unhealthy offspring. Sometimes, however, aversion can occur due to the brain misinterpreting or overreacting to a perceived threat.

If you're attached to a certain form of 'correct' behaviour, perhaps you perceive somebody you love deeply repulsive when she's drunk or unwashed; or you've a strong aversion to street dwellers, certain animals or foods, or other behaviours.

Aversion is a form of experiencing fear or anxiety, which expresses itself by pushing something away and hiding from it. But if you experience this emotion in one of this chapter's meditations, return repeatedly to your breathing and stay with it for a while, giving yourself the opportunity to ask whether your reaction is appropriate or misguided. The sidebar 'Discovering how to love again' shows that you can overcome misplaced aversion, but you don't need a big misfortune to feel aversion. Much smaller triggers can cause a similar reaction. For example, many older people find ageing itself repulsive and can't cope with the changes in their looks and abilities due to the passage of time.

Perhaps explore whether you feel aversion towards an aspect of yourself or others that your heart would prefer to accept. Consider whether your feelings originate in an attachment to, say, your youth or former health.

Understanding the importance of acceptance

Unless you discover how to let go of attachments and accept all of yourself – past and present, good and less good, the beauty and the beast! – you're going to struggle with life and other people. The human condition is one of imperfection, of ongoing change and challenge. Without gently moving towards accepting the whole lot, the light and the dark, you can never reside in a mental place of equanimity and peace. All your experiences, and the little or big scars they leave behind, shape who you are and so have all been important to some extent.

Acceptance of what is, rather than what you'd ideally want, is one of the biggest challenges and liberations you can discover through practicing MBCT. You benefit greatly from seeing that nobody and nothing is perfect and everything that people judge is dependent on the eye of the beholder. You can move towards peace if you can embrace this fact.

Letting go of the desire for quick fixes

This book contains enough stories, poems and real-life examples to help you see that quick fixes rarely offer the best solution. Also, if you're attached to dealing with your problems in a certain way that doesn't shift them, perhaps you need to give a new response a chance.

Every moment can be a new experience and open the gateway to change. If this is life – your life – you're best off being the owner of it all. Therefore, engage with any experience as fully as possible, and remember that not everything is what it seems: certain occurrences involve pain and exhaustion and yet lead to new joys and insights.

Discovering how to love again

A woman sought therapy because she'd developed a strong aversion to her husband's disability. She'd married a healthy man, but then a car accident left him with both hands missing. She developed an aversion to being touched by him and even eating at the same table with him. She felt repulsed and terribly guilty simultaneously. She wanted to love him again and overcome her aversion to him not out of pity, but because he was a good man and her deep love for him was still intact. Of course, she also felt it was superficial to reject her kind husband because of something that had turned his own life upside down as well.

Mindful awareness and compassion training helped a lot and she's getting a little bit closer to him as weeks of practice go by. In many ways the couple has grown closer, after she shared with him her initial emotional displacement as well as the meditations she was studying.

Jettisoning pleasant attachments too

Although the exercises in this section mostly relate to resolving unpleasant or difficult experiences, letting go of intense attachments to pleasant experiences is just as important.

You may be surprised by this statement and so here's an example. Imagine that you eat the most delicious ice cream while on holiday in Venice. It's simply divine and you go back to the ice-cream shop within an hour to purchase another delicious feast. The next day, you return to your home country. Alas no more ice cream of this kind until, if ever, you return to Venice. And even if you did, would you find that little store again that was in one of the hundreds of 'stradas' somewhere in Venice? So you may never have that ice cream again. Never ever.

After a while of ruminating on this lost experience, you may not even be able to remember the joy you had because the whole incident becomes tainted by a sense of loss.

Living in the moment really means just that: fully experiencing, without guilt or attachment, what life offers. And then, on purpose, moving on to the next point in your life's journey.

Reviewing Your Accomplishments This Week

At the end of week five of the MBCT course, please consider the following questions to take stock of your progress:

✔ How are you getting on with letting difficult thoughts and memories just be (as I describe in the earlier 'Allowing the Presence of Painful Thoughts, Emotions and Memories' section)? Don't worry if you're finding it awkward; give yourself time to become accustomed to what can be a discomfiting experience.

✔ Can you detect an improved relationship with difficult events in your life after using the exercises in 'Tackling Troubling Past Experiences' earlier in this chapter?

✔ Are you continuing to work on disengaging yourself from all attachments, including pleasant ones, as per the preceding section?

The Eastern mindfulness meditation masters spend a lifetime practicing this, so don't be too hard on yourself after just one week!

Chapter 9

Going with the Current – Week Six: Accepting the True Nature of Thoughts

....

In This Chapter

▶ Understanding your thoughts at a deeper level

▶ Disengaging from self-doubt

▶ Treating your mind with love and kindness

....

> *Serenity is not freedom from the storm but peace within the storm. What lies behind us and what lies before us are tiny matters, compared to what lies within us.*
>
> —Ralph Waldo Emerson

*L*ife brings difficult experiences to every single person on the planet – from the lowest pauper to the highest Hollywood celebrity – but as Emerson's quote implies, the amount you suffer is related to how you think about and respond to those experiences. Handling the events themselves is difficult enough, without compounding your problems by struggling against your own thoughts and emotions as well.

In this chapter you delve deep into the world of your thoughts, as I invite you to see them as mere events occurring in your mental mind (as opposed to the feeling or heartful mind that I describe in Chapter 8). The exploration of this thought-world is often called *awareness* and it lies apart from thinking. Rather, awareness is more like a container that can hold your cognitive and emotional thinking, allowing you to discover how to explore and understand the patterns and movements of your thoughts, while becoming increasingly aware that thoughts aren't necessarily the only truth with regard to what light they shed on your experience.

Awareness helps you to observe your thoughts dispassionately, finding out what kind of destructive thinking patterns are causing you problems and how to let go of them. Often such thoughts are the result of a trigger, after which they race away out of control on their own (the negative automatic thoughts, or NATs, that I discuss in Chapter 5). Better awareness allows you not to get tangled up with any particular thought, but to see it as just one of many possibilities.

I also show you how to detect your own most common *downward-spirallers* (in other words, the thoughts that trigger subsequent thoughts and moods that continuously build on top of each other and pull you down emotionally) and discover how you can look at them from a number of different perspectives, including kindness and compassion.

Getting Your Bearings on the Course

This week I invite you to investigate particularly negative thoughts more deeply. In order to do so, ideally you've been practising mindfulness for a few weeks. Specifically, please check that you're *au fait* with:

- ✔ My introduction to thoughts and fears (flip to Chapter 1).

- ✔ Your regular meditation space and position. Some of this chapter's meditations are longer and deeper than previously and you need to be comfortable with the basics (check out Chapter 4).

- ✔ Your preparation for dealing with NATs and observing troublesome thoughts. I describe the former in Chapter 5 and the latter in Chapters 7 and 8.

This chapter isn't the ideal starting place unless you're used to mindfulness meditation. I design it to help you tackle deeper issues and build on material in Chapters 4 to 8. Therefore, I suggest that you read these chapters before diving in to this chapter's longer exercises.

Demystifying Thoughts: They're Less Peculiar Than You Think

Your automatic, unwanted – but not necessarily negative –thoughts aren't mystical, fantastical, incomprehensible things. You can, perhaps, see them usefully as 'hiccups' in the brain, which is constantly active and vigilant, trying to protect its home: you.

If you've been practising the exercises in Chapters 7 and 8, you may be starting to understand that distant and recent experiences of thoughts and feelings on which you ruminate, and that used to appear irresolvable, can be or have already changed. Even if you're not aware of it, such thoughts and feelings are altered by passing time and any changes occurring during this time. Their intensity and power over you may have already diminished; you may have gained new insights or accepted that this is how a particular event presented itself to you and how it felt for you.

Here, I take a deeper look at what thoughts are (and aren't), how they can affect you and how to reclaim your mind from unwanted thoughts.

When negative thoughts and emotions constantly cascade through your mind and feel so overwhelming that facing them seems impossible, you can reduce the power they hold over you by watching them as if you were standing behind a waterfall. This lets you see them from a distance and a point of safety because the strong water torrent acts as a barrier and makes it easier for you to simply name them. For example, you can say to yourself, 'there is sadness/ fear/sorrow/guilt/anxiety/stress/frustration/ uncertainty', and so on. By not owning your thoughts and saying that they simply exist in your awareness, you don't risk being dragged down by their heavy sentiments, and you avoid being caught up with them. This waterfall technique is extremely useful and effective if you wish to stay concentrating on your chosen focus of attention, such as your breath. When you're able to look past all your thoughts in this way, you can see that what lies on the other side is the real you: the person who encompasses all your thoughts and moods, who can be self-contained and who can self-determine how things affect you.

Understanding how your thoughts affect your moods (and vice versa)

Thoughts and moods are different but strongly connected. Understanding this fact is useful in itself and for you to apply to your life. Here are a couple of linked examples. Please imagine that:

- ✔ **Scenario 1:** You're feeling quite low because you've just been told that 20 people in your department are going to lose their jobs in the near future. Suddenly one co-worker you really get on with rushes by you and doesn't even say hello. You now feel even worse; obviously that person isn't among the 20 and knows that you are.

- ✔ **Scenario 2:** You've been told that you're going to be promoted and feel chuffed with yourself. Suddenly a co-worker you like rushes by you and doesn't reply to your hello. You now feel a little sad on her behalf because she has obviously found out that you got the job and she feels upset or envious. You still feel quite happy though and plan to invite the person for a meal to make her feel better.

In both instances you jump to a conclusion and the hypotheses relate to you and your inner story. Although in both events you receive news and shortly after a co-worker ignores you, scenario 1 probably hits you harder, because your negative mood interprets the action of your colleague as proof for your uncertain future. In scenario 2, being ignored may well only slightly touch your mood, because your original state of mind was elevated due to good news. That existing mood even inspires you to do a good deed, because your compassion responds to what you thought to be the person's disappointment.

When you become more mindful, your ability to see the larger picture increases. You may start thinking of possibilities outside the 'me, me, me' box, for example that the person:

- Was on her way to an important meeting and was already late
- Had a stomach upset and was on her way to the lavatory
- Had just experienced a fight with her husband or somebody else and wanted to be alone

A multitude of possibilities exist as to why the person you tried to reach out for did not or could not respond. No doubt you can think of many other reasons that could apply to these scenarios.

Observing negative thinking patterns – such as jumping to conclusions or imagining the worst – that lead you to believe that everyone who ignores you must be against you, is important. Be mindful and aware when such thinking patterns arise in you, and query them. You must be your own protector and, like a scientific investigator, look at all the possibilities before you decide on an answer. Also consider whether you could actually just let it be and be patient with not knowing for now. If the same person keeps acting strangely, maybe then you could decide to find out why.

Distinguishing your thoughts from facts

Thoughts are just thoughts. Different people can differently interpret even thoughts based on facts, because everyone has a different mind and varying abilities to hypothesise.

Consider the following example involving a specific fact – a man abandoning his fiancée at the altar:

> A young girl stands at the altar to be married. She smiles at her husband to be, a man who's 25 years older than her. When the vicar asks whether anybody knows a reason why this couple shouldn't be married, the man says: 'I do. I won't marry this beautiful angel, for if I did she wouldn't get the life she deserves.' The woman is devastated and cries; the man leaves the church.

The thoughts and emotions surrounding this event can vary enormously depending on each participant's point of view. The man believes that his young bride would miss out on all the things that he, as an older man, can no longer do or does not want to do. The fiancée feels rejected, embarrassed and devastated. The vicar is confused and can't do his job.

What would you think, say or ponder on? Which thoughts or feelings are the correct ones? No single answer applies to this question, because it all depends on how you interpret the fact – how you think and feel about it.

For much more on discerning thoughts from facts, flip to Chapter 5 and the exercises I provide.

When you're disturbed by negative thoughts or emotions, use the coping breathing space meditation from Chapter 6. It can help you stop ruminating and focusing on negative thinking and sensing, bringing you back to a new focus of your life: just one breath after the other.

Relating to your thoughts in a new way

Please consider for a moment what is meant by being with thoughts. By setting apart the thinker and the thought, and simply being with your thoughts, you enter the space between them, a skill which is called *mindfulness of thought*. The Austrian poet and philosopher Rainer Maria Rilke put this difficult hypothesis into words:

> Be patient [and] try to love the questions themselves . . . Do not now seek the answers . . . because you would not be able to live them. And the point is, to live everything. Live the questions now. Perhaps you will then gradually, without noticing it, live along some distant day into the answer.

Rejecting thoughts may prevent you from comprehending that the dilemma is not the thought, but the thinker's attitude towards it. So, if you take the challenge of being with a thought (even a difficult one), that thought can eventually dissolve. The absence of thought that you then have is the awareness of space and silence, or as the Indian speaker, writer and philosopher Krishnamurti explains, 'freedom from thought'.

When you look at the nature of thoughts, they tend to have a positive or negative flavour. Negative thoughts drag you down. Helpful ones, however, can assist you to become more creative and support you in finding ways to overcome obstacles which you might otherwise try to conquer just by focusing and refocusing on them – probably unsuccessfully, leading you to enter a downwards spiral. Helpful thoughts assist you in unlocking your potential by allowing the more creative and emotionally driven parts of your mind to flourish.

You may not always come up with new answers to problems – but sometimes just understanding the problem, engaging patience and being with the problem is enough. In fact, apparent quick and easy fixes are often not helpful at all. If you always just order fast food whenever you're hungry, sooner or later you miss out on important nutrients! Your stomach may be full, but your body's still starving.

Building a new relationship to your thoughts isn't easy, because you've probably followed a particular way of interpreting the world for a long time. The part of the human brain that is used for cognitive processing starts as an empty hard disk, as it were. Humans have a lot fewer instinctive habits imbedded in them than other mammals.

By referring to the brain's *hard disk,* I mean all the areas of the brain where human behaviour and memory are stored. While certain elements we use as our minds begin to accumulate information are present at birth, we do not begin life with the ability to use them.

As this and other chapters show, you can relate to your thoughts differently when you no longer believe that they contain complete truth. If you implement the right sort of change, you can improve your wellbeing and liberate yourself from the shackles of negative thoughts, feelings and behaviours (see the sidebar 'Trying something new').

Ask yourself what fixed beliefs you have about yourself. Can you perhaps decide to let something go and start afresh? Even if it only works for a few moments, you can build and expand on that. Write down in your diary what thoughts and behaviours you want to shift.

Trying something new

For a long time the received wisdom was that office workers could only be trusted to do their work properly if they came into the workplace. Yet, over time, commuting became more and more cumbersome and not everybody thrived in open-plan offices. So a number of bigger companies experimented with letting employees work from home. Amazing results revealed that often more work was done, and of a higher quality, with less absenteeism.

During a recent illness, I had a lot of time for meditation and concentration. I saw an image that portrayed me doing various enjoyable activities. The strange thing was that I saw myself being creative in the late hours of the evening, rather than during daytime. I wondered what my subconscious was trying to tell me. Was I really being invited to try being creative at night? Night time was for watching the sky, having meaningful conversations or reading. But why not, I thought to myself, particularly as my life as an author seems to be rapidly expanding at the moment. So the next day I had my dinner, let it settle and started writing and drawing around 9:00 p.m. It was a miraculous discovery, and I now do this at least three times a week. Glorious freedom enveloped me – being creative when everything is still outside is a great gift.

Parting the Waves of Self-Doubt

Looking at your negative or limiting thoughts with the intention of not believing them can be quite challenging. Many of them have been long-term acquaintances and seem so familiar or even comforting, such as the following old friends, roommates and nosy neighbours:

- ✔ 'Better the devil you know.'
- ✔ 'I'm not good enough.'
- ✔ 'I only got this job because there was nobody else.'
- ✔ 'Just wait until they find out who I really am.'

In this section, you discover a few techniques and meditations that help you attend to or accept difficult thoughts.

Bringing awareness to your thoughts

Wouldn't it be great to start freeing yourself from unhelpful thoughts? Some Eastern traditions say that you're truly precious and worthy just because you're part of universal creation. Imagine how it would feel to believe that you're really special, wanted and worthy, and what it would be like moment by moment if everything was all right as it is: no worrying, no criticising, no wanting, no blaming – just accepting this moment of your life experience fully as it presents itself. Can you imagine such stillness residing inside you?

 Pause for a moment and sense what you're feeling and thinking when you read these words. Are you in disbelief? Do you think, 'When am I going to wake up?' For now just observe your reaction and if possible note it down in your mindfulness diary. Maybe, in addition, you can recall moments of total harmony with life recently or during your childhood.

All the practices that you explore in Chapters 4 to 8 can help you to deeply search and bring awareness to moments where you feel alright. The exercises you connect with in your dedicated meditation space and your everyday awareness exercises point you in the direction of just being, moment to moment. There will without doubt be moments, either during meditation or in everyday life, when you feel inner contentment and peace. Perhaps you can remember a moment where you sat down in a park and just listened to the wind and the birdsong and watched a butterfly land on your arm, for example. When you're surprised by joy, just because the beauty of a moment is a reality, you see that life offers many such possibilities. If you learn to observe them and pay attention to them when they occur, you'll see that individual moments of life can be totally precious; nothing is lacking, nothing needs to change.

Here are a few questions to ask yourself about your thoughts, so that you can attend to them productively, with interest and non-judgemental awareness, but while not becoming attached to them (as I describe in Chapter 8):

- ✔ Am I confusing my thought with an absolute truth?
- ✔ Am I thinking in all-or-nothing terms?
- ✔ Am I condemning myself completely because of one thing?
- ✔ Am I concentrating on my flaws and forgetting my talents?
- ✔ Am I blaming myself for something that isn't my fault?
- ✔ Am I setting unrealistic standards for myself, which can lead to failure?
- ✔ Am I mind-reading?
- ✔ Am I expecting myself to be or act perfectly?
- ✔ Am I overestimating disaster?
- ✔ Am I having double standards?
- ✔ Am I jumping to conclusions?

The defining stance to take with your thoughts is that of gentle interest, compassion and curiosity.

Although you may occasionally experience tasters of contentment and stillness that expand into periods where you want for nothing else, where nothing seems missing, expecting this outcome to happen isn't helpful. But I want you to know that a strong possibility exists of this occurring.

Performing the pebble meditation to consider deeper thoughts

I've really benefitted from and am still discovering a lot about my mind and my patterns of thinking by practising the *pebble meditation*, a practice that can help you explore and understand the many layers of your thoughts through employing the help of visualisation and metaphor.

You may often react to your initial thoughts about a person or event, and therefore act almost instinctively. However, when you take your time and respond from a more reflective stance, your responses are likely to be different from your very first reactions. Think of it as looking at the actors on a stage. The main actors on stage represent your automatic, instinctive thoughts; they are in the foreground and seem louder. In the background, however, are quieter thought-actors that nevertheless play an important role. The pebble meditation is a way to ensure that you can become aware of all these levels of thought that can occur and act from a place of greater insight and awareness.

In the pebble meditation, you imagine sitting on the edge of a metaphorical pond and throwing a pebble into that pond. The pond could be your mind, and the pebble a question or an insight. The pebble slowly floats down to the bottom but it also creates circles on the surface of the pond. These circles stand for the expanding awareness of your mind on the surface level. The deeper the pebble floats down, the more insight and understanding you may discover residing in your mind. When you repeatedly focus on the same question, different answers arise from the depths of knowing (that is, the pebble sinking deeper and deeper into your subconscious) and awareness.

To practice the pebble meditation, kindly sit down in a comfortable position, on the floor or on a chair:

1. **Visualise yourself sitting at the edge of a beautiful, clear pond.** The sun is shining and you can see some of its rays reflected in the water and feel the warm energy caress your shoulders. Around you are pond grass and water lilies; maybe you hear a frog croaking. Blue and green dragonflies circle around. Allow yourself to see this pond in all its glory and add any image or sound that comes up naturally in your imagination.

2. **Imagine yourself picking up a small, flat pebble and throwing it into the water.** Watch it float down a little – be still and notice what thoughts, feelings and sensations come up in your experience right now.

3. **Allow the pebble to float further down into the water.** See whether any of your sensations, images or feelings change by letting it sink deeper. Allow the pebble to settle at the bottom of the pond. Perhaps you can even see where it lies at the bottom of the pond.

4. **Consider what you feel, sense or think.** Are any messages arising from your deeper consciousness that you need to hear or perhaps bring to your awareness?

5. **Sit a little longer and just breathe, moment to moment.** Just take care of this experience, this moment.

After you complete this ten-minute meditation, please take time to note down in your mindfulness diary any insight you gained. Even if you can only come up with a few words or pointers, kindly jot them down.

Writing to yourself about your thoughts

This week, write yourself a letter about your thoughts – yes, really write with pen and paper! When you've finished your letter, address it to yourself and ask a good friend to send it to you – not immediately, but maybe a few weeks from now. When it arrives, you can read it with interest and notice what arises as an insight about how your mind works. Please start the process as follows:

1. **Prepare a steaming cup of tea or coffee.** Really notice when you pick it up how you guide it towards your mouth, how your lips curl around the rim and how you drink and swallow. Each sip is a mindful experience in itself.

2. **Sit down to write.** Notice your intention to sit, the movement of your body when changing from standing to sitting, and the connections you feel between your body sitting at a table and the surfaces it connects to.

3. **Bring awareness to how you pick up the pen.** Pay attention to how you hold it, such as the points of pressure in the various areas of the hand and finger connections.

4. **Start to write.** Allow each word to be a moment of stillness and contemplation.

5. **Write about this week's topic, which is relating to your thoughts.** You can write one sentence or one paragraph, as little or as much as you choose. What thoughts are residing in your mind right now? Write them down and reread each one of them before you continue with the next. Doing so lets you see thoughts in a less emotional and overwhelming way. Also, the pause between having the thought and writing it down can give you a moment to reflect on its meaning. Furthermore, you engage both hemispheres of the brain when you write thoughts down (touch, vision, thinking and maybe taste and smell when you drink your beverage). Engaging the whole brain often leads to you gaining a broader perspective, because you're approaching the activity from both a creative and intellectual perspective simultaneously.

Perhaps ask yourself:

- ✔ Did this thought just pop into my head automatically?

- ✔ Does it fit with the facts of the situation it refers to?

- ✔ Is something there that I can explore further?

- ✔ How may I have thought about it at another time, in another mood? You do not have to come up with a definitive answer (obviously you can never *know* what you would have thought); just engage your mind with the idea that you *may* think of things differently at different times and in different moods.

Approaching difficult thoughts in a longer meditation

This exercise calls for you to expand your sitting exercise (from Chapter 5) to as much as 40 minutes. This is an experiment, and if you really focus on each moment you're likely to lose the awareness of time. Because you are going to sit for longer, please be sure to sit in a posture that supports your spine and cover yourself with a blanket or shawl.

Can you recall ever reading a fascinating book or magazine, being deeply involved in a meaningful conversation or making love without having a sense of time? The principle in this meditation is total engagement. The invitation to you is to stay with the practice even if you find it difficult because moment by moment this may change. Sitting with difficulties is a way of trusting your own resourcefulness and strengthening your ability to be with whatever comes up. You will harness patience, trust in the practice of mindfulness and realise that everything changes at last.

You may have a particular difficulty that you decide to work with before the start of this meditation. I invite you, however, to be open to the possibility that an unexpected visitor may arise at the point of the meditation where you open up to the difficulty. Kindly do not fight this but go with the flow. It may be valuable to observe the difficulty that arises out of nowhere.

The point of this exercise is to discover that you don't have to resist difficulties. What you resist often persists, so you take a different approach. Invite the difficult: a thought, a memory, a physical or emotional pain and be with it instead of running and hiding. Then observe what changes in response to being open and accepting towards this difficulty.

 This meditation shows you that the typical activity of running a mile or pushing a problem down if it hurts isn't the best response. Go to your special meditation place and get ready for a longer practice. Cover yourself with a shawl or blanket:

1. **Focus on the sounds you can hear and your breathing.** Get a sense of your body as a whole.

2. **Begin to engage with your thoughts.** Look at them simply as mental events.

3. **Notice whether you start getting involved in a 'story'.** Kindly allow this thought and related ones to pass by, endeavouring to observe thoughts as if they were sounds – here one minute, gone the next, pleasant, unpleasant, significant, insignificant: just thoughts. When you become settled in looking at your thoughts without 'owning' them, you can move on to the next step.

4. **Introduce some difficulty into this practice.** It may be something you're feeling in your body right now or a thought, a memory even. Whatever it is, try simply to accept it, maybe adding words such as 'whatever it is, let me feel/experience it'. Stay in the eye of the storm, to get right close to it. As you stay with the difficulty, does it change with time? This process may happen in one sitting or in a repeated attempt but after a while you'll be able to really feel it: its temperature, its intensity, its stinging or

stabbing or numbing pain. Let go of being the victim and really study the difficulty. See what you can discover by doing so.

5. **At the end of the practice, please note any meaningful insights in your diary.**

To approach big issues with this practice, you have to be an experienced meditator or to do the exercise along with another person. Please start with baby steps, and most of all keep yourself safe, protected and calm.

Visualising problems and problematic people

In this exercise, the key point is to understand that you have the choice to identify less with your thoughts and thus relate to them differently. When you deeply accept this notion, problems and difficulties tend to feel lighter and easier to deal with. Please relax yourself and when ready:

1. **Sit down on a chair and close your eyes.** Connect firmly to the chair you're sitting on and feel your feet deeply rooted to the ground.

2. **Visualise walking into your workplace.** You see a certain colleague to whom you feel inferior and who tends to create in you a feeling of weariness and discomfort.

3. **Ask yourself, as a compassionate friend would, what is causing you to feel so low, anxious or unworthy when this person enters your space?** Has this person ever belittled you or put you down? If the answer is no, search deeper. Does the person in any way remind you of other people who competed with you or were praised when you weren't? If the answer is yes, use a compassionate phrase you could say silently to yourself. For example, you might say, 'I know he reminds me of Peter in sixth form who always got the better reports and who was praised publicly. But right here and now I want to let go of this old tape in my mind. I am good enough and the best I can be at this moment.'

4. **Imagine yourself standing in the middle of a circle made up of mannequins that represent this person.** Each mannequin holds up a sign which represents one of the feelings this person seems to make you experience (such as insecurity, envy, fear, and so on).

5. **Imagine stepping out of the circle and looking at these mannequins from the outside.** The mannequins and the feelings they represent aren't really the person you're thinking about. Kindly understand that at any moment you can let go of these negative attributes your mind has made up. If you're feeling particularly creative, perhaps imagine each mannequin coming to life, stepping into the centre of the circle, taking a bow and walking away before disappearing into thin air.

6. Let go! Maybe you begin to realise that all human beings have their fears and insecurities, but that these feelings do not define them, nor do they define who you are or how you have to feel.

As with all meditations, note down insights and discoveries in your diary.

Being Kind to Yourself

The exercises in the preceding section (and indeed many of those throughout this book) help you to gain a clearer understanding of the fact that you don't have to be limited by your thoughts. They're mental events, influenced by your upbringing, environment, what you've been taught, and so on; they weren't imprinted unchangeably on your original brain from birth. By understanding thoughts and their origin, you can choose not to be consumed by them; on the contrary, you have the opportunity and ability to change negative and debilitating thoughts.

A key part of this thought-changing process is showing yourself kindness. While remembering that old habits die hard, you can focus on what's beautiful, nourishing, generous and supportive in your life. As each moment is a new beginning, you can decide here and now to let go of destructive and limiting thoughts that weigh you down or cause behaviours that lead to negative actions.

It can happen to anyone

At the height of his fame, Burt Reynolds was one of the film industry's highest paid actors. He was beautiful, intelligent and wild. While filming the movie *City Heat*, in which he wanted to do his own stunts, a chair he was supposed to be hit with was accidently exchanged, and didn't break apart when it hit his face. Instead, he ended up with a broken jaw. This event changed his life.

As he didn't seek medical advice immediately, the condition never healed properly. He was in so much pain that he used a daily cocktail of anti-depressants, painkillers and sleeping pills to get through it. Within two months, he'd lost a quarter of his body weight and had become addicted to many of the substances. He regularly used such high quantities that he should have died. His personality changed, his marriage broke up and he lost regular access to his young son.

Recently, Reynolds said that one day he looked in the mirror and said to himself, 'Is this what you want to end up as?' From that moment he didn't touch another of those pills. Amazingly, he was stronger than what tied him down. A simple act of will changed his life. And even though he still suffers from daily pain, he's happy and has a wonderful relationship with his adult son now.

This story is a great example that any moment can be the start of a new you. Right now you can, if you want, change your life around. It may not work out so smoothly as it did for Burt Reynolds, but you can make a start.

In this section I introduce you to the loving kindness meditation. It was the last practice the Buddha taught to his students. So you may say it is the most important one of all. I ask you to look at typical self-doubting or self-criticising thoughts and to try and change them at least a little, step by step. Basically, I invite you to learn the language of self-kindness.

Treating yourself well with the kindness meditation

In order to achieve the kindness and compassion that you need to acknowledge your demons and leave them behind, you may want to use this section's meditation, which focuses on kindness and compassion. It's a little bit like a prayer and starts with the seed of intention. By practising and trusting that these words have supported millions of people before you, you simply do it and see what happens.

Read the following phrases and then repeat them a few times silently to yourself:

- ✔ May I be safe and protected.
- ✔ May I be peaceful and free of suffering.
- ✔ May I live at ease and with kindness.

Visualising yourself, vulnerable as you are, as an image of your face, as your name written on an image of your heart, or by hearing the sound of someone saying your name, can be really helpful. Maybe even put one of your hands on the centre of your chest (to soothe yourself) before you repeat these gentle phrases again.

If you don't like these words, by all means change them to something simpler such as, 'I want to be safe, healthy, peaceful and kind.' Or make up your own verse.

Each time you recite these phrases, you're inclining your mind towards what's wholesome, kind and nourishing. Each time, a new thought of kindness imprints itself in your brain, mind and heart.

Remembering real moods occurring during real events

Thinking about how you felt in certain situations and being completely honest about your moods and emotions can help you understand them and get more joy and contentment out of life. The human experience is one of constant change, but you can create the intention to minimise harmful thoughts and actions for your own sake and that of others.

Even when a mood returns that in the past caused you to react emotionally – for example, erupting in anger – with more awareness you can see it for what it is. Using mindfulness and perhaps the coping breathing space from Chapter 8, you can be with the mood and observe it. Eventually you may master the situation, at least sometimes, and ride the waves of your anger without the need to lash out. You still feel the mood as it really is (with bodily sensations and emotions), but you intentionally don't replay the whole story over and over as you did in the past. In other words, you change the resulting action.

I suggest that you write down a list of memories or stories that tend to start you spiralling off into fruitless rumination. Draw up a list of events that created particularly strong positive and negative emotions. Consider what you felt during and after the event. Please try your best to be completely objective and without judgement. Then look for patterns, and find those that keep you stuck in the 'if only' or 'poor me' mental state.

Please take a look at the following two examples of hypothetical events and the negative thoughts and responses that you might have that are connected to them. See to what extent you can adapt them to suit your own experiences:

✔ **Remembering the last evening of a holiday romance:**

- 'If only he hadn't been Greek and lived overseas, he may have been the love of my life.' (Attachment and all-or-nothing thinking.)

- 'Why do I never find any exciting wonderful women who are available and live near me?' (All-or-nothing thinking.)

- You experience a lump in your throat and a tightness in the chest; you feel tearful and sad, with thoughts such as 'poor me', 'life is cruel' and 'why me?'

✔ **Remembering a wonderful dinner in town with many of your old schoolmates:**

- 'Most of them looked so good and had such interesting stories to tell. I'd love to experience this feeling every day.' (Desire for an experience to be repeated, which can lead to unrealistic expectations and disappointment.)

- 'My stories must have been really boring.' (Crystal-ball gazing; do you really know this for sure?)

- 'Most of them looked so much better than me.' (Maximising the negative from your point of view and minimising the positive in regard to you.)

- You're tense all over, repeatedly checking in the mirror and looking at those aspects of your appearance you don't like. You feel low and despondent. You want to curl up in bed thinking, 'I'll never go again.'

Consider what you notice about the thoughts and reactions, and whether you see any patterns emerging. Here's how I see the process:

1. **Both scenarios start with a happy memory.**

2. **You then add attachments and rejection, plus negative automatic thoughts (NATs), quite arbitrarily and based on no evidence.**

3. **Eventually nothing positive remains in your emotional, sensory and thinking awareness; it's all doom and gloom, brooding, disappointed ambitions, 'if-only' thoughts, and so on.**

The main thinking error is that you're seeing everything in a highly generalised way. The more you see things in this way, the harder you find it to pick out what really made you happy, calm and joyful, and which aspects of experience really were painful or uncomfortable. When your mind enters this dark space, you open up to all the fears that your mind can conjure: not being good enough, not good-looking enough, not interesting enough, not loved enough. Of course some of these fears may be based on real experiences, but over-generalising from past events and everything happening now and in the future is emotionally unwise. Fear has the tendency to feed on itself and soon you end up in a never-ending cycle of defeat.

Scientific evidence proves that the more you remember events in a generalised way, the more you experience negative mood traps of brooding, all-or-nothing thoughts and a sense of being stuck. The more specific you can train your mind and memory to be, the less trapped in negative mood states you feel. Mindfulness practice is a great way to train your mind to be specific.

Here are a few practice points you can experiment with in your diary. Write them down and then answer them as accurately as possible:

✔ When did you last feel grateful?

✔ When did you last feel childlike?

✔ When did you last feel peaceful?

✔ When did you last feel upset?

✔ When did you last feel adventurous?

✔ When did you last feel stuck?

Although the list contains negative mood states, I guess that if you can answer the question precisely you won't end up ruminating about the situation for ages.

Avoiding self-criticism and -judgement

The Rumi poem 'The Guesthouse' that I talk about in Chapter 8 indicates that moods and feelings come and go like unexpected visitors. By encouraging you to welcome negative emotions, I don't mean that you're desperately waiting for them to come back. But if they do, I ask you thoughtfully to accept that this is part of the human experience and remember that they're going to leave again sooner or later.

Negative thoughts, moods and feelings visit everyone. You can learn from them sometimes, or deepen your compassion for all humans, but you're not to blame when they arise.

I believe that over-simplistic and excessive judgement is a real bane of the world. From the day people start school until they retire (and often still thereafter), they're judged by their usefulness and how well they fit into the structures that humans have developed over the centuries of living in bigger and bigger tribes. Although society is now arguably more supportive than in old tribal atmospheres, many of the same hierarchies still remain. Some of these structures may well be welcome and helpful, but on the other hand in many respects people often forsake their uniqueness in order to fit in. Consider your responses to these questions:

✔ How much do you feel you judge yourself and others on a regular basis?

✔ Are you prepared to give yourself and others the benefit of the doubt?

✔ Do you look beyond the first layer of truth and deeper into the why and how of situations?

Consider these situations:

✔ When you see a figure wearing a hoodie, do you expect the worst even when it's windy or raining?

✔ When you tell your boss that you can't complete this task because you've an appointment booked, do you feel guilty?

✔ When somebody cancels an arranged date, do you judge the person as unreliable or think of yourself as unimportant?

✔ When you see a beggar, what do you think of the person?

Please write down some of your most common judgements about yourself, other people and the world in your mindfulness diary. Leave space after each statement. Then sit a little with each point and see whether your mindful self can come up with alternatives. It may happen, or may not, but give it a try to expand your awareness.

Releasing unhelpful emotional habits

One thing I encourage you to do is to plan your escape route for every potentially difficult situation – your figurative rope ladder that allows you to climb down from a heightened state of negative emotion when it seems to entice you to act aggressively and destructively. The platting of the rope ladder is your ongoing practice of mindfulness.

The platted rope – sometimes also called a safety net or a parachute – refers to the fact that mindfulness needs to be woven deeply into your unconscious so it can be an effective support in challenging times. It won't suffice if you use it like a headache-pill or a plaster to cover a scratch. Frankly speaking, if you practise mindfulness only occasionally, in times of trouble, it may not be helpful at all. It's a skill that you need to know by heart, so you can access it even when you're stewing in adrenaline and most rational thinking and decision-making fails.

Please consider writing a list of negative actions that you want to let go of, bit by bit. The point of this list isn't to make you feel guilty, but to create a reminder of what work lies ahead. Here are a few examples, but please note down your own little errors if they aren't contained in the list (avoid mentioning any big or grandiose mistakes you've made, and concentrate on the little things that can make all the difference):

- ✔ Shouting at somebody who made a mistake or to vent frustration.
- ✔ Belittling somebody for a weakness.
- ✔ Being overcritical of others even when they've given their best.
- ✔ Letting others down because you don't feel like doing something.
- ✔ Taking advantage of someone's kindness or vulnerability.
- ✔ Being greedy and/or lacking in generosity.
- ✔ Being short with others when they need a listening ear.
- ✔ Not offering your seat on public transport to somebody who needs it.
- ✔ Judging others who seem to be wasting their time – for example, people who live on the street.
- ✔ Finding logical excuses for not giving to charity.

No doubt you can think of other little deeds and acts of meanness that you can easily give up, as much for the sake of others as for yourself.

Recent research on the brain shows that self-compassion feeds outward compassion and vice versa. In all the above instances, kindness meditation helps you to let go of unhelpful habits and increase your awareness of kindness towards yourself and others.

Finding inner peace by sitting with your thoughts

Here, I describe another way of sitting with your thoughts and inviting them to arise in your awareness (to add to the methods in Chapters 6 and 8). This exercise differs from allowing random thoughts to engage you in a longer thinking process. You're going to watch thoughts as if you were outside yourself looking within. You observe the events of your mind without judgement and let them go. No response is expected or required.

The start of this practice may be familiar to you from Chapters 6 and 8:

1. **Settle into your preferred starting position in your meditation practice space.** Make sure that you won't be disturbed and that you feel warm.

2. **Feel the connection points of your body and the surface you're sitting on.** Shift into a dignified upright posture, using your breath or sound as your focus of awareness.

3. **Bring your focus to your body.** Some areas of your body tend to feel strong sensations. The invitation here is to bring friendly curiosity to this experience. If at all possible, go even further, softening and opening to the experience of discomfort and observing whether this makes any difference to the experience.

4. **Say to yourself: 'What is this feeling I'm experiencing about? Does it feel like fear or more like anger?'** Many thoughts are tightly linked to feelings, so experiment with observing the root of the feeling more closely. Again, dare to get really close to any destructive emotion or thought so that you understand the intrinsic parts of it and may with time discover that you can let it go earlier and earlier and more and more.

5. **Finish the practice after 30 minutes by returning to your breath, grounding yourself and eventually opening your eyes.** Sit for a little while before you get up.

Here are further ways in which you can vary this meditation:

✔ See your thoughts or feelings as dandelion heads that are ready to be blown away. Get familiar with them and before you enter the realm of the story you are about to tell yourself, blow them away.

✔ View your thoughts or feelings as snowflakes falling from the sky. Try to catch them, and as soon as they're caught, they dissolve.

✔ Visualise yourself standing on top of a big bridge over a motorway. Each vehicle that passes by carries a thought or feeling, which you briefly get a glimpse of before it disappears from sight.

Reviewing Your Accomplishments This Week

Whether you're following this course sequentially and have now completed week six or you've read only this chapter, please use these questions to help review your efforts:

✔ Do you feel able to relate more effectively and positively to your thoughts after reading this chapter? If not, perhaps consider taking another look through the earlier section, 'Demystifying Thoughts: They're Less Peculiar Than You Think').

✔ Are you managing to disengage from your thoughts a little more easily after practising the exercises in the 'Parting the Waves of Self-Doubt' section, earlier in this chapter?

✔ Can you look upon yourself with more compassion, perhaps giving yourself the benefit of the doubt a bit more, as I describe in the earlier section, 'Being Kind to Yourself'?

Chapter 10

Coming Into Port – Week Seven: Looking After Your Own Wellbeing

- -

In This Chapter

▶ Being proactive in your own treatment and restoration

▶ Handling everyday negative experiences

▶ Bringing enjoyment into your life

▶ Protecting yourself

- -

*N*o doubt you know just how easily you can get caught up in the whirl of daily duties and activities, leaving no time for yourself. And when you do get a moment to relax, the temptation is to spend it in non-productive or even unhealthy ways, such as slumping in front of the goggle-box. As a result, you need to ensure that you create time that's quite deliberately reserved for your wellbeing, because if you put things off until time appears miraculously, you're going to have a long, long wait!

The key aim of this chapter is to encourage you to reconnect to activities and interests in your life that you may have given up or put on hold in order to create more space for work and responsibilities. I ask you to review your daily activity and work schedule, decide which actions drain and which recharge you, spend a few minutes each evening on those that positively benefit you and work on accepting that you've no reason to beat yourself up just because you're taking a little time for yourself. I also provide some great practical exercises for dealing with everyday hassles and problems and encourage you to have fun and enjoy mindful living throughout the day.

If you feel resistance – perhaps thinking that you've no time to spare and can barely fit in your daily meditation as it is – please don't give in to the urge to avoid reading any further or to drop this book accidentally into the bath or leave it on the bus! This chapter is an essential part of your mindfulness practice, so remember to observe any such reactions mindfully so that you can catch yourself before you make any rash decisions.

Ahhh, that's NICE!

The UK government created NICE in 1999 to lessen the discrepancy in the accessibility and quality of NHS treatment. In brief, NICE is a kind of watchdog, making sure that the NHS offers and recommends only safe treatments. As part of its duties, NICE makes recommendations for healthy living and prevention of disease.

Kindness, compassion and mindful living reduce the probability of ill health and increase a sense of wellbeing, connectedness and belonging within yourself and to the world around you. The mindset I ask you to adopt in this chapter is one of nourishing and replenishing yourself with kindness, generosity and patience. Take great care of yourself, and remember that your wellbeing is vital to a great life!

Getting Your Bearings on the Course

If you started your mindfulness programme because it seemed the 'in-thing' to do and looked straightforward, by this point in the eight-week course you no doubt know that mindfulness isn't as effortless and uncomplicated as you thought. Your mind wants to keep busy all the time and tends to lean towards and connect to pointless ruminations. A wise American psychologist once said that 'negative thoughts are like Velcro and positive thoughts are like Teflon': you attach to the negative thoughts all too easily! The problem is that these ruminative patterns rarely concern themselves with the joy and adventure of life.

For this chapter to yield the best results, you should already trust in mindfulness enough to implement it into your life, because only regular practice allows you the chance to feel equanimity and peace. As part of this preparation, I suggest that you:

✔ Design and set up a personal, designated, conducive meditation space, as I describe in Chapter 4, in which you can feel calm and be left undisturbed. Also, find and stick to the best time of the day to meditate for you.

✔ Become familiar with the idea of 'non-doing'; in other words just being with the breath and scanning your body mindfully (see Chapters 4, 5 and 6).

✔ Read Chapter 7 and work on gaining an understanding of stress and how mindfulness can combat it.

Taking Positive Steps to Look After Yourself

What you do with your time, moment to moment, can affect your general welfare and your ability to respond competently to the challenges you inevitably come across in the course of your life. Amazingly, many people truly believe that they don't have time to pamper themselves or look after themselves as they would look after a friend, child or pet. I'm not talking about ruining yourself through excessive gratification or reckless over-indulgence, but instead that common belief that you shouldn't do something you enjoy doing – at least not too often. Often, this belief causes guilt to arise when you do something you want to do.

Evidence shows that mindfulness helps people to recover from burn-out and illnesses of both body and mind. This evidence is why the National Institute for Health and Care Excellence (NICE) Guidelines and the Mental Health Foundation (UK) promote and encourage people to develop mindfulness skills, so that they can prevent illness or help themselves to heal more quickly (check out the sidebar 'Ahhh, that's NICE!' for more details).

Taking a break: Fixing your focus mindfully

Throughout this book I describe a good number of meditations and daily mindfulness exercises for you to practise in your everyday life. Rather like brushing your teeth, having a shower or eating regularly, the need to engage in your chosen mindful routines is important.

MBCT – more than it first seems

Significant and repeated research indicates that mindfulness-based cognitive therapy (MBCT) can reduce the recurrence of depression. Two randomised controlled trials came to the same result: individuals who tended to suffer from recurrent depression halved their relapses when regularly implementing MBCT. However, evidence also suggests that MBCT can be helpful in other areas too: it can improve sleep, increase self-acceptance, increase immune functioning and reduce dependency on alcohol and illegal drugs. More than 10,000 research papers on the subject have been published during the last decade. More and more neurological research indicates that mindfulness practice also improves certain areas in the brain responsible for memory and compassionate behaviour, for example.

Here's an extended version of the ten-minute mind-movie viewing meditation in Chapter 6, which you can do anywhere, at any time, in any position. This time, I invite you to choose something that initially appears to have no particular interest, such as a blank wall, a curtain with a repetitive pattern or a piece of rubbish like an old cloth. These viewing objects do not present any beauty or interest at first, but see what you can really make out when you look more deeply. Even if you find nothing outstanding, check whether your body sensations or emotions vary from the beginning of the practice to the end of it. Consider thinking about whether the simple act of watching something can change the experience of the present moment and the energy flow in your body.

When you feel ready, please:

1. **Ground yourself by feeling into your body.** Focus on three points of contact: your big toe, the little toe and your heel, which together act like a strong tripod of safety. Bring your awareness to your body sensations and emotions and mentally note down what you find there. Are you calm or excited, joyful or irritable? Are you feeling tension anywhere in your body or do your muscles feel loose? Remember that no right or wrong way of being exists. Simply acknowledge what you find without attaching any value or judgement to it.

2. **Locate a window frame, a plant or an object at home or in your office; or stop in front of a shop window, a tree, bush or any other interesting item.** Now resolve in your mind that for the next few minutes you're going to gaze only at this one chosen viewpoint.

3. **Resolve not to let your eyes wander.** See how much detail you can find in this one area of focus. Sometimes things change within the frame much more that you may expect (for example, when you look out of a window frame, different visitors come and go). Even if you choose an empty white wall, you can still find little cracks, dots, shadows and so on. Bring patience and curiosity to this practice and don't force your eyes to deal with an overload of information.

4. **Re-ground yourself before finishing the exercise.** You may well feel more grounded and connected to life and in yourself. You may even experience a sense of solidity, a tingling sensation or feel as if you've had a weight lifted off your shoulders.

As always, I suggest that you write down your personal experience of this practice in your mindfulness diary. Not only does this activity deepen your brain's neuro pathways of wellbeing, but it also gives you an opportunity to see and compare how this way of being is developing in your life.

This meditation can be an important step to caring better for yourself. Taking a few minutes to allow your sense of seeing to rest on a small detail of life relieves your eyes from the relentless overload of technology and visual stimulation.

Maintaining and developing your practice for your benefit

Your mind wants to keep continually busy with thoughts and worries, and so on. But these ruminations often revolve around what you have to do or think you have to do, the things that went wrong and the things that may go wrong. Regular mindfulness practice offers you a whole new experience of life; a kind of childlike curiosity and connectedness with being alive and a moment-to-moment encounter with tiny little aspects of life.

Regular practice is crucial here, as is noting down in your mindfulness diary what changes you observe in your daily life, behaviour, thinking patterns, use of language, and so on. For some examples, take a look at the sidebar 'Noting progress for motivation'. Let these examples inspire and motivate you. Write down a list of your own ideas about changing everyday behaviour and actions by applying mindfulness to them.

Be patient and kind to yourself, because nobody manages to carry out all their good intentions. Any single one is a step in the right direction.

Noting progress for motivation

People who practise mindfulness regularly report the following positive changes – perhaps a few tie up with your own observations:

✔ I eat more slowly and have experimented with foods I wouldn't have touched before.

✔ I drink tea or coffee with much more aware-ness and joy. I bought a special mug and feel its texture and weight, look at its beautiful colour, try different types of tea/coffee and have a real break from everything, just by doing this one thing. Not only does it taste better, but I feel more relaxed when I finish.

✔ I don't run after a bus or a train anymore. Another one'll be along soon. I walk more slowly and see the world rush by. I prac-tise mindful walking or queuing and feel at peace. Every minute of my life is worthy to be experienced; actually, it's precious.

✔ I listen more carefully to what my partner/colleague has to tell me. I'm also more mindful of how I respond and what words would best express what I am feeling.

✔ I have a mindful bath or shower where I no longer make mental to-do lists; this activity is almost like being in a spa on holiday.

✔ I treat myself to a massage or facial because I really enjoy being looked after.

✔ Many people have noticed that I'm more joyful and interested in life; some think that I seem to have more patience and am less fussy or critical.

These possible results of mindful living are just a few examples; you can undoubtedly think of more.

Beginning your day with a treat

In Chapter 6, I suggest that you start your day with a delicious mindfulness breakfast with your favourite options and your own ingredients. To help you generate ideas, peruse my personal idea of a mindful breakfast:

Here's how to go about creating a French breakfast at home. For the perfect *café au lait* you need fresh ground coffee, a cafetière, a small pan, an electric whisk (to froth up the milk), an ideally fresh croissant and brown sugar:

1. **Prepare the coffee, making sure to smell the ground powder before adding hot but not boiling water to it. Breathe in deeply and enjoy!**

2. **Heat the milk (semi-skimmed or full cream) and just before it boils, take it off the stove.**

3. **Put the croissant on top of a toaster and keep turning it over so it gets crusty but doesn't burn; continue until it smells lovely and irresistible.**

4. **Start frothing the milk in the small pan – always start with the top layer and work your way down.**

5. **Pour the coffee into your favourite mug, add sugar if you want and then, spoon by spoon, add the milk into the mug, stirring it in gently and at the end add the frothy part on the top.**

6. **Add a crown of powdered or grated chocolate on top of the frothy peak if you desire.**

7. **Find a perfect seat in the kitchen or dining area and bring in the *café au lait* and croissant.**

8. **Dunk the croissant mindfully into the coffee, let it soak up a bit of the brew and immediately bite off a chunk soaked in frothy coffee and still crusty at the top.**

9. **Chew and soak up the flavours of coffee, sugar, frothy milk and crispy croissant.**

10. **Really taste each bite – it's a heavenly concoction; enjoy the smell and notice how you're feeling in your body while engaging in this joyous ritual.**

If you can start every day with a mindful breakfast – joyfully engaging with it, using all your senses and tasting it in an unrushed way – the likelihood is that you can take this sentiment and energy into the rest of your day. Yes, maybe you need to get up 15 minutes earlier, but it really is worth it.

Please don't forget to write down your experiences in your diary.

Story of a mindful dishwasher

Some twenty years ago I was told the story of a young mother who was always listening keenly to the tales of her girlfriends who had started yoga and meditation classes. She was a single parent of three young children and couldn't afford babysitters, so had no way to attend classes. All she could do was to offer visiting yoga and meditation teachers from India or Sri Lanka a guestroom in her house. One of them was a very well-known yogi and would have been happy to guide her in a sitting practice every morning. However, each time they tried one of her children suddenly needed attention. She was so sad not to be able to learn directly from this wonderful teacher.

One day, the yogi simply asked her what chore she spent most of her time doing. 'Washing the dishes, of course', was her immediate answer. So he went and stood next to the sink and instructed her while she was washing up. He invited her to be really present in the here and now and said: 'Feel the temperature of the water, the movement of your hands, how you pick up a bowl or some cutlery. Watch how you hold your body and what you can see, sense and smell. Bring mindfulness to everything and every action you encounter when washing the dishes.' She really entered a space that was totally connected to the moment. How you connect to the here and now doesn't really matter, and this was her best option for now. In this way, the washing up became her practice for many years until her children were old enough and she could go to meetings and retreats.

If you are one of the many carers, mothers, fathers and other people who have very little time for formal practice, kindly try your best to make an everyday activity into your formal practice.

I hope that this story shows that you can live life mindfully moment by moment, and the formal practices are only the preparation for leading a mindful, peaceful and compassionate existence.

Rebalancing Your Daily Life

Sometimes you can have sincere intentions of introducing a new idea into your life, but fate seems against you. Hindrances of all different kinds can prevent you from practising mindfulness effectively. Well, here's the good news! There's no right or wrong way of doing it, only your way!

Think about an everyday chore that you can engage in mindfully. Choosing a repetitive activity that has to be done can become a fertile practice ground. For example, having to shred hundreds of pages of paper can be a time to connect to your breath, to a sense of your body as a whole and to check how you're feeling in general. Don't hold back; let your imagination run wild – you can take the rubbish out mindfully, wash the car mindfully, change the cat litter tray mindfully.

Mindfulness is so adaptable that you can use it to rebalance your life more positively and even to remove the hindrances that get in the way of you practising mindfulness. How convenient!

Identifying your daily drainers and possible rechargers

Often you can feel listless because all your energy is invested in the things that 'matter': work, status, bonuses, and so on. From time to time, you may ask yourself, 'is this really it?'

In all likelihood, you always feel like you've too much to do in too little time. People nowadays have longer working hours, longer commutes and still have to deal with everything concerning the family home (in the past people often lived in union with grandparents, aunts, uncles, and so on and everybody chipped in). The relative wealth in monetary terms has a high cost in relation to day-to-day living. You're also constantly challenged by technological advances which, although assisting you in many ways, require you to use more time and energy in order to use them effectively than you're likely to save.

And the best place to start changing is right here with the person who's known and cared for you all your life: you! (Have you met?)

In this exercise, I ask you to find out which aspects of your life are feeding and nourishing you and which are draining and depleting you. Kindly do this activity in a quiet place where you won't be disturbed:

1. **Write down on a sheet of paper or in your mindfulness diary a list of your daily activities, including the time of day that you performed them (be as specific as possible).** Begin with waking up in the morning, continue through your day at work and go all the way through to the evening when you go to bed. Please try to keep this daily log of activities to no more than 20 entries.

2. **Draw an image or a symbol next to each activity, indicating whether you like it and find it nourishing, feel neutral about it, or feel negatively about it or that it depletes you of energy and positivity.** For example, J for positive, L for negative and 0 for neutral – use whatever symbols make the most sense to you.

3. **Go back and mindfully ask yourself which negative activity (or indeed neutral one) you can change into a positive one without too much effort.** For example, perhaps you can make waking up more enjoyable: count your blessings, think about something you're grateful for, and go to the window and open it, taking a few mindful breaths of fresh air.

4. **Think about what other mindful activities you can implement to increase the nourishing aspects of your day.** You can perhaps decide to walk to work mindfully, and let any sound be the sound of mindfulness inviting you to stop and take a mindful breath. Or you may be able to have a proper lunch break in silence or take a co-worker with you and explore nearby lunch options. A brief walk, fresh air, natural light and actually eating when you're supposed to be eating can be a real mood-lifter.

Table 10-1 shows what your daily activities log may look like.

Table 10-1	Sample Daily Log of Activities	
Time	*Activity*	*Reaction*
7:00 a.m.	Wake up	L
7:15 a.m.	Get up	L
7:30 a.m.	Shower, brush teeth, get dressed	0
8:00 a.m.	Eat breakfast	J
8:30 a.m.	Drive to work	L
and so on	and so on	and so on

This exercise can help you re-evaluate those activities that you may consider necessary but for which you can pay the high price of stress, depression and burn-out, and immune disorders and other physical forms of illness. I describe the physical illnesses in more detail in Chapter 7.

Sometimes you can help relieve the pressure on you by completing a simple task that has been looming over you for a while. This task doesn't have to be anything big, perhaps just paying an outstanding bill or making a quick phone call to sort something out.

Alleviating feelings of anger

Emotions of all kinds, good or bad, can trigger thoughts and vice versa. You may be surprised to discover that I suggest you invite in any guests – even malice, shame and dark thoughts.

Accepting such negative emotions as part of you may be a little odd, but the truth is that humans become angry and bad-tempered. In a recent interview, the Dalai Lama admitted that he'd occasionally been trapped by anger and bad-temper. He was still his usual self and laughing when he explained that his team knew well how he sometimes displayed these destructive emotions. Perhaps he laughed because he's so very much aware of his humanity.

So before you can accept something and then respond wisely, the first step is always to know that it exists. Then, if anger and bad-temper occur more regularly than usual, you can take it as a sign that you're stressed or mildly depressed. Allow your awareness to use these emotions as a guide, and then mindfully search for alternatives within your heart.

Please read the following lovely piece of writing a few times. Ask yourself why I include it in this section. Now see whether somehow you can embrace the fallible, angry you. The fact that 'you are' suffices. Just because humans have a more developed brain that other animals and can ask 'why', doesn't necessarily mean that you need to ask permission or display perfect behaviour to deserve your place in this world. Try to get your head around this proposal: even if you make mistakes (join the club!) you're worthy to be here as a wonderful expression of creation.

Just For Me

What if a poem were just for me?

What if I were audience enough because I am,

Because this person here is alive, is flesh,

Is conscious, has feelings, counts?

What if this one person mattered not just for what

She can do in the world

But because she is part of the world

And has a soft and tender heart?

What if that heart mattered,

if kindness to this one mattered?

What if she were not distinct from all others,

But instead connected to others in her sense of being distinct, of being alone,

Of being uniquely isolated, the one piece removed from the picture

All the while vulnerable under, deep under, the layers of sedimentary defence.

Oh let me hide

Let me be ultimately great,

Ultimately shy,

Remove me, then I don't have to. . .

be . . .

But I am.

Through all the antics of distinctness from others, or not-really-there-ness, I remain

No matter what my disguise

Genius, idiot, gloriousness, scum

Underneath, it's still just me, still here,

Still warm and breathing and human

With another chance simply to say hi, and recognise my tenderness

And be just a little bit kind to this one as well,

Because she counts, too.

—Anon

Stabilising your mood

In order to (re)balance your mood, you really need to balance your daily activities: ask yourself how you can take care of yourself, limit activities that bring you down and accept areas in your life that, at least for now, you simply can't change. Here are a few other suggestions for those difficult moments:

- ✔ When you feel overwhelmed by demands, follow the coping breathing space meditation from Chapter 8.

- ✔ Ground yourself when your brain seems to shut down. Feel your feet firmly rooted; sense three points of contact – your big toe, your little toe and your heel. This grounding helps to give you a sense of steadfastness and solidity. You're likely to feel much clearer in your thinking and more in control of the situation.

- ✔ Ask yourself, when the going gets rough, how will I feel about this situation tomorrow, in a month in a year from now. Perspective is a great healer.

- ✔ Book a home treatment (such as massage, Pilates or reflexology, for example) or personal training session – many complimentary therapists and personal trainers are nowadays perfectly happy to come to your home. It can be so lovely not having to go out again after a treatment or training session, particularly if you've a long commute to work. You can stay put and yet still engage in a healthy activity.

✔ Call, or even better, invite round a friend. Humans are pack animals and socialising and meeting others is important.

✔ Do something manual and creative such as kneading dough, arranging plants, drawing a picture or playing a musical instrument. Stimulating the creative mind balances out the overactive left hemisphere of your brain.

✔ Ask yourself whether a challenge can wait until tomorrow.

✔ Look at photographs you've collected over the years.

✔ Just take care of now – this moment is precious if you really allow yourself to think about it; the present moment is part of your life.

Having Fun for Fun's Sake

You can use only one of your two nervous systems (which I describe in more detail in Chapter 7) at any one time:

✔ **The sympathetic nervous system:** The 'fight-or-flight' system that releases stress chemicals and is essential for survival.

✔ **The parasympathetic nervous system:** The 'peace' system and the one in which ideally you want to spend most of your life.

Laughter automatically switches on the second system, thus making humour a great stress releaser: you laugh and feel a little better.

Wellbeing has a direct connection to good humour and mood. Try it out: think about what makes you giggle and thus nourishes you, and note it down in your diary.

Laughter is the best medicine

In his book *Anatomy of an Illness* (as well as in a movie about his story), Dr Norman Cousins describes how he was suffering from an untreatable degenerative disease. But he discovered that laughter gave him periods of being pain-free and eventually was one component of his self-developed treatment plan that helped him return to good health. He watched funny films and read funny books and jokes; doctors were perplexed as to how he reversed not only his illness but also the damage it had already done to his body.

Treating yourself

Have a 'Happy Unbirthday' (as Lewis Carroll says in *Alice in Wonderland*) 364 days a year. Every day is worth celebrating – as indeed is every moment.

Consider what gifts you can bestow on yourself and what treats you can organise for yourself in order to feel good and special. Write down a list of possibilities, including things you used to do and want to restart or things you always wanted to do but never dared (or got around) to – perhaps hobbies you really enjoyed in the past or adventures and holidays you'd enjoy.

Simple actions are a good start, like having your first hot drink in the morning and taking real time to enjoy it, while looking out into your garden if you have one. Or having a hot bath or massage, going to a movie or out for a lovely meal, or walking in the countryside.

And don't forget being generous towards other people, such as taking time to help in a soup kitchen at Christmas or donating to a good cause. Kindness nurtures kindness.

Not overindulging

Here's a little pinch of wisdom: looking after yourself is great, really! What isn't helpful, however, is to make any of your chosen tension-releasing activities absolute must-haves.

If you book a massage and suddenly receive a text telling you that the masseuse is unwell, rather than feeling stroppy and letting self-pity ride you, try to be mindful of your disappointment and think of an alternative activity. Or perhaps find a simple act right there and then that gives you a sense of wellbeing, such as putting your feet up and reading a novel in the middle of the day, even if loads of housework still needs to be done. You know what? It'll still be there in half an hour.

Furthermore, bear in mind that pastimes such as gambling with friends, video games and watching television can also become unhealthy attachments. You aren't going to disappear in a puff of smoke if you can't watch this one favourite TV programme, or eat the chocolate you put in the fridge that disappeared because another family member has eaten it!

Whatever you do, remember that anything that holds you prisoner is, in the long run, not healthy.

Dealing with Threats to Your Wellbeing

Over time, and with continued mindfulness practice, you become more and more able to respond wisely to unexpected occurrences. Don't worry about turning into a perfectly functioning machine (as you know, machines also malfunction), but do notice as you move beyond being a prisoner of your old patterns and fears. You can truly build enough new, compassionate, moment-to-moment patterns of thinking and behaving that can guide you in taking the right actions. Nobody else has to tell you what to do and how to respond. Your wise mind (in other words, your brain and heart in unity) guides you.

When you have even a sniff of this experience, you don't want anything to disrupt it. So, in this section I provide tips on tackling impediments to your wellbeing.

Remembering the good

If you feel that your mental and/or physical health is beginning to deteriorate, your first point of action needs to be the coping breathing space meditation (in Chapter 8). It can help you to see deeply what's amiss, what feels out of balance and how you may proceed.

Your next point of action, once you have started using regular mindfulness interventions, is to focus on your 'EGS', which stands for Enjoyment, Gratitude and Satisfaction. Ask yourself the following questions for each category:

- ✔ **Enjoyment:** 'What did I enjoy today?' For example, 'I enjoyed birdsong, a nice meal, a hot bath, making my friend laugh, a lovely sunset or rainbow', and so forth.

- ✔ **Gratitude:** 'What am I grateful for?' For example, 'I'm grateful for my legs, my eyes, my home, this apple, my friends', and so on.

- ✔ **Satisfaction:** 'What am I satisfied with?' For example, 'I'm satisfied with polishing my shoes, taking out the rubbish, getting rid of old clothes or newspapers', and so on.

Satisfaction isn't as significant as achievement, but it points at a small action that in itself was useful enough to remember. All the little things count, just as every moment does.

Write down your regular EGSs every evening (a minimum of one per category) and immediately in times of need. Doing so helps you to incline your mind towards that which is wholesome, nourishing and energising.

I recommend that you write them down by hand in your diary because:

✔ Writing things down by hand stimulates both brain hemispheres.

✔ If you write things down last thing at night, it closes your thinking process on an optimistic note.

✔ In an emergency, you still remember those exercises you practise most regularly (that is, the coping breathing space and EGSs).

✔ Your diary helps you to remember all the good things in your life even when life is tough. Everything passes at last and rainbows often follow storms.

Finding the right response

Life is unpredictable – joy, suffering and equanimity are all available to you, but never on demand. Therefore, being with 'what is' is really important. Becoming disappointed about something not arriving or occurring is only natural, but chewing over the why, how, when, and so on only deepens the ruminative downward spiral towards despair.

Adapting to and accepting the unexpected is a skill that's wonderfully supported by mindful awareness. When you sit in mindfulness meditation and watch your thoughts – good, bad, indifferent – but don't get caught up in their web, you can at times experience a sense of peace and oneness.

Linking your actions to your moods

Linking your actions to your moods can only be helpful if you understand that everything is transient and passes in time. Feeling upset because your friend doesn't show up for an arranged meeting, for example, is generally understandable. Shouting at her when she eventually manages to get in touch may prove to be the opposite of what's helpful for gaining perspective towards what really happened. What if her mobile had run low and she was involved in an accident, hopefully only as a witness. She may not share it with you if she feels you've already judged her.

So let mindful action and speech be your guides. When she turns up or phones, focus mindfully on your breathing and ground yourself by feeling your feet firmly connected to the surface you're standing or sitting on. Then listen with awareness and compassion to the story she has to tell. Thereafter decide, ideally without judgement, whether her actions make sense to you or whether you need to tell her how worried or disappointed you were. She's likely to listen more readily if she feels you haven't jumped to a conclusion and is likely to respond empathically to your pain if she can really hear it rather than your self-pitying tirade!

Even if your mood has been affected by a long, uncertain wait, as best as you can, apply non-judgemental compassionate awareness. And even if you don't manage to, you can always practise it next time. This experience is part of the human condition, the human experience. Maybe, at the next opportunity, you can apply a mindful response.

Improving how you feel through what you do

When you cope with mindfulness as your guide in all interactions with others and also yourself, you find more often than not that the heavy cloud of low, anxious or angry mood lifts and your dealings with fellow beings appreciably improves.

It does take time, but moment by moment you notice a softening towards your own flaws and those of others. With this softening, you may also observe a gentle but ongoing embrace of life's experiences, even those you may not have handled well in the past. There's no guarantee of significant change, but there will be a general tendency towards kindness.

Boiling over with personal frustration

In the past, before I had started to meditate regularly, I remember being a lot more easily upset and frustrated when others got things wrong (in my not so humble opinion). I suppose I had a lot of judgement, but also a fear of others not caring enough for me.

One day, an Austrian friend who'd recently come to visit me in Wales had the lovely intention of making tea for us. She filled the kettle and put it on the electric stove. Soon there was a burning smell and smoke, and the fire alarm was set off. She was almost in tears because she'd ruined my electric kettle (which in the 1980s weren't available in Austria). She just sat down and trembled and cried while I was opening the windows, turning off the stove, removing the melted kettle and

telling the fire brigade that it was a minor household incident. They were so kind and laughed heartily when I told them what had happened. I then had to use a pan to boil water and make tea.

When I joined my friend on the sofa, she was still completely stunned. When I asked her why, she told me she was waiting for me to explode. She explained that exploding is what I usually did when people acted unthinkingly. I then shared with her how kettles worked differently in the UK and that I had been the one who was unthinking because she'd just arrived and couldn't possible know what 'hi-tech' advances the UK had accomplished! In the end, I gave her a big hug, and she relaxed and we both laughed. She's still my friend now 30 years later.

Sitting with spacious awareness

This exercise, which you can also listen to in Track Eight, is also often called 'choiceless awareness'. In this practice, you don't anchor your awareness in any particular way. It's a free-flowing meditation, which has its own beauty and is also different every time you practise it. You can see it as allowing the mind to observe whatever surfaces during the meditation. Issues that have been deeply repressed may begin to rise to the surface, providing you with the opportunity to address them consciously. By recognising your self-destructive patterns, their power to control your behaviour diminishes.

Choiceless awareness may create a quality of mind that's free from making judgements, decisions or generating commentary as it meets with sense experiences. It assists the mind to respond to each new moment without the burden of its past history or of making future projections. When the mind no longer clings to anything, not even to the idea of 'not clinging' (non-attachment), you may realise, suddenly or gradually, that you already are truly what you've been searching for.

Buddhists believe that nature resides in everyone already. In layperson's terms, this belief means that all you are (even the imperfect, stumbling actions you engage in) already holds the key to beauty and kindness. This concept may be an odd one to grasp, but think of it as having the intention to achieve a greater sense of spaciousness and sitting with determination, while also being open to different 'anchors of attention/awareness' (a concept I describe more in Chapter 4).

To practise this meditation, please:

1. **Try to let go of any specific focus of alertness – just sit with awareness.**

2. **Allow whatever thoughts and so on arise simply to be here, now, in this moment.**

3. **Notice any messages or insights that arise, and if you choose make a mental note of them without taking it any further right now.**

4. **Observe recurring patterns of actions and reactions of the mind (thoughts and emotions) and the body (such as aversion or tensing up).**

5. **Return to the breath as an anchor if your mind feels too unsettled.**

6. **Finish when it feels right, trusting your inner clock as to how long this meditation lasts.**

Reviewing Your Accomplishments This Week

Please take a look at the following questions to help you appraise your well-being practices:

- ✔ Have you been able to accept the importance of proactively looking after yourself and put the lessons into practice too (as I discuss in the earlier section 'Taking Positive Steps to Look After Yourself')?

- ✔ Are you continuing to practise the exercises in the earlier section 'Rebalancing Your Daily Life' to assist you with everyday experiences?

- ✔ Are you managing to bring more moments of pure fun into your life (see the section 'Having Fun for Fun's Sake' earlier in this chapter)?

- ✔ Do you feel more confident about protecting your wellbeing after reading the preceding section 'Dealing with Threats to Your Wellbeing'?

Chapter 11

Looking Beyond the Horizon to the Rest of Your Life – Week Eight: Living Mindfully

In This Chapter

▶ Beginning the rest of your life
▶ Continuing to practise
▶ Living a daily mindful existence
▶ Taking your life into your own hands

This chapter (which covers week eight if you're following the course in order) is all about assessing your practice, if necessary addressing any specific aspects that you decide need your attention, and maintaining your motivation. This way you ensure that you continue to benefit from mindfulness into the future, whatever life throws at you. Think of it as being rather like brushing your teeth regularly and not just prior to visiting a dentist; you're brushing and flossing to achieve mindfulness meditation and daily mindfulness in regular life!

My aim is to prove that you can continue regular mindfulness practice even when you seem too busy or times are hard. I relate a few inspiring stories of how mindfulness helped other people and how much benefit they reaped from developing and practising this life skill on a regular basis. I invite you to add compassion to mindfulness, so that you allow yourself the occasional lapse into old unhealthy patterns but still know that every moment is a new beginning. I also provide a 'manual' for a mindful day, which is rather like a home-based mindfulness retreat.

Mindfulness can become second nature to you with practice and by maintaining a mindset of openness, childlike curiosity, adventure and patience. To help, I describe a number of attitudes that can help you move towards a gentler and kinder way of being. You can discover and work on these attitudes by practising mindfulness meditation.

Getting Your Bearings on the Course

As you approach the end of the eight-week course, I hope that you're managing to reserve a special 'out time' for yourself. If so, you may have realised how a little bit of stillness – moment by moment – can do wonders for your mood, energy and general wellbeing.

Please consider the following aspects as you begin the final week and implement any that you believe may help you:

- Think about which meditations are particularly working for you. Perhaps pausing for a breathing space (see Chapter 6) is proving helpful or just sitting with your breath is your all-time favourite. You may also like the body scan (check out Chapter 4), which can be a great practice to still the chattering mind and prepare you for sleep.

- Move mindfully during the day and feel the wonderful tension release when you open your chest and let your shoulders drop. Perhaps attempt mindful walking and decide whether you prefer indoors or outside. Try walking with bare feet and feeling how you imprint the soles of your feet onto the carpet or ground, noticing the lifting, shifting and placing of your foot. Turn to Chapter 6 for more on physical awareness and mindful walking.

- Consider how you arrange your meditation corner or room. Add little rituals, such as lighting a candle or ringing a bell, to help your body and mind remember to sit with dignity and kindness for the upcoming meditation (flip to Chapter 4 for more).

- Use the same shawl or blanket for your meditation each time so that it collects some wholesome energy with each practice as you increasingly associate it with sitting peacefully. Don't forget your 'Do not disturb' sign on the door. Make sure that you've a way of letting others in your home know that you're practising mindfulness. And remember that you *are* allowed to switch off your phone for a while!

Embracing a Mindful Life in Good and Bad Times

As I describe in Chapter 8, visitors in the form of events and situations come and go in your life and they aren't always pleasant or enjoyable. These visitors include illnesses and diseases that knock sufferers and their families for six. In this section I show that whatever challenges life throws at you, a little space for mindfulness helps you cope a lot better.

As just one example, research suggests that mindfulness exercises can help people caring for those with autism, enabling them to cope better with the challenges of leading a meaningful life. Mindfulness skills assist in reducing anxiety, obsessive behaviours and aggression. Read the sidebar 'A very special boy' for a specific inspiring instance.

A very special boy

Here's a story about a mother and child who were visited by a health challenge that took them on a long journey that had many rough moments. This is my story, and that of my son. I never thought we would get through as well as we did but, on this journey, I discovered mindfulness and it became my survival tool. This story shows that you can use mindfulness to help turn around difficult circumstances by continuing moment by moment, without giving up, kindly and patiently.

At about nine months of age, my son started singing and humming tunes. Any tune he heard was stored forever in his memory and he could hum it beautifully. People called him 'the little nightingale'. He learned to walk when he was about a year old and never wanted to drink out of a bottle or use a dummy. After stopping nursing, he went straight to drinking from a beaker.

Unfortunately, however, he still hadn't uttered a single word even when nearing his second birthday. In addition, he began experiencing anxiety with other children because he couldn't understand what they were saying or respond to them. He started spitting, screaming and hiding in corners. He engaged in obsessive rituals, such as straightening all the shoes in the hall and getting really upset if anybody moved them. He screamed his head off when he heard a vacuum cleaner. He only allowed me and his dad to touch him and hissed at other adults – even his grandmother, who was very upset at this behaviour.

We had no idea what to do or where to go. I went to Hong Kong (we were living in Beijing at the time) and visited a child psychologist, who initially suggested that my son was deaf, even though music was his life and loud noises drove him crazy. The psychologist then said that he was developmentally delayed, because he couldn't answer a single question correctly in the test she administered to him. I hired a speech therapist and gradually his attention span increased. He learned his first word at over two years old: his mother's name. But then he suddenly called all adults by this name.

Eventually, my son was diagnosed with ASD (Autism Spectrum Disorder) – a developmental disability that affects social, communication and imagination skills. People with ASD seem disinterested in the social world and struggle with non-verbal communication, such as interpreting facial expressions. I was heartbroken, and began to ask myself how he would ever be able to fend for himself.

When he was 6 years old, he managed to string his first sentence together. Around that time, I hired instructors for violin, piano and voice. The music centre in the brain is near the language centre and the strong stimulation through music most probably helped him with his language. He attended school with an assistant who worked with him at his own pace. At 19, he took his A-level exams and at 22 he finished university. I continued practising mindfulness after my son's diagnosis and I swear that it helped me to remain patient and compassionate. Even though my life was challenging, the gift of mindfulness changed my private and professional life. I discovered how to embrace life and all the guests who come and visit – the welcome and less welcome ones alike.

Two great figures for inspiration

His Holiness, the 14th Dalai Lama, was picked for his role of duty around 3 years of age. So he grew into the life of mindful meditation at an early stage of his development as a human being. Nevertheless, he still remembers some of the things he missed when no longer living at home: boiled eggs and pork, for example, which the Dalai Lama wasn't allowed to eat, for no reason that he's ever managed to find out. His family moved very close to his new royal residence and his dad used to tell him whenever this food was on the menu at home and the little monk sneaked away for a forbidden feast!

When he shares this anecdote and others, he shows not an iota of guilt. He's a real inspiration for people, because he's so at ease and at peace with others and himself. Of course, he also meditates for around five hours every day; the correlation between the two should be self-evident.

Another great role model is the philosopher Socrates. He was observed walking through the market in the centre of ancient Athens carrying a lit oil lamp at noon. Now, oil at that time was very expensive. Some of his students became worried that the famous eccentric was losing his mind. They asked, 'What are you looking for?' Eventually he replied, 'I'm looking for a Human Being.'

This story shows why Socratic questioning is a method still used in cognitive psychotherapy. Socrates intended his disciples to find answers by questioning and looking deeply inside. Through an extravagant form of lighting and seemingly wasting a precious commodity, he was making the important point that although the daytime market in Athens was riddled with beings, could any of them claim to be truly human?

Creating regular mindfulness practice is like bringing up a baby. As soon as you think that the child's routine is settled, it changes again; loving parents need to find out how to be patient with their newly arrived gift. Similarly, when you're creating a new lifestyle, even if it takes up only 40 minutes a day, you need to appreciate that challenges remain ahead.

Go about your practice as if only this moment matters, and treat every instance as a new beginning. Ask yourself and people you know well whether changes in your attitude or behaviour have been noticed. Perhaps you've become more sensitive to injustice in the world and the suffering of others. See which bell of mindfulness rings loudest for you. In the end, what matters most is your ability to apply mindfulness to your daily life – the changes will come, sooner or later.

The term *bell of mindfulness* refers to aspects of life that trigger new attention in you: the kindness you wouldn't allow, fearing it may be exploited; the awareness of human suffering; and the fact that all humans are in the same boat. These observations are wonderful details to record in your mindfulness diary.

Pledging to Practise

Everyone finds their enthusiasm and commitment to regular practice fading from time to time. In this section, I provide some tips and ideas to help you continue your practice for many years into the future.

Motivating yourself

A great help in maintaining your mindfulness motivation is to recall from time to time why you originally bought this book. Consider whether somebody told you about it, or just about mindfulness-based cognitive therapy (MBCT), or whether someone inspired you (check out the sidebar 'Two great figures for inspiration'). If you had particular hopes in respect of acquiring the skills of mindful living, think about how things look now. Ask yourself what you've found out about yourself and the practice of awareness, and what benefits you've discovered from practising meditation.

Here are some other questions to help you assess your progress:

✔ Are you ready to commit to mindfulness practice for a lifetime?

✔ What can you gain as against what you need to invest?

✔ Are any obvious obstacles preventing you from going on with this voyage?

✔ Have you considered strategies that may assist you when you feel stuck?

✔ How would you have responded to life if you'd been allowed to remain mindful, aware and in the moment, as children naturally are?

Remember those moments when you felt surprised by joy for no apparent reason; when you were totally involved with eating an ice cream, stroking your cat or dog or watching clouds passing, and not feeling guilty about not 'achieving' anything.

Here's a thought: if every single person on this planet added a sprinkle of mindfulness and a dash of compassion to their daily actions, how do you think our planet would be affected? Not everybody can be a Gandhi, a Martin Luther King or Aung San Suu Kyi, but little actions multiplied by many participants make a difference. Maybe you could think of that little gift you could offer.

Creating action plans

As part of exploring and practising mindfulness, you may have written down action plans to help you create space and willingness for regular meditative practice. Sometimes, however, even when you pencil the plans into your diary, you can find yourself not implementing them. If so, read the following account of an interesting psychological experiment that may help you to stay inspired and return to mindfulness meditation, even if you briefly lapse into your old pattern of living.

A researcher visited an old people's home to test whether using mindfulness or awareness would make a difference in the participants' lives. She chose two groups of people in their eighties and nineties. One group followed their normal routine but to another group she gave three awareness exercises to practise every day for one month: looking after a plant; getting dressed by themselves; and making one cup of tea or coffee for themselves every day.

After one month the group with the mindful tasks demonstrated extraordinary changes, which were apparent in their wellbeing and behaviour:

✔ They were more extroverted and started to create friendships; some even started dating again.

✔ Their mood was more sanguine.

✔ They had better skin-cell renewal, better immune responses and less stress chemicals in their blood.

✔ Their lungs worked more efficiently and they had an improved breathing ability.

How interesting what a little bit of mindfulness can do for you!

If this story inspires you, please consider thinking about what you plan to engage in mindfully and regularly from now on. Here are a few ideas:

✔ Connecting with nature in some way, such as gardening, getting new house plants or helping in a local project

✔ Showing kindness to your body, such as with mindful baths and showers, lovely lotions and potions, an Indian head massage or any other body treatment, buying a lovely soft nightgown or pajamas

✔ Starting a new hobby or renewing interest in an old one

✔ Going to the movies, theatre or opera, or watching a stand-up comic

✔ Meeting up with friends or people you like

> ✔ Joining a group that voluntarily offers something to the world and its inhabitants
>
> ✔ Eating and doing housework mindfully
>
> ✔ Travelling mindfully – not just on holidays, but every time you need to
>
> ✔ Engaging in a daily meditation practice of your choice
>
> ✔ Surprising strangers you meet by offering your seat or holding the door open for them – just because you care

Keeping a progress diary

If you haven't started keeping a mindfulness diary, it's never too late! At this stage, make it playful and stimulating so that you keep your practice going. You can create one with a lovely cover page, for example. This way your diary will not simply be a clinical collection of practice-related thoughts and observations, but something deeply personal to you; a physical embodiment of the playfulness and creativity you are discovering through your mindfulness practice.

Perhaps find some photos of beautiful snowbells to stick on the cover of your first diary; they symbolise the beginning of spring, a new start that repeats itself every year. Then every time you look at the diary or write in it, you feel inspired to write down new ideas and reread old entries. Choose whatever tickles your heart and helps you to persist.

Examine whether you're aware of blocks keeping you from engaging with your diary, such as:

> ✔ Oh no, I can't be bothered to do any more writing today.
>
> ✔ I thought mindfulness was all about 'being' and yet writing a diary reminds me of 'doing'.
>
> ✔ I'm so tired and relaxed now; I'll write it down later.
>
> ✔ I hate diaries – I hate my handwriting – this is all too much.

Make a point to notice your mind's tendency to focus overly on problems and avoid looking at benefits. See whether you can come up with advantages for writing things down in your mindfulness diary. For example:

> ✔ It will help me remember my journey.
>
> ✔ I can reread it when going through a rough stage in my life in the future.
>
> ✔ I may re-engage with my creativity: instead of writing I can draw.
>
> ✔ I'll write down a few bullet points – I can and want to manage that.

Having a Mindful Day, Every Day

In this section I introduce you to the possibility of carrying mindfulness through every moment of your day. Even if you find doing so too difficult just yet, perhaps you can pencil in one day a week where you experiment with mindfulness step-by-step from morning to night.

Waking up

When you wake up, and before you get up, kindly bring your attention to your breathing. Just watch the in-breaths and out-breaths for a little while. Feel the rising and falling of your chest. Maybe you can even notice how the air is cooler around your nostrils when you breathe in and warmer when you breathe out. Bring awareness to your body and mind, noticing how you move from lying to sitting, to standing, to action.

When you engage in your regular bathroom routines, such as brushing your teeth, showering, shaving, washing your hair – fully enter the experience. Allow all your senses to feast on the moment (smelling the shampoo or shower gel, tasting the toothpaste, feeling the warm water on your skin) and leave the planning of the day for after breakfast.

Breaking your fast

Many people leave out breakfast altogether or wash down their coffee while chewing the last bit of toast on the run. If you recognise this pattern in your life, try something different and celebrate breakfast like a king, really giving yourself time to enjoy a new day and a delicious meal. I describe preparing a full mindful breakfast in Chapter 6, but even if your breakfast's a tiny meal, mindful eating helps to make it last.

Now, give yourself time to plan your day by making mental notes or writing in your diary a few bullet points to help you remember.

Journeying mindfully

If you travel to work, be mindful of the little surprises the journey offers. Ensure that you don't need to rush – maybe leave ten minutes earlier than usual. Feel the air on your face, arms or whatever as you walk – or from your car's heater or air-con or through the bus or train window.

Your body thanks you for not getting stressed: doing things more slowly and mindfully helps you stay in your parasympathetic nervous system of soothing, equanimity and calm (see Chapter 7 for details). The more time you spend in this mode, the better your immune system and brain function.

Taking regular breathing breaks

Whenever you hear a sound – a car, voices, sounds of nature – use it as your call of mindfulness. Truly listen in an aware manner.

Throughout the day, seize a few moments to bring your awareness to your breath and connect with it. Are your in-breaths and out-breaths of the same length or not? Where do you feel the breath in your body? Do you notice the short pauses after each breath? Try a few deep and long breaths, really filling your lungs and breathing out slowly, because doing so helps to slow down your heart rate and makes you feel calmer and safer.

Performing mindful daily actions

Whenever you have a meal or drink, connect with your food/beverage and appreciate that it's linked to things that nourish development: sunlight, rain, the earth, the farmer, the shop where you purchased it. Bring awareness to consuming this food consciously for your physical health: really see your food, smell it, taste it and chew it. Even dwell with the taste in your mouth as a reminder of what you've just enjoyed.

Whenever you're waiting in a queue, kindly use this time to notice your standing and breathing. Take a moment to bring awareness of the contact of your feet with the floor and how your body feels. Notice any tense areas and gently stretch or breathe into them. Bring attention to the rising and falling of your abdomen. Focus on whether you're feeling impatient.

Kindly bring wakefulness and gentle awareness to all your daily activities – combing your hair, washing up, tidying up, dressing and putting on your shoes, ironing and working.

Communicating mindfully

When listening to people, try to do so mindfully without agreeing or disagreeing, or preparing what you're going to say next. Otherwise, you may miss out on important information. When speaking, see whether you can speak without overstating or understating. Kindness and patience are such wonderful states of mind that assist you when you want to get a message across and feel heard.

Going to sleep

This time of day may be best for your EGS (enjoyment, gratitude and satisfaction) practice that I describe in Chapter 10. Before you go to sleep, bring your attention to your breathing again. Close the circle of a day as you started it. Feel your body relaxing into rest and peace.

Embracing your experiences

Awareness and mindful living offer an uncomplicated but potent way for getting yourself back in contact with your instincts, with your innate inner wisdom and sense of truth – who you are beneath the restrictions and pressures placed upon you by your gender, class, religion and environment. All you need to be is yourself, not copying anybody else.

Re-engage with what you can call the 'true you', not worrying whether everybody agrees with or likes this original version of you. If you reconnect to this primal, unspoilt version of yourself, you quite naturally connect to mindfulness, for only this moment matters and counts.

Exercising mind and body

Remain aware of any tightness in your body throughout the day. Breathe into it and, as you exhale, kindly let go of excess tension. If you still feel tension – for example in your neck, shoulders, chest, stomach, jaw, knees or lower back – try some stretching exercises or practise the Alexander Technique, Pilates, Tai Chi, yoga or mindful walking once a day (I discuss the latter in Chapter 6).

Developing Mindfulness Attributes

Finding kindness and patience in your frenetic life can be challenging. So many things are out of your control: transport, noise, pollution, the weather, people's reactions to you, work demands and changes, and so on. But you *can* strive to be in charge of how you respond to each challenge and how you approach dealing with it. This voyage into awareness offers its own tests, but just remember that another moment is always around the corner for you to start again. Let kindness be your guide always.

This section describes the attributes that you develop by engaging in mindfulness meditation and everyday mindfulness, and which I ask you kindly to seek to cultivate and explore throughout your life ahead.

Remembering non-judgement

Mindfulness grows and expands as you increasingly take the position of an unbiased observer of your life experience. You need to become aware of the steady flow of judging and reacting thought patterns to your internal and external experiences. You may even feel trapped by them at times. However, through mindfulness, you can discover how to move away from them and almost like a backdrop on a theatre stage keep them on the outer edge of your experience.

When you start paying attention to the hyperactivity of your mind, you may be surprised by how frequently you judge everything. You aren't to blame, because you're taught to label and categorise what you see, hear, taste, smell, touch and think.

Notice also how you judge the value of each experience. You judge some aspects as good (perhaps they earn you a reward of some sort) and condemn others as bad (maybe they cause you discomfort). This constant evaluation can lock you into unconscious reactions. These judgements often take over your thinking, which in turn leads to a lack of peace and tranquillity within.

Kindly observe how often you're worried about liking something or being liked by someone. If you really care about yourself and go on the quest of finding peace, bring awareness to your favourite automatic judgements. This way you can slowly acquire the skill of seeing through your own prejudices and anxieties and freeing yourself from this judgement trap.

Here's a way to combat judgement of your meditation practice:

1. **Imagine that you're practising listening to sounds.** Again and again you become aware of thoughts referring to this practice as cumbersome or unnecessary, or you even think to yourself 'when will this be over?' These judgements simply arise uninvited.

2. **See these judgements for what they are and let them pass – even if they arise hundreds of times.** Every time you notice them, kindly return your attention to the sounds – your anchor of awareness.

3. **Remember that even if you perceive this listening practice as not exciting, that's absolutely fine.** From a mindfulness perspective, neutrality and equanimity are welcome states of balance. Nature is at its best when in balance. Also bear in mind that thoughts, just like sounds, arise and pass through your awareness. They only stay for longer if you start ruminating on them.

Having patience

Persistence and patience are wise attributes that indicate you comprehend the need for things to unravel in their own time. Consider situations in your own experience that required space and patience to unfold, such as a project at school that came from a mere idea. You may still have this piece of creation at home. If so, look at it and remember the hours of thinking and doing that went into bringing it into existence.

Try to develop patience towards yourself and engage with mindfulness. Remind yourself occasionally that impatience doesn't serve you well. You simply feed tension and fear when you obsess and demand a certain outcome within a certain timeframe. To grow and expand, you need to allow yourself to have the space and time for exploring life experiences mindfully. So treat yourself gently, like you would a vulnerable pet.

Also observe your mind's way of wandering into the past or the future and ruminating about things that you can no longer change or foretell. Thoughts can be versatile and enticing – whether enjoyable, anxiety-provoking or neutral – but they tend to draw you away from being in the moment. A calm mind is a friendly and open mind. You don't have to be intellectually active all the time; that's just a habit that you can unlearn and so free your mind for creativity and equanimity.

Patience enables you to be open to whatever occurs in the now, kindly receiving the richness each moment offers and allowing life to unfold moment by moment.

Using childlike curiosity: Beginner's mind

Children, particularly preschool-aged ones, have this wonderful ability to be amazed by little things. I remember taking my 3-year-old son to the zoo to see a rare white tiger. It was a beautiful beast, but my son pulled me away because he'd just seen his first real-life ladybird and was excitedly exclaiming 'ladybird, mummy, ladybird!'

Such moments can be rich and enriching. Ordinary things can be just as extraordinary as a white Bengal tiger, if only you look and really see the intrinsic beauty of each small pebble or raisin. Even diamonds look just like rough stones before they're cut.

The *beginner's mind* is one willing to see all things afresh. Bringing childlike curiosity to each mindfulness practice helps free you from expectations, because each moment is unique, fresh and new. No moment is the same as any other. Simply be with it as it occurs.

Apply this attitude to the regular experiences of everyday life. Try seeing your partner with new eyes, or yourself with less critical tendencies and the eyes of somebody newly in love. You may be astonished. Perhaps experiment with somebody you meet regularly and see whether you discover aspects of them you'd never considered. You can also experiment with inanimate objects – anything and everything.

Trusting yourself

I ask you to trust yourself to engage with mindful being and live as so many millions of people have done before you. Just be and experience: it's practically your birth right. Even though you need to earn a living and get involved in other activities, you can still find many moments to simply experience.

Furthermore, trust in your own unique experience. You will stumble on the way but walking your own path is best. Allow your feelings to guide you because they express your innate wisdom. When practising mindful movement, for example, listen when your body tells you that a particular movement is unhelpful: there's no point in hurting yourself. The practice of mindfulness ultimately leads you to become more true to yourself. Teaching materials can guide you but in the end the decision is yours and your own depth of commitment is what enables you to change (see the sidebar 'Practice trumps evidence').

Practice trumps evidence

Today, you have the privilege of neuroscience and other research methods that prove why mindfulness works, how it changes your brain structurally and alters your biochemistry. That means you can read scientific evidence to support your journey. But the ancient wisdom is what's carried on over thousands of years and continues to teach awareness, kindness and compassion to help people really live their lives fully.

Working on non-striving

Usually, you engage in activities to achieve something. Mindfulness, however, encourages you to, say, walk just for the sake of walking, or experience how you breathe because your body is doing it anyhow. Switching off the doing programme and moving into just being requires attention and diligence, and that you trust yourself simply to be human.

This challenge of not feeling under pressure to do your meditation practice requires you to deliberately refine the attitude of 'non-striving', which can lead you closer to accepting yourself just as you are, now.

Be with tension, pain, self-criticism, boredom, fear, and so on and refrain from judging yourself. Instead, give yourself permission to experience your life simply as it unfolds at this very moment. You may at times notice a change or a shift in your habitual moods and responses, but everything occurs in its own time.

In other words, try not to strive (but don't strive too hard not to strive!)

Accepting things the way they are

Acceptance means *seeing things as they present themselves now:* the good and not so good, the beautiful and the less beautiful, the ache, the joy – the full catastrophe of life! Doing so isn't simple, because you tend to add stories to events; interpretations that may or may not be accurate. Accepting yourself as you are now is the point from which you make change possible. During meditation, try to accept every moment as it arises without adding your own 'shoulds' and 'oughts'.

Feel what you feel, see your thoughts for what they are and remind yourself to be interested in and open to whatever occurs. By intentionally accepting what is, even something difficult, you create the opportunity for you to respond positively rather than react automatically – to move on and heal instead of staying stuck in a struggle.

Letting go

You may notice that your mind gets caught in the same way as the monkey in the nearby sidebar 'Catching monkeys', which is why developing the attitude of letting go is so important. Fortunately, this ability develops naturally when you practise non-judgement, curiosity, acceptance and the other attributes that I describe in this section.

Catching monkeys

Here's a metaphor for letting go that describes an ingenious method of trapping monkeys with just a coconut and a banana. Cut an opening into the coconut just big enough for a monkey's hand to get in. Place the banana inside and tie the coconut firmly to the branch of a tree. The monkey comes along, discovers the precious gift and immediately grabs for the banana. But the hole is too small for the fist and the banana to come out. The monkey refuses to let go of this delicious meal and you simply catch the monkey.

You then comprehend why you need to let go of certain expectations and outcomes. I encourage you to 'be with' whatever occurs while you meditate, so that you can overcome the desire not to stop a great meditation or call a premature halt to a less pleasant exercise.

The whole point of meditating is to see that life is unpredictable and that you can be with whatever comes up.

When you notice judgement arising, let go of such thoughts. They can be present one moment and gone the next; it's up to you. Practising letting go in meditation helps you to apply the same attitude in regular life situations where it may be helpful. After all, letting go isn't all that unfamiliar. You do it every night when you fall asleep: you lie down and let go. If you hold onto your thoughts, for example, you don't fall asleep. If this happens to you, check out the relaxing tips in Chapter 6.

Accepting the importance of commitment, self-discipline and intention

Like any change you want to apply to your lifestyle, this eight-week MBCT course requires dedication and a good portion of willpower to keep trying and restarting every time you lapse. Compare it to training for a marathon: you need to run regularly whether you feel like it or not.

A lovely lady I know trained six times a week for a whole year to complete a marathon to support cancer research. You can benefit from a similar attitude; give it your best and after the eight weeks you can decide whether you want to continue or not. You may need to rearrange aspects of your life to create the space necessary for regular meditation, such as reducing the time spent watching TV, reading the newspaper or surfing the Internet. You can gently adapt your daily timetable in hundreds of ways. Perhaps use your mindfulness diary to explore the possibilities.

For the first time

I wrote the following poem on a morning when I felt intensely alive. This feeling happens to everyone at times. These moments of joy come unexpectedly and so welcome them with an open attitude and really notice the colourfulness of life. Maybe you can focus a little more on the gifts you've been given and less on the challenges.

Imagine one day

Really waking up

And just seeing it all

As if for the first time

The view from your bedroom window

Bushes, grass, the little wooden bench

There is the tall Japanese cherry tree

In full bloom

The pond with one white water lily

Magical beauty

And just hearing it all

As if for the first time

The magpies, woodpigeons

Larks, finches and even

Excited parakeets

A lawnmower the

Background of the orchestra

And smelling, tasting and touching it all

As if for the first time

Freshly baked bread and honey

Ground coffee just brewed

Gorgeous sensations

Luscious sustenance

Allowing joy, amazement and most of all

Gratitude to arise

Stepping into life

As if for the first time

by Patrizia Collard

Keeping it simple

Think about mindfulness as being like cooking: what's the best recipe for garnishing your life with mindfulness? Like a master chef before he becomes experienced, just start and do it with curiosity, gentleness and a sense of purpose and adventure. To make a delicious grilled cheese sandwich, you need only bread, cheese and a grill – and voila! Similarly, start your voyage into mindfulness with a simple breathing practice from Chapter 4 and a mindful cup of tea as I describe in Chapter 6.

Each journey starts with a single step. Moment by moment you can direct your attention to what's actually happening. Your life is your own, so be really present to see how your mindfulness adventure unfolds.

Giving yourself a reason to keep practising

You may at times ask yourself, 'Why practise, why add another duty, another goal?' But if at all possible, approach being mindful completely differently from other things you have do. Awareness is all about being, rather than doing. Unfortunately, this attribute isn't widely promoted in the goal-orientated Western society. Telling your friends or colleagues that you've embarked on a journey towards non-doing or just being can sound rather unusual. And the journey is unusual because, alas, it's not the 'done thing'.

If you need a reminder of why mindfulness can be so beneficial to you, just watch a TV programme about nature or look at a bird or a squirrel focusing on the here and now. Deep inside your brain your instincts know that you need to simply be every now and again.

Doing so helps you continue on the quest of bringing more peace, kindness and patience to yourself and the people that you meet. You gain a new point of view on the old trip; as if you're starting at the beginning of your life journey, for the first time looking out beyond the horizon.

The beauty of mindful living, when you truly commit to it, is that you can dedicate every moment of your life to a fresh start. It's never too late to let go of unhelpful patterns of behaviour or thoughts. Even if you have to start a million times, so be it. Just begin again.

Reviewing Your Accomplishments This Week

This chapter contains quite a few questions to ask yourself to help maintain your motivation to practise regularly. To see the fruits of your self-assessment, what you've discovered over the eight-week course and how you plan to continue your mindfulness practice, consider the following points:

- ✔ If you doubt that mindfulness can assist you during difficult times, read the earlier section 'Embracing a Mindful Life in Good and Bad Times'.

- ✔ If you're struggling with your motivation to continue practising mindfulness, take a peek at the tips in the earlier section 'Pledging to Practise'.

- ✔ Have you managed to complete a full mindful day, and if so, how did it go (see the section 'Having a Mindful Day, Every Day' earlier in this chapter)? If not, try to schedule one now.

- ✔ Have you considered the personal attributes that I describe in the preceding section? See which ones you think you possess and which ones you perhaps need to work on.

Part III
Developing Different Treatment Practices

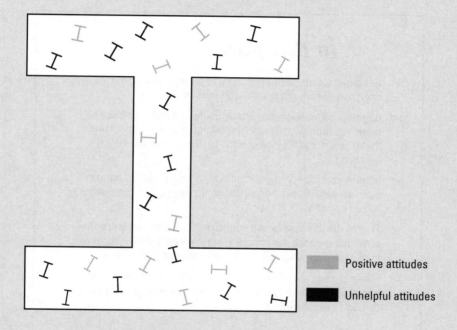

Positive attitudes

Unhelpful attitudes

In this part...

- ✔ Get clued up about successfully applying mindfulness-based cognitive therapy to the varied areas of your life.

- ✔ Regain control over your life by using mindfulness-based cognitive therapy to tackle the addictions and compulsions that blight it, such as addictions to drugs, alcohol, eating or gambling.

- ✔ Inspire confidence in yourself and in your ability to cope with pain, anxiety, stress and suffering through using mindfulness-based cognitive therapy.

- ✔ Employ mindfulness-based cognitive therapy to help you rediscover the purpose, meaning and joy in your life when you have to cope with a terminal condition and/or the onset of old age.

- ✔ Re-energise your life and your relationships – both personal and professional – and bring calm and satisfaction to your life through living mindfully.

Chapter 12

Stopping the Cycle of Depression

*D*epression is a growing malaise of the 21st century. People's lives are getting faster and more pressured, with longer working hours and stressful commutes causing exhaustion. Experts estimate that one in five people in the UK are going to suffer an episode of clinical depression. So if you're standing in a queue of ten people waiting for a bus, the chances are that two of them are suffering or have suffered from depression; if you're one of those two, at least you know that you aren't alone.

My aim in this chapter to is to show you ways of thinking that you can use to help overcome depression. I describe the nature and causes of depression and some of its different forms and manifestations. In addition, I encourage you to investigate your own personal type of depression; that is, what occurs emotionally in your thoughts and how depression manifests itself in your life. I also explore how you can use mindfulness-based cognitive therapy (MBCT) to shorten and lighten episodes of depression and reduce/prevent relapse in the future.

I guide you through a number of mindfulness interventions to practise regularly in order to stabilise your mood and act as an anchor when the going gets tough. To a large extent, these meditation exercises come from the eight-week course that forms the basis for Chapters 4 to 11, and so where necessary I direct you to other relevant chapters. In particular, your mindfulness diary (which I describe starting and maintaining in Chapter 4) proves highly useful in showing how specific practices affect you and what insight you gain by exploring them.

MBCT is particularly useful for preventing depression relapse, and it works best when you're no longer severely depressed. Why? One problem with depression is that it affects the areas in your brain that you need for learning new tools and skills and retaining new information – your memory function is inhibited when you're depressed. So if you are currently depressed and feel vulnerable please see your GP or a psychiatrist and accept medication if they prescribe it to you. The time when you come out of the black tunnel of depression and begin to see light again is the right time to start learning MBCT.

Staring into a Black Hole: Understanding Depression

An episode of depression involves a state of very low mood, and can affect your physical wellbeing, your sleeping pattern and your motivation as well as your emotional stability. Depression is often brought on by feelings of stress and/or anxiety, and can occur as early in life as 12 years of age; the earlier you have your first episode of depression, the more likely it is that you'll also experience reoccurrences later on in life. Sometimes, people go on to experience bouts of depression throughout the course of their lives, and it is for these people that MBCT can act as an extremely effective and comforting coping mechanism.

Many people trying to explain their own understanding or experience of depression tend to use analogies, such as being stuck with no way out, receiving a visit from *the black dog* (Winston Churchill) or 'feeling the blues'. People equate certain moods and mind states to the image of somebody curling up in the back of a cave in darkness and waiting in limbo until something happens. Initially, no light is visible on the other side.

One vivid and insightful description of depression is an account by the talented writer Jeanette Winterson. In a BBC documentary on her life, she describes how she was totally unprepared for it (read the nearby sidebar 'Jeanette Winterson on depression'). Winterson's experience reveals that in the end the only option is to surrender to your suffering and pain and start afresh. The human experience is one of joy and sorrow, and in essence people experience less suffering if they can accept this fact.

Jeanette Winterson on depression

The novelist Jeanette Winterson endured a traumatic, abusive childhood and coped by escaping into her mind and telling herself stories.

But in 2007, a long-term relationship ended unexpectedly and she was suddenly thrown into the abyss of despair. Her depression felt like a physical blow to the stomach and chest, even bringing her to her knees. At this time of need, the language that had sustained her forsook her and left her in an abandoned place. She speaks about how even beginning to describe what she was going through was difficult. Her mind was in agony; she often curled up and waited for the pain to pass. Mostly she was unable to share this frightening experience with others, as if she felt ashamed for having negative emotions. How could she possibly justify being so miserable? After all, she was a successful writer, without financial worries and with many wonderful friends.

But during this time of darkness she was unable to access her life's benefits or feel or be in touch with the positive, ever-curious and adventurous self ('the space that was me'). She had the strong desire to be gone rather than carry on this 'lukewarm existence'. She pondered that she couldn't escape the 'fire' of her breakdown and subsequent depression. Things were getting worse but she refused to see a doctor because she didn't want medication. She says that her 'life before was gone forever' and she decided to end her life.

She locked herself into her garage and turned on the car engine. But one of her cats had been accidentally locked in with her. She was unconscious when the cat started gently scratching her face, seemingly calling her to stay. She stirred, dragged herself outside and they both survived. She explains how, at that moment, 'I literally came to my senses . . . and watched myriads of stars in the sky.'

Kindly read or reread the poem 'The Guesthouse' (in Chapter 8) and remember that uninvited guests may come but that they also leave. You sometimes need to accept your struggle mindfully and then start again. I invite you to trust that each moment is a new beginning and after accepting what is, even if this acceptance is a most difficult thing to do, you can then move forward and respond wisely to the challenge.

In this section, I look at the nature, experience, causes and symptoms of depression.

Becoming depressed: You're not alone

Human beings become depressed in many different ways. It can initially start with you feeling a little down because of the weather or even your body fighting a cold virus. You may also feel lethargic and a bit pessimistic. Slowly but surely your thinking engages in negative ruminations and downward spirals (problems I describe in Chapters 4 and 9, respectively) as well as catastrophic predictions, as if you're locked in a bad dream. Everything loses its spark.

The more often depression occurs, the more likely you are to get depressed again. Each episode of depression increases by 16 per cent the chances that you're going to experience another instance. Therefore, developing mindfulness skills to avoid relapses is an urgent priority.

Knowing the common symptoms of depression

The diagnosis of *clinical depression* indicates that you suffer from a minimum of five of the following symptoms for two weeks or longer:

- ✔ Difficulty concentrating or remembering
- ✔ Dramatic decrease/increase in weight
- ✔ Experiencing a sense of dread first thing in the morning
- ✔ Feelings of guilt, worthlessness, anxiety, irritability
- ✔ Indecisiveness
- ✔ Lack of interest and pleasure
- ✔ Loss of desire for intimacy
- ✔ Reduction in personal hygiene and looking after yourself
- ✔ Sense of being without hope or purpose
- ✔ Sleep disturbance – early morning waking or sleeping much longer than usual
- ✔ Thinking about ending your life – wanting to disappear into thin air
- ✔ Tiredness in general or upon waking; loss of energy
- ✔ Particularly low mood; becoming upset for no specific reason
- ✔ Withdrawal from the world around you

Depression in numbers

Here are some cold, hard facts about depression:

✔ Typically, a first episode of major depression occurs between the ages of 18 and 44. Yet, sometimes it can happen as early as 14 and as late as after retiring.

✔ Sometimes the depression persists even if treatment is attempted: 15–39 per cent of cases may still be clinically depressed one year after the onset of symptoms and 22 per cent of cases remain depressed two years later.

✔ Depression is three times more likely to occur in women than men, at least among the reported cases. Men tend to try and ignore it, hoping it'll go away. Often, however, depression doesn't. So kindly remember that help is at hand if you go and seek it.

✔ The highest suicide risk is for separated, divorced and recently widowed people who are experiencing depression. So having friends or a life partner is vital in managing depression.

Identifying the causes

Depression arises for all sorts of reasons. More often than not it's caused by a big blow, such as losing a job, feeling rejected by a partner, close relative or friend, or making a mistake for which you can't forgive yourself. The following list contains some other triggers for depression. See whether or not you've experienced these triggers or think that they may apply to you (if so, consider how you reacted and make notes in your diary):

✔ **Assertion skills:** If you can't assert yourself at home or work, you may end up doing things that you've no time for or that aren't part of your job description. Doing compassionate acts to help out in areas outside your expertise is fine, but if you do this too often you can end up exhausted and depressed.

✔ **Biological factors affecting brain chemistry:** High levels of stress chemicals can spiral you down into *burn-out,* where all desire and energy disappear. When depression follows, it can be the body's way of hibernating in order to regain balance for returning to active life.

✔ **Genetic predisposition for depression:** Maybe you're aware of relatives who are or were depressed. Perhaps mental health problems run in your family. While these situations may mean that you're prone to the causes and effects of depression, you are by no means destined to have the same experiences with it as your family members. You may even be able to find more support and compassion from them than you first expected, as they will know what you're going through.

✔ **Learned predisposition for depression:** Maybe you picked up behaviour patterns from a close relative when you were too young to distinguish between wholesome and destructive ways of being. If your parents or other close adults always thought the worst if, say, somebody was late for dinner, or always complained about what a horrible place this world was, you may have bought into this belief and now carry it on yourself. Like any bad habit, however, you can be weaned off the tendency to bring depression upon yourself, and MBCT can be very helpful in doing this.

✔ **Loss, decrease or absence of rewards, or inability to obtain rewards:** You may have a boss or partner who doesn't praise you when you do things well. Maybe they're introverts who find giving compliments to people awkward or they simply don't realise that you need it (everyone does really).

Try to start the praise cycle by mindfully observing your boss or partner and giving them praise occasionally. This way they may come to appreciate positive feedback and start giving it back.

✔ **Perfectionism:** The 'healthy pursuit of excellence' (as coined by psychotherapist Albert Ellis) is a commendable attitude. But perfectionism makes you 'drive in fifth gear' without ever achieving the 101 per cent you're looking for. No human being is perfect.

✔ **Poor problem-solving skills:** If you simply don't have the skills you need to solve recurring problems in your life, compassionately ask yourself how you can expand your knowledge. Watch how others do it, read up on it or attend a course.

✔ **Relationship factors/loss of a relationship, feeling unwanted or taken for granted, lack of intimacy:** If you lose somebody you love through death or separation, your world can be shattered. Similarly, you can feel this way if your family takes you for granted or your partner seems no longer interested in being intimate with you. In these cases, try to speak up mindfully for yourself and express your needs.

Loss has a timeframe of its own and you have to support yourself with kindness to 'be' with it rather than denying it. Check out the meditation on being with difficult thoughts and experiences in Chapter 7. Also, meditating on your loss regularly can be helpful. However, don't attempt to deal with recent bereavement by yourself; seek the help of a qualified bereavement counsellor to guide you through this process. The most helpful elements of MBCT at this point are those that help to expand your awareness of the world around you, outside your grief, such as going for a mindful walk or practising the sound meditation.

✔ **Skills deficits:** If you're struggling at work because you lack important aptitudes, consider sharing this problem with the Human Resources department, who can treat the matter confidentially and may well offer you courses. Or perhaps a kind colleague can help you. And of course *For Dummies* books are available for almost everything you may want or need to know. For example, perhaps you want to learn better time management, assertiveness skills, communication skills or self-presentation skills.

If you continue working without the skills you need, you're in danger of losing your job or getting highly stressed, which can ultimately lead to depression.

✔ **Specific stressful life events:** Two of the most stressful events in life are changing jobs and moving home. As well as the obvious possible disruptions and challenges, you may also have lost the kind colleague at work or the neighbour who always offered a listening ear and a cup of tea. In general, people take a year or so to get used to a new job, a new home or being able to accept that a loved one is no longer with them.

Depression can also arise slowly and not be caused by one single event. The onset can be so gradual that you can't pinpoint exactly what caused it in the first place. A negative mood is fed by negative thoughts, which feed into more negative thoughts (check out the later section 'Overcoming Unhelpful Thoughts').

Observing the effects that feed depression

Certain ways of being and thinking can deepen and worsen your symptoms of depression. If you already have a sense of inertia or lack of interest in life, the worst you can do is to do nothing. The following list itemises certain depression feeders, so that you can be alert for them and nip them in the bud before they take over your life:

✔ **Biological changes:** The more stressed you become, the more changes take place (the more stress chemicals are released), which can make things worse, causing heightened emotions, thoughts and sensations.

✔ **Negative thoughts:** Your thoughts play a powerful role in controlling depression, which tends to focus your mind on being unlovable, inferior, worthless, defeated and trapped. Getting caught up in a ruminative thinking loop only gets you more stuck (see the later section 'Deleting the Depression Loop').

Discovering how to see your thoughts for what they are – occurrences or hiccups in the brain rather than facts – can be the first and best step on your way out of depression.

✔ **Procrastination:** Not making decisions you need to make can affect your work and home life negatively and eventually result in more problems.

For example, postponing a dentist appointment can cause the need for a simple filling to develop into losing a tooth.

✔ **Self-blame:** Blaming yourself can activate more stress and guilt and therefore more symptoms of depression.

✔ **Withdrawal from life's activities:** Often this withdrawal becomes a self-fulfilling prophesy. Less people get or keep in touch with you if you don't make the effort, which leads to a deeper sense of being alone or forsaken.

Breaking Down Common Symptoms: Your Personal Narrative

In the earlier section 'Staring into a Black Hole: Understanding Depression' I state some common manifestations and signs of depression, but of course the list isn't (and can't be) complete. You probably have other significant personal signatures that are particular to you, and which you need to discover and observe in order to tackle your own depression.

Searching for your personal signature

Do you perhaps self-medicate by drinking excessive amounts of alcohol or using other non-medical drugs? Do you find yourself having loads of short-lived relationships, or constantly changing jobs or homes in order to get to the greener grass on the other side? These behaviours and many others can be distractions or cover-ups for depression.

Before you can truly come to terms with your depression and gently work your way out of its doughy nature, you need to understand your personal concoction of depression. Here are a few questions to ask yourself:

✔ Why has your subconscious resolved to enter a state of depression?

✔ What is your depression really about? Is it about avoiding pain (letting go of something or getting through something) or even inviting pain?

✔ Are you punishing yourself? If so, what for?

✔ How much of your depression has been brought on by your lifestyle and how much is biological (for example, through stress hormones) or inherited (for example, through a genetic biochemical imbalance in the brain)?

✔ How much is the healing process under your control? Do you want to get better and feel balanced again, when that may mean having to re-enter busy life again. Perhaps hiding under the duvet appears much safer right now.

MBCT can help you find answers to many of these questions. Mindfulness research and clinical experience shows that practising MBCT regularly can significantly decrease the chance of relapsing into depression. Unless you try it, you'll never know.

Engaging in mindfulness exercises increases awareness and enhances creative thinking, memory, patience and curiosity. Every human being is unique and so no single answer or prescription exists for your depression, but the power of your mind and awareness can lead you in the direction of wellbeing, especially if you're open-minded and write down in your diary everything that comes up as a possible explanation for why you're depressed and how you can best beat your blues.

Another important ingredient is to observe patiently all aspects of your sadness, and trust that, even though it may seem impossible at first, a way out is available. And don't forget to show yourself a little compassion as you start moving back into the adventure of life.

Consider the following points and, if appropriate, put into action the relevant intervention:

✔ **See whether you recognise any of the following examples of depressive thoughts or something similar.** 'I'm a complete idiot and nobody cares for me. I'm lazy and no good and even if I try I'll only fail again.' Identify the terms you use to describe yourself in these situations, and investigate deeply what these negative evaluations do to you; thoughts aren't facts, but they can still hurt you if you believe in them.

✔ **Consider whether you tend to hold on to the same old thinking spirals or patterns, fully knowing that they're neither true nor helpful.** If so, see the thought as just a thought and let it pass away like a balloon you can let go of, or a cloud in the sky that passes by. (Check out the sitting with difficult thoughts meditation in Chapter 7.)

✔ **Ask yourself whether any advantages or disadvantages exist to holding on to or changing this particular belief about yourself.** What evidence may support your belief? The advantages may be that staying with the 'devil you know' is easier. The disadvantage would be continuing to be in mental pain and distress for longer and longer.

✔ **Design appropriate experiments to prove to yourself that you're not an idiot, lazy or a failure.** The fact that you're reading this book and experimenting with the meditations is definite proof that you aren't any of these negative self-concepts. As an experiment, you could choose one part of your job description you find difficult and ask colleagues and friends whether they do or would find it easy. If they do, ask them how they go about it. Now choose part of your job that you find easy. Again ask other people how they feel about this particular aspect of your work. You may find that some people don't find it as easy as you do, but that doesn't make them stupid. Nobody is perfect in everything.

✔ **Consider how you'd see yourself if you weren't depressed.** Ask friends, family or other people how they perceive you. What do they like about you?

✔ **If you've been depressed before, you probably remember when depression gently lifted like a veil and life looked more colourful again.** If so, ask yourself: 'How do I see life when I'm well and how do I see life when I'm depressed?' Also, how may this period of unwellness look three months from now?

When you've developed an idea of the causes and symptoms of depression, focus on each symptom and see which ones sound all too familiar to you. Perhaps you know some of these low moods well but never saw them as signals of your depression. For example, changes in eating patterns, such as over-eating, can signify the onset or depth of depression. Similarly, changes in sleeping patterns are often an aspect of depression.

Write down the symptoms that fit your experience in your diary, perhaps giving them a funny name. Doing so can help bring a little lightness into the dark depressive cave.

Noticing how depression affects you

In this section, you get to know your particular and personal depression triggers and manifestations. I ask you to slip into the role of a master detective (such as Columbo, Morse, one of the cool CSI detectives or anybody else who takes your fancy). The idea is to remember the minute details that trigger or prolong and deepen your personal experience of depression.

Please go to your meditation place and get into a comfortable and dignified position, as I describe in Chapter 4:

1. **Focus on becoming grounded.** Feel your feet on the floor and your sitting bones on the chair, and then focus on your breathing. Allow it to continue as usual and bring your awareness to your breath (acting as your anchor of attention – see Chapter 4).

2. **Say the following words to your inner self when you become settled or even calm: 'Let me see you, depression. Let me remember you in all your detail.'** Keep breathing and notice any information that arises in your awareness: single words, sentences, feelings, sensations, colours, shapes, and so on.

3. **Notice each piece of information as it arises.** Let it pass by like a bird flying into the deep sky of your mind.

4. **Return to your breath as your anchor of awareness when the information starts to repeat itself or stops.** End this meditation when you like.

Now pick up your diary and note down all the information gained through this exercise. When you get going, you may even remember more details about how depression manifests in your life. Each person is unique, and so each experience of depression is different.

Lacking drive or energy

When you aren't depressed, you most likely enter each day's activities without thinking about it. Depression, however, tends to take the wind out of your sails. Hence, in this section I invite you to decide to do certain things even if you really don't feel like it.

Setting realistic goals that you can achieve is extremely important, because the danger exists that failure can result in you feeling even lower than before. So make an appointment with yourself to practise a meditation, and engage mindfully in regular activities.

Mindful breathing

Your breath is always present and you can access it without too much trouble. Kindly carry out the breathing meditation in Chapter 4. Afterwards, write down in your diary what comes up, what you notice and how you're feeling.

In order to expand your awareness of breathing even further, see whether you notice the in-breath being cooler around your nostrils and the out-breath warmer. Focusing on such minute details really hones your deep awareness skills.

Mindful walking

The tiredness of depression has nothing to do with ordinary tiredness so, to activate yourself, try fast mindful walking. Find a spot where you can walk up and down swiftly for about 20 steps:

1. **Stand in the mountain posture (from Chapter 6).** Place your legs hip width apart, grounding yourself by sensing three points of contact (heel, big toe and little toe), letting your shoulders hang loosely and keeping your head and spine upright.

2. **Let your gaze focus on one spot ahead.** Avoid looking at your feet.

3. **Start walking with vigour.** Your anchor of awareness is each step on the ground. Focus on your breathing too, noticing its intensity rising with each 'lane' you complete. Continue for around 20 minutes.

You can also listen to this exercise in Track Nine.

Brief body scan

You know how wind often changes lingering unpleasant weather? Well, here's a chance to help your system free itself from damp sadness!

Please read the instructions for the body scan meditation in Chapter 4. This time, however, consider sweeping through your body more quickly. Pay attention to each body part in a less detailed way than in the long body scan, breathing into each part and imagining a strong gust of wind sweeping through it. Hold the intention of cleansing the whole system. Experiment so that the body scan becomes more active and invigorating while still attending to yourself with kindness and patience.

Feeling helpless

In the past you may have felt helpless when you began to notice depression visiting for the first time, or again. Depression tends to be a place that doesn't let the light in, that crushes you down and seems to be at the end of time. Feeling helpless is so frightening and without end: often feelings of forever more and ultimate pain are all around you.

Biochemically you're producing none of the wellbeing chemicals at such times, whereas the adrenaline-fuelled fight-or-flight response increases your focus on all that's negative and appears threatening. When you understand that this reaction is merely your brain and body doing their jobs (helping the species survive), you may be able to bring a kind of soothing awareness to this. Consider grounding yourself by feeling your feet connected to the floor and see whether you can gently expand your breathing.

The first intervention is always the emergency breathing space meditation (from Chapter 6). After bringing awareness to what you're thinking, feeling and sensing, you've already left the state of helplessness. Then you may want to reread this chapter and the notes in your diary that describe how depression manifests in your personal experience. Seek to understand and know what your depression is and how you can intervene, while remembering that everything passes eventually.

Understanding why some people self-harm

At times you may feel like harming yourself, whether by overusing alcohol or drugs or physically hurting yourself. Sometimes strong physical sensation can be a way of getting in touch with the pain of depression or a distraction from it. *Self-harming* is a particular method of expressing extremely deep distress, of conveying anguish that seems beyond words. Whatever the reason for self-harming, most people still find excuses for visible signs of self-harm ('Oh, I just fell over' or 'I burned myself cooking') or perhaps they hide the obvious marks away. Excuses and denials like these show that an inherent feeling of embarrassment is attached to self-harm and not being able to cope, which makes it even more difficult for people to seek help or be offered it.

Self-harming behaviours include:

- Scratching, cutting or burning yourself
- Banging your head or fists against hard surfaces
- Taking an overdose or swallowing/putting sharp things inside yourself

Less obvious ways are taking unnecessary risks, remaining with an abusive partner, developing an eating disorder, being addicted to substances or just not looking after yourself (in other words, *self-neglect*).

Self-harming on screen

The Piano Teacher is an extremely disturbing film based on the novel by Elfriede Jelinek, who received the Nobel Prize for Literature in 2004.

Erika is a piano teacher at a music conservatory. She's around 40 years old and not only lives with her controlling mother, but also shares a double bed with her. Viewers find out step by step about Erika's private life. Although professionally successful, she's sexually repressed and her low mood leads her, among other extreme behaviours, to cut her genitalia. Each time she engages in self-harming, she seems temporarily relieved. But her depression soon returns and causes destruction in a number of other people's lives as well as her own.

The film portrays the near-fatal consequences of hiding one's pain rather than facing and dealing with it, in a fascinating yet deeply disturbing way.

When you understand why you self-harm, you can try a new way of dealing with depression as follows:

1. **Know what depression is and that depression is usually transient.**

2. **Bring awareness to your tool kit (see the earlier 'Lacking drive or energy' section).**

3. **Work on accepting that the human condition means that you're sometimes going to experience suffering, but also that mindfulness can shorten the stay of this unwanted visitor.**

Overcoming Unhelpful Thoughts

The eight-week MBCT course in Part II offers clear insights into the nature of thoughts. Although they can seem real and permanent, in reality they may be figments of your imagination, incorrect interpretations, conclusions you've jumped to or just mental irritations based on no facts whatsoever. In this section, I take a look at a couple of particularly insidious thoughts.

Imagine for a moment that you're thinking: 'I haven't been in a relationship for two years now; this means I'm utterly unlovable.' Ask yourself, does it really? Kindly mull over the following two statements and see how you feel then:

✔ What would you say to your best friend if she made such a statement?

✔ How would you see this situation if you weren't depressed?

Consider your responses and write down in your diary how your perspective has changed, if at all. Plus, add a pinch of compassion to the part in you that's hurting. Maybe you can tell yourself: 'I know I feel lonely right now but everything passes eventually. What can I do for myself to accept that right now I'm hurting? Maybe I can ring a friend.'

Thoughts are by no means reliable. If you give them too much time and power, unhelpful negative ones can spiral out of control in depression. This is a key insight to understand – and only you can do it for yourself.

'Snapping out' of it

Earlier in this chapter (in 'Searching for your personal signature') you discover the benefits of observing and getting to know your own manifestations of depression and what you can do when they threaten to come back. Therefore, you may well feel annoyed when well-meaning friends or relatives suggest that you attempt to 'snap out of it'. After all, you know your depression and its disguises and how it can creep up on you. The sad fact is that people who've not experienced depression often show little empathy towards sufferers.

Don't take such advice too seriously and if at all possible ignore it and try not to succumb to anger. Easier said than done, of course, but honestly . . . they simply don't understand and anger only feeds your negative mood.

Instead, get in touch with your black dog of depression. Perhaps say to it, 'I know you only too well, but this time I'm not going down this road with you. This time I choose another route.' If doing so proves impossible this time, bring kindness in as your aid. No use in simply slapping yourself in the face. Allow yourself to take the time you need.

Believing that you're against the world

Obviously everyone's experiences in life are unique – no one can completely understand what you're going through. But that doesn't mean that you're totally isolated and can't find ways of communicating with others during this time – you never know who can help. Kindly accept the company of those who are open or offering to assist you and remember not to dump your problems on others or blame them. Instead, bring a kindly curiosity to a conversation about depression. Compassion is a two-way street – if you wish your friends to show you compassion, you must offer compassion to them.

Here are a few more suggestions for communicating your way back into joining the world:

- ✔ Share your experience with close friends or relatives; be interested in their own experiences of low mood and how that relates to what you're going through.

- ✔ Talk to your GP and see whether any local self-help groups are available for you to join.

- ✔ Ask your Human Resources department at work whether your employer offers any free counselling to employees.

Deleting the Depression Loop

Research shows that, during depression, certain aspects of emotions, sensations and thoughts join together. On their own they may be manageable, but as a combined force they appear and feel overwhelming, forcing you into a depression loop. In this section, I describe the ways in which mindfulness can assist you with breaking this cycle.

A *depression loop* is a particular circle of events that feed on one another and eventually, like quicksand, take hold of you and drag you down.

Encountering a depression loop

Here's an example of a depression loop. You've had your annual review at work and it was quite outstanding and positive in most parts. One particular criticism, however, rankles with you: your team-leader writes 'tends to arrive late a little too often.' Now, negative thoughts are like sticky tape and stick in the forefront of your memory, overshadowing all the positive ones, even if they're smaller in number. As a result, all you can think about is the one criticism.

You rerun mentally all the times you were late, trying to find proof that you're being unjustly held responsible for the bad public transport service. Then you add some other negative thoughts about life: all the stresses you face, and how useless everything is, including you.

Soon, you're feeling anxious, irritated and upset. You may even have one too many drinks or start over-eating. Doing so affects your sleeping pattern and makes things worse and voila! – you're in a depression loop. One negative thought causes a negative feeling, which causes a negative behaviour. The more often you travel down this alleyway, the quicker your loop ends up in a full-blown depression relapse.

At any point in this example (or, rather, your own version of it), you can try to intervene and do something different. Immediately following the event, you can carry out a breathing space meditation (from Chapter 6) to take stock, observing and identifying your thoughts instead of believing that they're 100 per cent correct. Then you can look mindfully at the particular negative experience more objectively, accepting the rising anxiety or unrest and gently breathing into it. You may be able to stop the loop from completing and taking hold of you. As a result, you probably experience a low afternoon or day rather than a full relapse of depression.

You really do benefit from regularly committing to MBCT practice. The fact is that your mind and body need looking after. No quick-fix, once-and-for-all solution exists; the answer is regular practice, but don't be scared by this! When you establish a routine of meditating mindfully, you may even miss it when you don't sit down to practise. Ideally, give mindfulness a good eight weeks before you decide whether to continue or not.

Making time, not finding time

Like most people, you aren't simply going to find more time, like an old choc-olate bar that slipped down the back of the sofa! You only have 24 hours in a day, like anybody else. Instead, you have to take responsibility for *making* the time to meditate to help you avoid relapsing into depression. So make a point today of asking yourself what you can reduce or give up in order to make room for regular mindfulness: what times of the day offer you the best opportunities to do everyday activities mindfully and to create a space for a longer meditation?

Your mind and body are too important to take second place behind other things. You can't function properly without looking after yourself, so please don't take yourself for granted or think that overcoming this obstacle isn't as important as your work, watching the news or having time for your hobbies. In fact, right now, overcoming your depression may well be the most impor-tant thing.

If giving mindfulness practice a proper space in your life allows you to avoid painful and long periods of depression, you gain plenty of time in return: 40 minutes a day can save you weeks of beating the blues later. Plus, brain research shows many more benefits of meditation, such as better memory, a more efficient immune system and a more compassionate mind and heart (see Chapter 3 for many more benefits).

Following up on your progress

If you're the type of person who initially commits to things full of enthusiasm before the old lethargy returns and takes over again, maintaining a mindful viewpoint of your daily meditation practice is vitally important.

Kindly recall the benefits of sticking to a daily routine, such as carrying out the body scan and focusing on your breath (Chapter 4), sitting with a sound (Chapter 5) or engaging in mindful movement (Chapter 6). And don't forget everyday mindful activities, such as having a mindful shower rather than making to-do lists in your head while all the pleasure of hot water and won-derful scents passes you by. Ensure that you make the effort to notice any changes. After a week or so of daily practice, do you feel that making the time for mindfulness is easier? Keep a written record of your progress and discov-eries because it really does help.

Thoughts like a broken record

While you're depressed, you experience a negative mood and thoughts, and physical sensations of listlessness and tiredness. Even when the episode is over, your brain retains the memory of these various symptoms. Afterwards, a relatively small amount of negative mood can trigger larger negative thoughts such as 'I'm a failure', 'I'm useless' and 'I'm never going to get better'.

The depression loop is like a broken record asking constantly, 'What's gone wrong?', 'Why am I always the victim?' and 'When will all this suffering end?' These ruminations don't help you find an answer, but instead prolong and deepen the negative mood you feel.

Using MBCT to prevent depression relapse

Two clinical trials in the UK and Canada show that MBCT is helpful in stopping depression from recurring in people who've suffered several previous episodes of depression. It helps to combat the worrying reality that if you've been depressed once, the amount of triggering required for subsequent episodes is lower each time (see the sidebar 'Thoughts like a broken record' for more).

Even when you feel on top of the world, your brain has developed memory pathways that link negative mood with negative thoughts, and this ticking time bomb can go off at any time. So keeping practising mindfulness is undoubtedly beneficial even when all's going well. This way you find out how to keep mild states of low mood from escalating out of control.

Believing that things can and will improve

A real evidence-based strong possibility exists that you *are* going to beat depression with regular MBCT practice. The UK National Institute of Clinical Excellence (NICE) has recently approved MBCT as being an effective treatment for prevention of relapse into depression. Research has proven that people who've experienced clinical depression three or more times (sometimes for twenty years or more) greatly benefit from the eight-week MBCT program. The evidence indicates that the program reduces rates of relapse by 50 per cent among patients who suffer from recurrent depression. I hope that this fact helps you to want to put your trust in this approach and in yourself.

Even if depression returns, it may not stay as long as before and you may experience fewer volatile symptoms. The only truth is that everything is constantly changing and that nothing remains forever. Even your depression has a sell-by-date! Kindly trust the power of your positive thoughts: if you believe that things will get better, *they will get better!*

An old Yogic saying goes as follows: if you want to learn, read; if you want to understand, write; and if you want to master, teach! If any of your friends share low moods and feeling down, introduce them to the mindfulness lessons you discover. Educating others strengthens your own new ways of thinking even more quickly.

Chapter 13

Breaking Free from Addiction

When you're addicted to a substance or behaviour, you often feel as if you've lost control over what you're doing, including whether or not you want to consume the substance or engage in the action. Addiction includes dependency on drugs and/or alcohol, but almost anything can lead to addictive behaviour patterns: gambling; having sex with many partners; overusing the Internet; feeling a compulsion to exercise daily for two hours or more (unless it's your profession); or eating too little or too much (the latter can be followed by self-induced vomiting).

Fortunately, you can use mindfulness-based cognitive therapy (MBCT) to overcome addictions and compulsions. This chapter provides useful insights and practical mindfulness meditations that you can use to tackle all sorts of addictive behaviours. I take an in-depth look at alcohol addiction, because alcohol is such a common destructive habit, but the mindfulness interventions and techniques I describe are transferable to most addictions to help you regain control over your life.

A core thread running through this chapter is discovering how to *be* with cravings without falling under their spell, and the kind of mindset to develop to free yourself from addiction. I give suggestions as to what to expect or be prepared for when escaping from these destructive habits.

Suddenly trying to stop some types of addiction by yourself can cause discomfort and weariness, and maybe headaches too. Other types of addiction, though, may cause extreme distress and physical withdrawal symptoms, so I caution you from walking this road on your own. Please seek the help of a medical professional if you intend to tackle an addiction to alcohol, medication or other drugs.

Discovering the Realities of Addiction

The term *addiction* refers to a physical dependency on substances such as alcohol, nicotine, cocaine ingestion, and so on. But it also includes any physical state in which someone compulsively engages in an action that eventually destroys their lifestyle and health, including gambling, shopping, eating disorders and body dysmorphic disorder (see the later sidebar 'Severe bodily addictions'). The focus of the habit isn't what's important; what matters is the fact that addictive behaviour is often the only form of stress-release the person knows. In fact, people with an addictive temperament or predisposition frequently switch addictive actions from one type of addiction to another. A person who gives up nicotine, for example, may switch to eating compulsively instead.

Whatever the addiction, the crucial insight is to acknowledge that addiction is rarely a search for pleasure, but a misdirected coping style. Initially, it may have been pleasurable, but the ongoing continuation becomes compulsive and interferes with ordinary life responsibilities, such as work or relationships, as well as personal health and wellbeing. Often, sufferers aren't aware that their behaviour is out of control and causing problems for themselves and others. In this section, I discuss addiction, including its causes and symptoms.

Filling a void – why people get addicted

Many people who resort to addictive behaviour (that in the long run leads towards self-destruction) initially believe that the same behaviour can save them. For example, if you fear giving a talk in front of others, flying on a plane or engaging in conversation with a person you very much like, you can feel the need of a crutch so you select a drink. And voila, it works! You make the speech successfully, enjoy the flight or get your dream date. Next time, when the fear returns, you rarely tell yourself 'I can do it, just like last time.' No, you've developed a belief that all will be well if only you have that little something . . . and so it starts and goes on. Soon you avoid any discomfort or anxiety with a little help from your 'friend', and you need more and more. Sooner or later, you're stumbling over your own feet and life begins to unravel around you.

Many people initially use alcohol to self-medicate for anxiety, loneliness and depression, only to find out that their miraculous aid becomes the bane of their life.

Whatever the addiction you're struggling with, please write down in your diary what event the substance or activity first helped you with. When you're aware of what you needed it for, you can retrain your way of thinking and use mindfulness to help you be with your anxiety and loneliness and help you let go of the destructive habit.

Severe bodily addictions

Body dysmorphic disorder (BDD) describes an obsessive tendency with one's looks. Sufferers perceive parts of their face as being distorted, ugly and therefore unacceptable to live with. Frequently the disorder leads people to save all their money and undergo numerous operations in order to achieve the perfect look. Of course, this look is never achieved, so sufferers often work just for the next surgical intervention. Yet to other people the reason why the forehead, nose, chin or whatever is deemed so unattractive by the individual that it needs changing is totally unclear.

Connected to BDD, and one of the most difficult forms of addiction, is *anorexia nervosa* in which people perceive themselves as overweight. This perception can refer to only one part of the body; for example, the tummy is seen as needing to be flatter and more concave. Sufferers largely stop eating and add diuretics and severe exercise regimes in order to lose even more weight. *Bulimia nervosa,* on the other hand, tends to encourage sufferers to overeat and then be sick and/or use diuretics to rid themselves of the unwanted food intake. Both conditions (which sometimes occur simultaneously) cause great danger to mental and physical health.

Looking at common factors of addiction

Several factors are common to people who become dependent on addictive behaviour. This section is important because it shows you how easily addiction can happen, and also that you aren't alone or untypical:

- ✔ **Biology:** The tendency to become addicted can be inherited. If you have relatives who are or were addicted, you may be more likely to develop an addiction yourself.

- ✔ **Emotional conditions:** Depression, bipolar disorder, anxiety or post-traumatic stress disorder can increase the risk of addiction if you remain undiagnosed. For example, you may be self-medicating repeated emotional pain through alcohol abuse.

- ✔ **Environment:** If you grow up in a home with parents or other significant elders who display an addiction, you're more likely to think that, say, drinking alcohol or smoking is okay. This belief increases your odds of developing an addiction.

- ✔ **Mistreatment:** If you've experienced physical, emotional, psychological or sexual abuse, you're more likely to develop an addiction. Your addiction may be the only way to cope with the ongoing negative emotions, trauma or flashbacks.

✔ **Low frustration tolerance:** Perhaps you get easily upset over everyday stress factors or when life doesn't work out the way you want it to. This tendency can lead to a desire to escape.

In order to develop mindful interventions so that you no longer need the substance or activity that has been your support, you need to explore the root cause of your addiction. Remember that your addiction doesn't define you. It may have taken over too much of your life, but you can reclaim every aspect of it by being honest and investigating its origins.

Turn to Chapter 9 and read the pebble meditation, which is wonderful for uncovering deep layers of the unconscious and perhaps the hidden causes of your addiction. Consider exploring it on several occasions and writing down any insights that help you understand why you resorted to addiction when you did. You may find that the substance served as a crutch, or you wanted to be part of the crowd or you followed the example of a parent or significant elder. Gaining insight helps you continue letting go of disappointment and anger and move towards acceptance and compassion, though the process can take weeks or months.

For an example of how knowing the why and what can be a step towards liberating yourself from addiction, read the sidebar 'Martin's story'.

Martin's story

Martin had no idea why he needed to drink all the time, although he initially thought that it was a bad habit developed at university. He lost jobs and relationships due to his habit, but then met Bee, a lovely woman who showed enormous empathy for his addiction. He felt that she was holding back from fully committing to him and realised that if he wanted to be with her he needed to stop drinking so heavily. He tried, but somehow it never worked for long.

When he experimented with the pebble meditation (see Chapter 9), however, he slowly began to see what alcohol was covering up. His mother used drink and sleeping medication regularly. One day, he came home from school as a young boy and she was lying naked in her own vomit, not breathing. He found an empty bottle of

whiskey and an empty bottle of sleeping pills. He washed his mother and covered her with a clean blanket, because her face and hands had never felt so cold. When his father came home and called the ambulance, it was too late. She was dead. Martin never knew whether she may have lived had he called the ambulance immediately.

He realised that shame, guilt, loss and a genetic predisposition lay behind his addiction. He told Bee, who cried with him and helped him see that he did the best a 7-year-old child could. He also talked to his dad, who assured him that his mum had been dead for several hours before the ambulance arrived. Now Martin regularly practises the kindness meditation (see Chapter 9) to find a way back to the lost child, to rebuild his confidence and to work through his grief.

Wanting to Stop: The Process of Change

Before actually starting to make a change, you may find yourself in a state of *pre-contemplation,* where you think about change and maybe even consider how and what methods you might need or want to engage in. Precontemplation is however still quite removed from actually starting to change your behaviour and rebuilding your life.

The first actual step to breaking free from an addiction is resolving to make a change, because you know deep inside that your obsessive relationship with the substance or behaviour is destructive and causes more problems than it resolves. But you need to gather resources to stop.

Here are the main stages in the process of changing:

1. **Contemplation:** Through which you decide that you have a problem.
2. **Determination:** You have a real desire to change.
3. **Stopping:** Physically bringing a halt to the behaviour.
4. **Maintenance:** Staying free of the addiction.
5. **Mindful awareness:** To help you when relapse seems the only viable option.

For all these stages of change, a number of mindful interventions are available to practise as soon as you need them:

- ✔ Mindful scanning of your body (see Chapter 4)
- ✔ Mindful walking (see Chapter 6)
- ✔ Mindful breathing (see Chapter 4)
- ✔ Mindful eating (see Chapter 6)
- ✔ Mindfully carrying out any other everyday activity (see Chapters 4, 5 and 6 for ideas)
- ✔ Mindfully coping with stressful situations and arguments (see Chapter 8)

The more mindfulness you can bring to the experience, the more you support yourself on the journey to recovery. Being mindful moment-to-moment may also help you foresee moments where you may be at risk of using your old friend (or enemy) again.

Entering the sea of change

As the preceding section implies, you need to get from the stage of pre-contemplation to contemplation, determination and action.

When you enter the arena of change it very much depends on your personality as to how you want to go about it. If your addiction is so severe that your life is in danger, please look for support when you start engaging in change. If, on the other hand, you have less dangerous addictions you want to free yourself from, then it may be best to start with the least difficult in order to get a sense of achievement and empowerment for continuing on to the next hurdle.

In order to feel strong and able to endure the process, the mountain meditation from Chapter 6 is a wonderful companion on your journey to change. Consider practising it daily and bring awareness to the fact that, although many changes take place around it (different seasons and types of weather), the mountain endures them all and remains strong.

Similarly, a lot of changes may occur in and around you while you're trying to beat an addiction. Here are some common types of changes and problems and how you can deal with them:

✔ **Cravings:** A habit you've engaged in for years doesn't just go away overnight. Areas of your brain are waiting to be satisfied. Cravings are like strong memories and can be so overwhelming that hardly anyone on their own can resist giving in to them:

   • **Bring compassion to yourself:** The addiction isn't your fault; it's been conditioning your brain over years or decades.

   • **Share what you're experiencing with a compassionate person, if at all possible:** Doing so can help you get through the worst.

   • **Reduce triggers:** Cravings reduce over time, particularly if you do your best to reduce actions that stress you or contact with people and places connected to your addiction.

   • **Observe the pattern of your cravings with childlike curiosity:** They rise and fall, like waves in the ocean. Visualise yourself surfing on the waves rather than being overwhelmed by them.

✔ **Dealing with stress and anxiety:** You may be used to stilling fear with your addiction, to help get rid of the discomfort. In Chapter 8 you can read about accepting, allowing and letting be. Life is a combination of moments of pleasure, neutrality and pain. By accepting this fact, you significantly reduce the suffering you otherwise create by resisting this fact. What you resist, persists. If you can accept that pain is sometimes going to be present in your life, you suffer less when it visits you.

Use a practice such as the breathing space (Chapter 6) or sitting with the breath (Chapter 5) and notice this new way of reducing the discomfort of stress or fear.

✔ **Kindness:** Be kind to yourself and accept kindness from others. Have a massage, take a hot bath, go for a nice walk or watch a cheerful film. Treat yourself!

✔ **Loneliness:** You have to choose not to return to places and friends associated with your addiction. But watch for loneliness, which can trigger a relapse. Gently persuade yourself to meet new people, perhaps ones who share your journey or want to use mindfulness meditation in some way. Check out the next section for more.

✔ **Shame about the past:** The past is gone, the future is unknown; the present moment is the time for living. Bringing awareness to this moment and being the best you can be now is the only way forward.

Meeting with others

Although your journey is in one sense always going to be personal and empowering, meeting with other people can be helpful. Cultivate new and *non-dependent* (that is, where neither of you feel the need to lean on the other; you just enjoy each other's company) relationships. Of course, you need to be able to stand alone too, but meeting like-minded people can be like a breath of fresh air. Here are a few suggestions for you to consider:

✔ **Reconnecting with or starting a new hobby that gets you in touch with others, and maybe with nature and keeping healthy too:** Walking, running, tennis and table tennis, gardening (having an allotment, perhaps), hiking, cycling, and so on.

✔ **Joining a group of people battling with addiction and supporting each other:** Plenty of support groups are out there for people to stave off loneliness and help each other.

✔ **Participating in a regular meditation class:** Alternatively, perhaps go on a retreat for a few days.

✔ **Cultivating breaks/lunch/tea with people you work with:** Doing so helps you (and them) to reduce stress and feel connected.

✔ **Getting in touch with distant relatives or old school friends:** Meet in a safe place that doesn't remind you of your addiction, but instead helps to build new relationships or bridge forgotten ones.

Accepting who you really are

You're *not* an addict; your addiction isn't who you are. The circumstances led to the addiction that you have to deal with. You need to accept yourself and that you have weaknesses and faults: everyone does. Furthermore, accept that you've already taken steps to get over your addiction by buying this book, which shows that you have strength! Most importantly, accept that everyone with an addiction tries to delude themselves that they don't have a problem. Honestly looking at what is and accepting the truth can be a great challenge. So show loving kindness to the fallible person you are and remember that you're still worthy of love. Resolve to keep yourself stay safe and protected, to be peaceful and live at ease and with kindness! (For more on this practice, see Chapter 9.)

Writing down insights in your diary can be helpful. It's for your eyes only and rereading the journey you're on can be most inspiring. Your diary also helps you to notice those areas of your life that may be repetitive stumbling blocks. You aren't looking for perfection, only a wholeness brought on by acceptance of who you are, warts and all. Awareness is the first step to that wholeness.

Kindly consider all the aspects that come together to make up you:

1. **Use a large sheet of paper and write down a huge 3D letter 'I'.** Fill the page with it and make sure that the letter is big enough for you to write little letters or facts about yourself inside (see Figure 13-1).

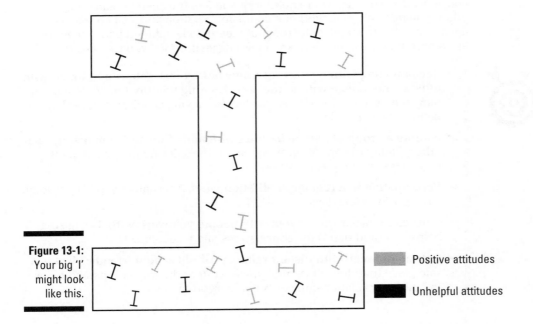

Figure 13-1: Your big 'I' might look like this.

Positive attitudes

Unhelpful attitudes

2. **Choose your favourite colour and a colour you don't like.** In the big 'I', please write down in your favourite colour as many little 'i's as you can, each representing an aspect you like about yourself, including actions, abilities and positive outcomes you've experienced in your life. Also include little 'i's in the colour you don't like, representing nega-tive experiences, actions or areas of your character or behaviour that

need improving. The big 'I' symbolically portrays all that you are at this moment.

3. **Notice the mix of the two colours – evidence that you can't define yourself by one single attribute.** Somewhere is a little 'i' that represents your addiction; a little 'i' that says you can't handle, say, alcohol. But that doesn't make you an alcoholic overall. I hope that you can see that your addiction is only one aspect of the whole that makes up you. Having visual proof in this way can be a big help.

By all means, take days to complete this project and feel free to invite others who care for you to add their own insights too.

Believing in yourself

At the end of the day, how much faith other people do or don't have in you doesn't matter. Most important is ensuring that you see the hero in yourself, the person who can make the difficult journey successfully. Only you can decide whether or not you're strong enough to make the tough decisions. Believe that you are, approach them all mindfully and you'll see how successful you can be.

I call this exercise 'the hero who lives in your heart'. Kindly repeat it as often as possible while you're trying to break your addiction:

1. **Go to your meditation room/corner and adopt a comfortable and dignified posture:** For tips, flip to Chapter 4.

2. **Close your eyes gently and start to use the breath as your anchor of awareness.** Breathe in and out until you feel quite settled.

3. **Imagine opening a door or a box (or any symbol you choose) and find information about all the good things you've been involved with, the times when you felt good about yourself and had moments of joy.** Also remember triumphs in childhood and adult life. Don't make them smaller than they were. Let them shine!

   Sooner or later the mind throws in negative stuff too, as is its wont: mistakes, ugly scenes, actions you're not proud of. Just look at them briefly, accepting their presence, and let them pass by like birds in the sky. No need to struggle – simply allow the mind to shine a light on whatever virtuous engagements come into your awareness, which is all that you need to see.

Letting go of addiction, mindfully

An addictive mindset that triggers unwholesome behaviour needs rewriting in order to get it to a point where it can truly open up to the possibility of a free and largely wholesome way of thinking and acting. In other words, you need to let go of negative thought patterns (as I discuss throughout this book but particularly in Chapter 9).

This exercise helps you to let go of self-doubt and thoughts of failing:

1. **Start the practice in your special meditation corner.** Sit with dignity and close your eyes.

2. **Focus on grounding yourself.** Then follow the simple action of breathing.

3. **Open the mind's gate of all doubts when you're ready, including nasty self-deprecating thoughts, fears, and so on.** Visualise them written on faulty goods on a conveyor belt, which leads all these trapped thoughts into a huge waste barrel that's then disposed of.

Here are a few typical nasty thoughts that can be particularly persistent:

✔ 'You've done so many bad things that you don't deserve another chance.'

✔ 'Come on, look at yourself; you'll fail again just like all the other times.'

✔ 'You'll be so lonely without drink; your only true friends are waiting in the bar for you.'

✔ 'You'll never enjoy parties again – you boring party-pooper.'

✔ 'What's wrong with [add your addiction here] – what doesn't kill you makes you stronger.'

Of course, you have your own version of these challenging thoughts, but just remember that they're caused by fear of failure and loneliness. So with as much compassion as you can muster, drop them in that barrel and let them go once and for all.

Mistakes are part of every journey

Think about people who redeemed themselves and became kind and good, such as Ebenezer Scrooge from Charles Dickens's *A Christmas Carol*.

Here's an example. Franz was a spoilt rich young gentleman who never showed responsibility or compassion for the poor. He became involved in a battle and survived but was seriously ill. After recovering, he gave away all his belongings and travelled to many countries teaching compassion, kindness and generosity to humans and animals. Today he's known as Francis of Assisi, patron saint of animals.

Perhaps you know people who changed paths and made a difference.

These thoughts have had a long residence permit, so don't be surprised if they've procreated and their offspring return! Just repeat the above exercise until you feel that they've given up.

Starting afresh, now

Even if you're still wading through muddy waters, your intention to stop is the most important point to remember. Please don't think that you have to completely get over the addiction before you can begin afresh; your new life starts the moment you decide firmly to make a change.

Remember that you need support on this adventure, so consider how you're going to help yourself on this new journey. What other support can you give yourself? What gifts and benefits can you receive from giving up a destructive way of living? Here are a few ideas:

- ✔ **Find joy in the little things:** A bird singing, a beautiful flower, a smile from a loved one – bring mindfulness to every moment.

- ✔ **Gratitude:** Instead of remembering all your flaws and tragic past events, focus on the gifts you've received. Write down a list of your own and do it every day so you incline your mind towards all that's positive and beneficial: the food you receive, the home you may have, and so on . . . the list can never be too long.

- ✔ **Mindfulness practice:** Let meditation be your daily ritual for cleansing your mind and soul.

Staving Off Relapse

Even if you manage to give up your addiction for a significant time span, no guarantee exists that you're safe from it forever. You have to find the means of continuing with the new healthier way of being when the going gets rough. A famous alcoholic writer is supposed to have said that stopping is the easiest thing on earth, but staying sober the hardest.

You can be particularly vulnerable if a big change or loss occurs in your life. Whether you've slipped already or are experiencing a strong urge to do so, please try the following:

- ✔ Note down the situation, the emotions and any other important insights in your mindfulness diary.

> ✔ Consider what went wrong, what you may not have been aware of and where more mindfulness may have been able to guide you through with less harm.
>
> ✔ Allow whatever you become aware of to be your guide for the future.
>
> ✔ Share your experience with other people, so that any lapses can bring increased awareness for you and others.

With time, mindfulness makes you more attuned to the ups and downs of living. As a result, more and more often, you will be able to see problems coming and turn away from falling back into the deep dark hole.

Mistakes and errors are part of the human experience and the meditator who has never failed and failed again is yet to be born! So, be kind and understanding with yourself, because compassion and forgiveness are brother and sister.

Losing Control: Understanding Alcohol Addiction

Addiction often feels like a loss of control over yourself, as you become dependent on a substance to cope with daily life. Alcohol addiction is one of the most common destructive habits in this regard, so in this section I look at this specific problem: the destructive facts of alcohol addiction, the signs that tell you how to recognise addiction and the difference between a bad habit and full-blown addiction. Remember, however, that you can adapt and use much of the information contained in this section to help with other addictions as well.

When you're addicted to alcohol, you experience feelings of helplessness, fear and shame. Tell-tale signs for alcohol addiction are hiding alcohol in unusual places, such as behind clothes, under the PC, and so on. People who don't know about addiction can assume that weakness is to blame, but research shows that certain humans are more likely to become addicted than others (see the nearby sidebar 'Alcohol facts and figures').

Considering the symptoms of alcohol addiction

If you have three or more of the following symptoms, you've already developed alcohol addiction:

✔ A strong desire or urge to drink alcohol regularly

✔ Reduced ability to be able to stop drinking after you've started

✔ Physiological signs for withdrawal (shaking, lack of focus, stomach pain, vomiting), which you eliminate only by drinking more alcohol

✔ A gradual expansion of your intake of alcohol in order to achieve a level of functionality in your everyday life

✔ An increasing neglect of hobbies, interests or friendships that used to be important to you

✔ Ongoing consumption of alcohol, even though you're aware of the destructive nature of your habit

Alcohol which reaches your brain through the bloodstream is perceived by the brain as a toxic substance. The brain can only cope with a small amount or else it may experience damage. In order to avoid long-term damage the brain grows receptors that soak up any surplus alcohol. Each time you drink over the limit of your receptors, more grow to avoid damage. At first glance this is a good thing. The only problem is that once you start drinking, these receptors behave like little hungry birds and cause a huge amount of craving until they're all satisfied. You may not realise when this level is reached and over-drink, which causes more receptors to grow. This so-called receptor trap is a vicious circle.

Alcohol facts and figures

More than 29 per cent of adult men and 10 per cent of adult women drink alcohol regularly, even daily. But health suffers significantly from regular over-drinking, with alcohol addiction leading to 20–25 years of reduced life expectancy. Annually, 2.5 million deaths are directly linked to the over-consumption of alcohol, according to the World Health Organisation. This figure is the equivalent of 4 per cent of all deaths worldwide per year and much higher than the number of deaths from AIDS, tuberculosis and malaria.

Genetic predisposition tends to determine how well or otherwise you tolerate alcohol, though men usually tolerate a higher intake than women (which is why women who drink regularly can usually cope with consuming only a smaller quantity and tend to get addicted more speedily, particularly post-menopause). Some individuals have developed high levels of enzymes for the digestion of alcohol and so transform and dispose of alcohol faster. Such individuals have a high level of tolerance and can develop a habit without becoming technically addicted.

A number of mental conditions can be caused or exacerbated by alcohol addiction, such as depression, anxiety and sleep disturbance. Alcohol is often seen as a quick form of self-medication for these conditions (read Chapter 12 on depression and Chapter 14 on anxiety).

Discovering the dangers

If you see yourself reflected in the preceding section, you need to know that regular heavy drinking, as well as alcohol addiction, can lead to serious physiological damage, even if you never feel inebriated. Some alcohol-induced diseases are:

- Bowel cancer and perforation of the bowel due to dehydration
- Breast cancer
- Cancer of the mouth and oesophagus
- Circulatory problems leading to raised blood pressure
- Dysfunction of the immune system
- Fatty liver, cirrhosis of the liver and liver cancer
- Heart attack
- Impotence
- Korsakov syndrome (on-going severe short-term memory loss)
- Memory loss (short-term)
- Weight gain
- Stroke

Furthermore, habitual drinkers are like tightrope walkers. Any major life crisis, such as the loss of a beloved person, of status, of their own health or difficulties with a significant other, can tip them over the edge. If you belong to this latter group, you can overstep your limit again and again until eventually you become addicted (at least in a psychological way).

The good news is that you can overcome addiction or heavy regular consumption and develop the ability to regain control mindfully. Each individual is unique so you need to find out which approach is best for you. Whether your goal is total abstinence or significantly reducing intake, the most important outcome for you is probably not to feel ashamed of yourself, to no longer endanger yourself and others, and to find joy and purpose again.

Challenging the misconceptions

Many a good friend may want to give advice, such as to simply drink less. To be honest, this advice is as useless as telling depressed or highly anxious people to pull themselves together. Instead, you need to have all the knowledge necessary to make an informed decision.

Keeping a drink diary is a good first step, because you tend to forget what and how much you consume on a daily basis. So, for a week or so, write down the following in your diary (note that, roughly, a unit is a small glass of wine, half a pint of beer or a single spirit):

- ✔ How strong is your desire to drink, from 1 (low) to 10 (high)?
- ✔ How long can you resist this urge (craving)?
- ✔ Does it pass if you resist? If so, after how many minutes?
- ✔ How many units do you drink on a regular basis?
- ✔ When do you drink, and how long for (starting time and, if you can remember, the time you finish)?
- ✔ How do you feel after drinking one unit?
- ✔ How do you feel after three units, and can you stop now?
- ✔ How do you feel upon waking up the next day?

This record helps you gauge whether you're already addicted or merely drinking too much habitually.

Worryingly, research shows that most people have been battling with addiction for seven years before they seek help. How many good reasons do you have to stop or reduce your drinking now? Please write them down in your diary.

Here are some common examples of false or unhelpful ideas that can get in the way of overcoming your alcohol addiction:

- ✔ **I don't really have a problem.** Please read the preceding pages again and write down anything that applies to you.

- ✔ **I simply love the feeling of freedom and relaxation I feel after the first few sips.** If so, note down how you feel after the first, second or third glass, after the last glass, and the next morning.

  Also consider experimenting with other ways to relax, such as a regular body scan after work before you do anything else (see Chapter 4), mindful movement or going for a mindful walk (I describe both in Chapter 6).

- ✔ **Nobody suffers because I'm a little tipsy.** Ask your partner, friends or colleagues for their honest answers. Please write them down.

- ✔ **I'm still in control and can stop anytime.** Really? Have you tried? Take a few days off or reduce significantly and write down how you feel when you're truly sober.

- ✔ **Everyone in my family drinks. It would look weird if I didn't.** Is this statement true? How many relatives have suffered from their regular consumption, and how? Kindly note the answer in your diary.

> ✔ **I have other thoughts of resistance.** If you like movies, maybe watch *Leaving Las Vegas* with Nicolas Cage portraying a man who loses everything: job, home, wife and kids. He completes his journey of destruction in a cheap hotel room in Las Vegas.

Believing that the problem is out of your hands

Alcoholics Anonymous works miraculously for many people, and if it works for you, that's fantastic. But that model isn't always helpful for everyone. The MBCT approach for addiction offers you a different path, and is very concerned with this moment in your life, such as the fact that right here and now, you can decide not to drink, just for a few minutes.

Cognitive behavioural therapy avoids labelling individuals for their actions or illnesses (so no 'alcoholics'), because labelling yourself with the disease can make you feel that it has become part of who you are forever, whereas in fact you're only addicted to a certain drug or behaviour right now. Negative thoughts and patterns arrive but aren't invited to become permanent residents, and you alone have the power to say to them 'Time to move on!'.

Step one of your recovery is to believe that you can empower yourself to change your mind and actions at any moment, because every moment is a new beginning.

As an exercise, begin by performing the breathing space (Chapter 6) and then put your hand on your heart, silently repeating the comforting words that I suggest in the kindness meditation in Chapter 9. By doing so, you're asking for, and so opening the possibility for, protection and safety (write down how the answer to this plea manifests itself in your mind). Furthermore, asking to remain peaceful implies that you're no longer feeding negative assumptions, but trusting that peace is possible.

Living with ease and kindness starts at home, so do away with this tendency to degrade yourself and to think that you'll never be good enough. All beings deserve to be at peace and ease and live with kindness. Maybe the greatest gift you have to give is that of your own self-transformation.

Going cold turkey

Putting too much pressure on yourself, by believing that you can just give it all up immediately, rarely works. Depending on the level and intensity of your alcohol addiction, you can trigger delirium tremens.

Never too late to quit

A former client had been drinking excessively for as long as he could remember. He promised that he'd stop when his unhappy marriage was over. When his wife passed away, he immediately stopped drinking and smoking, and managed for a couple of months.

One sunny evening he returned to his old inn and met up with his old mates. He lit his first cigarette and was treated quickly to his first beer. Many, many rounds later he managed to get home, but before he reached his bed he collapsed with terrible pain on the floor. A day later he was found by his son and taken to hospital. His stomach had perforated, he was diagnosed with lung cancer and had secondary tumours in his spine. When he woke up with a colostomy bag and heard all this news, he wondered what he had to live for. A nurse told him that he'd almost died, but that he wasn't dead yet. She suggested that he live for now. He experimented with doing just this – one moment at a time, no more, no less.

He's now 81 years old and has been sober for five years. Of course, he's not always happy but he is experiencing life in all its shades of colour. So it's never too late to start anew. Even if you have to start a thousand times, so be it. Every moment can be a new beginning.

Delirium tremens (DT) is a medical emergency that can cause death: if you experience its symptoms call an ambulance immediately. DT can occur when you stop drinking alcohol after a period of heavy drinking, especially if you don't eat enough food and avoid mindfully reducing unit by unit. It happens most often to people who drink more than a bottle of wine or more than eight pints of beer daily for a number of months, and can affect you if your regular habit has been going on for over ten years.

Symptoms of DT most often occur within 72 hours of your last alcohol consumption. However, they may occur up to a week after the last drink. Observe yourself patiently during the first week of alcohol reduction. Seek medical advice if some of the following symptoms occur. Here is a list of symptoms, which can start mildly and then get worse quickly:

- Agitation, irritability
- Body tremors and irregular heart beat and chest pain
- Changes in mental function
- Deep sleep that lasts for a day or longer
- Disorientation
- Fatigue
- Feeling jumpy, nervous, shaky
- Hallucination (seeing or feeling things that don't exist)
- Headache
- Increased activity, restlessness, irritability or excitability

- Insomnia (difficulty falling and staying asleep)
- Loss of appetite
- Nausea, vomiting and stomach pain
- Pale skin
- Quick mood changes
- Seizures
- Sensitivity to light, sound, touch
- Sweating on the palms of the hands, the face or having a fever

In order to avoid DT, start your withdrawal with the help of a medical support person or in a withdrawal centre. If your drinking history isn't as excessive as described or hasn't been going on for such a long time, you can experiment with the help of your drink diary to reduce your alcohol intake gradually, and mindfully observe any unexpected symptoms.

Remembering Helpful Lessons

This section helps you create a prescription for when life is tough and danger looms round the corner (yes, it can seem like this every day).

Please consider going through this chapter and your diary and noting down the ten most important points you want to remember. Here's an example, but please create your own and print out ten copies to pin up in the bathroom, kitchen, bedroom, office, toilet, sitting room, and so on. Believe me: mindful repetition really helps!

- Rediscover the magic and purpose of your life.
- Engage in mindful moments throughout the day.
- Let go of shame and guilt and reclaim your hero.
- Write and read your mindfulness diary every day.
- Express gratitude for everyday living and moments of joy.
- Learn from and share the awareness that grows from mistakes.
- Establish a solid meditation practice.
- Connect with other people, nature and your deepest self.
- Work at living, loving and making your own decisions.
- Live moment by moment, making a fresh start in every moment.

I find these topics interesting, but they aren't definitive. Consider sitting down and meditating on your own ten points to remember.

Chapter 14

Relieving the Strain of Anxiety

· ·

In This Chapter

▶ Understanding the nature of anxiety

▶ Dealing with various forms of anxiety and fear

▶ Coming to terms with your personal anxieties

▶ Accepting that anxiety is a part of life

· ·

Mindfulness-based cognitive therapy (MBCT) can help to prevent the onset of anxiety and stress, and tackle the associated symptoms, whether you're experiencing a particular type of anxiety or suffering from a number of different manifestations. Anxiety can often be like an infectious disease: if you don't cure one aspect, it soon spreads into other areas of your life. Knowing the real nature of anxiety is part of winning the battle, so the key aim of this chapter is to lift the veil of this mysterious disease, which so often hides from common understanding.

I also offer you clear and detailed interventions to reduce the impact of general and individual anxiety as much as possible. I guide you towards a level of acceptance where you can honestly say 'I'm still feeling the fear, but I'm not going to let it stop me from leading my life'. And you never know – when anxiety loosens its grip it may get bored altogether and leave you be.

 If you tend to suffer from regular panic attacks, visit your GP and have your blood pressure, blood sugar and cholesterol levels checked. Panic attacks may be a symptom of something else, so get a professional medical opinion on their possible cause.

Coping with Pressure

No other species on Earth surpasses humans when it comes to creative and intellectual thinking, and yet physically they're a rather weak creation, with no large claws, big teeth, heavy fur or strong scales to protect them. In this sense, people are really vulnerable and have always had to be on high alert to avoid being attacked.

The stress response in action

Imagine that you're walking through a dark wood and see a long slim object on the ground in front of you. Before your higher brain centres can get into action, the amygdala (the human brain control centre) activates your complete response centre and you stop in your stride, pant heavily, feel your heart racing and your sense of hearing sharpen. Only then do your higher brain functions process all the information you're facing. 'Is the long thin 'stick-like' object moving? Is the front bit slightly bigger and the back bit pointed? Does it make a sound – maybe even hiss?' The answer each time is 'no', and so you're pretty sure that it's just a stick and not a snake. You notice your breathing slow down and even creativity move in as you pick it up or poke it or make sounds to see whether it moves. Only then, when you're certain that it isn't going to harm you, do you carry on walking. A lot of palaver for nothing, perhaps, but what if it had been a poisonous snake?

As you can see, your fight-or-flight stress response is pretty awesome, but if it gets triggered too often or you can no longer step out of anxious mode, you suffer from anxiety. Unfortunately, this highly functioning warning system recalls individual moments of threat so precisely that, say, you remember getting stuck in a lift once instead of the 100,000 other times you didn't.

Mindfulness trains you to perceive things as they really are, so that your threat centre doesn't get over-activated and lead to constantly feeling anxious.

Although their natural predators have reduced significantly, humans now face new versions of savage animals that cause their brains to go into overload! These new threats are machines, technology, speed, overpopulation, daily commuting, and so on.

Unfortunately, the human threat-detection system isn't highly evolved enough to know the difference between a demanding project you may feel inadequate for and a wild, man-eating animal. A few anxious thoughts and short breaths are sufficient to activate the whole fight-or-flight response. All that has really changed over the millennia are the triggers. So far, evolution hasn't assisted people in feeling calmer and less anxious when under pressure. As Paul Gilbert wisely points out in his book *The Compassionate Mind* (published by Constable & Robinson in 2010), Mother Nature was purely focusing on helping the species survive, not on how to chill out and have a good time.

In this section I take a look at how stress works and some of its common manifestations.

Knowing the stress chemicals

The two most prominent chemicals involved in stress are adrenaline and cortisol. The former's role is to activate a higher heart rate (to bring more blood to essential areas such as limbs so that you can run faster or hit harder), increase breath intake (to provide the body with more oxygen) and initiate sweating (to keep the body cool).

Cortisol immediately mobilises glucose stored in the body for extra energy, inhibits the immune system where it's not needed and enhances it around areas where your enemy would potentially harm you (for example, your throat). Short term, that's exactly what you need to survive an attack, but long term it can lead to depletion (burn-out) and disease (the immune suppression can cause serious illnesses).

Understanding how anxiety manifests itself

If you're interested in how anxiety activates the stress response in detail, kindly go to Chapter 7 (week four of the eight-week program). In brief, the important information that you need to know is that the sympathetic nervous system gets activated when you interpret a situation as potentially dangerous. The trigger can be something as simple as your neighbours harassing you again because you repair a fence panel to stop their delightful bull terrier from soiling your garden. Intense neighbours, relatives, clients, workmates, and so on can all start off the stress-reaction process.

When you're floating in your stress chemicals, you take much longer to regain your mental balance. Not only that, but you may suddenly become aware of numerous aches and pains as your body functions in fifth gear, and the fear about an unknown invading disease can continue to feed any anxiety that arises. Your brain control centre is now on full alert like a rescue team in a hijacked plane; anything that moves gets shot. So you need to grasp that body and mind work in union in order to survive any perceived threat (please remember the importance of the word 'perceived'!).

Differentiating between the types of anxiety

The anxiety loop that I describe in the preceding section can eventually lead to general anxiety disorder (GAD) and other anxiety-related disorders such as obsessive compulsive disorder (OCD), phobias, hypochondria, agoraphobia, and so on.

Physical symptoms initially include sweating, change in body temperature, feeling sick and nauseous, increased sensitivity to sounds, strong heart palpitations, and digestive and urinary tracts becoming overactive. Long-term anxiety or repeatedly triggered anxiety can cause raised blood pressure, headaches, muscle aches and sleep disorder as well as lowered immune response. The latter can lead to irritable bowel syndrome, skin diseases such as psoriasis, frequent stomach upsets and inflammation, urinary and respiratory tract inflammations, and viral infections.

Here are a few more details:

- **GAD:** Living constantly with a sense of non-specific dread, which is uncomfortable and drives sufferers into staying in their homes. Associated symptoms can include chronic muscle tension, fatigue, getting easily upset (even aggressive) and disturbed sleep.

- **Hypochondriasis (health anxiety):** Excessive fear for one's own health set off by ordinary bodily sensations; for example, a stomach ache, which may be caused by stress, is interpreted as a stomach ulcer or even cancer. Ongoing fear leads sufferers to attend hospital more frequently, which can compromise their immune system because hospitals tend to expose people to more germs and viruses than they'd normally encounter.

- **OCD:** Forces the sufferer to check things or have certain thoughts (obsessions) repeatedly. To try to control these obsessions, sufferers feel an overwhelming urge to repeat certain routines, rituals or behaviours (compulsions). In extreme cases, OCD can take over your life. If it takes you four hours before you think your desk is sufficiently sorted or before your teeth are clean, you aren't going to have enough time to follow a career or a relationship.

  People with OCD can have extreme difficulty challenging these behaviours. Read the later sidebar 'A short case study on OCD' for an OCD anecdote.

- **Panic attacks:** Sudden fear or dread that leads to numerous symptoms of anxiety simultaneously, which again feeds into health anxiety. Panic attacks can also be triggered by trauma or overuse of caffeine.

- **Phobia:** Usually manifests itself by an unhealthy preoccupation with a particular thing or action, usually to an extent that you can't tolerate being near the object or action that causes your high anxiety response. Here are a few common phobias:

  - Agoraphobia: Fear of open spaces (going outside or leaving a space of safety).

  - Arachnophobia: Fear of spiders.

  - Claustrophobia: Fear of tight, enclosed spaces (as well as tunnels or transport systems that lead through such spaces, for example the London Underground).

  - Social phobia: Fear of people, particularly larger gatherings.

A short case study on OCD

A young Muslim woman came to see me about her OCD. She had been to many highly recommended therapists and yet her symptoms persisted and got worse. She had to check all electrical equipment at least seven times prior to leaving the house and also lock and unlock her entrance door seven times. All therapists had tried to make her see that her behaviour was illogical and that checking everything once or twice would suffice (that is, what people usually consider sufficient).

I became interested, however, in what she was avoiding by this compulsive checking. Instead of focusing again on changing her behaviour, I decided to talk with her about her life in general. She slowly revealed that she wanted to be an obedient Muslim and that her religion demanded that she was soon to marry a man that her parents had chosen for her. But not only did she find this man totally unattractive, even worse (so she thought), she found all men undesirable. In fact, the truth was that she felt drawn to a particular woman at work. She felt 'something like love' for this woman. The concept of entering a same-sex relationship and disobeying her parents was totally outside her mental boundaries. The more she thought about her future fate, being with a man she didn't even like and in a physical relationship with a man,

the more anxious she became. Only her rituals covered the pain of her severe anxiety.

Her subconscious mind resorted to using those rituals so she could avoid having to think about her sexuality, religion and family traditions and obligations. The more she focused on finding a resolution that would help and satisfy everybody involved, the more she realised that it was an impossible task to achieve. She was a lesbian woman, attracted to other women and in particular to one woman for whom she had feelings of love and desire. This was incompatible with her tradition, her family and her faith. She knew deep down that as long as she was not 'normal' enough to get married (that is, free of her OCD) she wouldn't have to face making decisions that would either ruin her life or possibly that of her family.

I am sorry to say that although these insights were helpful to her in the short term, in the long run she took the option of staying with her mental disorder. OCD seemed the easier option.

In a case like this, you can mindfully conclude that there would have been emotional pain and unhappiness whatever option she chose to take. The human condition of suffering cannot always be resolved in an easy or straightforward way. Sometimes you just have to accept that there is no easy answer or resolution.

Tackling Your Fears with Targeted Interventions

The central aspects of MBCT really come into their own when helping you to deal effectively with anxiety disorders, such as those I discuss in the preceding section.

Developing a coping plan

From a behavioural perspective, one important intervention is to reduce your repetitive safety behaviours and mindfully increase healthy, but presently suppressed, normal behaviours.

As an example, imagine that you suffer from a form of public speaking anxiety. The problem is so severe that it doesn't merely affect you speaking in public, but extends so far that you can't write (even just to sign a cheque, for example) or eat in public. You have a deep desire to re-engage with such activities but simultaneously feel extremely anxious even thinking about doing any of them. Such anxiety is sure to make every day a trial.

To make it easier to be with the anxiety you experience, whatever its specific nature, think about using some of the following mindful actions:

✔ Start each day with a short breathing practice (check out Chapter 5 for details).

✔ When you get out of bed, feel your feet firmly on the ground. Take a few mindful breaths and smile a genuine smile.

✔ Sit up and give yourself a mindful hug while breathing with awareness for a couple of minutes.

✔ Rub your hands until they feel hot and put each hand over one eye, relishing the soothing warmth radiating from your hands. Take a few mindful breaths.

✔ Write a list of all the activities of the day that may make you feel anxious.

✔ Visualise coping with each individual action mindfully, as follows:

  • Taking a second to stop what you're doing every so often and 'arriving' in the present moment, feeling connected to the surface you're standing on and with the space around you, before continuing with whatever you were originally doing.

  • Grounding yourself with a breathing space meditation (see Chapter 6).

  • Staying with each activity when it occurs and only dealing with this particular challenge (not thinking ahead).

✔ Make your motto 'One step at a time'.

✔ Add compassion and patience to your daily list. Remember that each experiment has a new beginning, a chance to start afresh.

✔ Visualise yourself carrying out an action that you find traumatic.

✔ Use humour to get through an awkward situation, even if your mind throws up the possibility of not getting it right. For example, if you spill your drink while giving a talk, say to yourself: 'Am I nervous or what?' Or just wipe up the spilt drink and continue as if nothing happened. After all, is it really so terrible?

✔ Finish each day by remembering all the little details you enjoyed, appreciated and were satisfied with.

Changing unhelpful thoughts

As I repeat throughout this book, your thoughts aren't solid, universal truths, so their power over you is no more than you grant them.

You only deem people or actions as dangerous when you apply an anxiety-provoking meaning to them, for example: 'If my hands tremble when I sign the cheque and the bank clerk notices it, I'll look stupid and feel like a total idiot.' If you don't have this thought, you either don't tremble at all or simply accept that your hands sometimes tremble. Both of these options are versions of a rational and helpful mindset, which doesn't lead you towards a state of high alert.

You can invite all sorts of healthy thoughts to your thought party, such as: 'Even if I shake a little, who'd even notice?', 'If anyone does notice, they may feel sympathy' or even 'Let them think what they want, at least I'm brave enough to do whatever suits me. I don't need anyone's approval.'

Write down your five most difficult scenarios and let your mindful and supportive voice assist you in getting through them.

Ask people you trust what they'd think about those situations. Most likely, you'll realise how unrealistic your thoughts or worries sometimes are. Plus, even if you have such thoughts occasionally, it hardly makes you a total fool. A compassionate approach is accepting the irrational nature of your thoughts and then practising new varieties of them, slowly creating new helpful thinking patterns for yourself.

Consider generating a list along the following lines:

✔ **Anxiety provoking thought:** 'I'm such an idiot for having shaking hands!'

✔ **How true do I think this is about myself?** Ninety per cent.

✔ **How true would most people think this is about me?** Ten per cent.

Apart from creating a list of desired behaviour and emotional changes and then practising those new activity patterns, ensure that you keep rehearsing the new helpful thinking patterns. You help yourself by creating the right mood environment where new thoughts can be tested and allowed to grow permanent roots.

Intervening mindfully

Unfortunately you can't simply stop being scared. Instead of being hard on yourself, use several interventions when you feel anxiety coming on and for long-term 'stress-fastness'.

Breathing exercises

One of the most common responses that anxiety provokes is *hyperventilation,* which is when you're breathing too fast and experiencing a number of uncomfortable symptoms, such as tingling face, hands, muscle tremors and cramps, dizziness and double/blurred vision, difficulty breathing, tiredness, chest and stomach pains.

Whatever the particular situation you're in, when you notice shallow breathing, kindly focus on the tip of your nose, feeling the airflow on the in-breath and out-breath. You probably notice cooler air entering your nose and warmer air leaving your nose. Simply focus on this in- and out-flow.

Another method of reducing this type of speedy breathing is to inhale through your nose and exhale through your mouth, imagining holding a spoon with hot soup that you're trying to cool down and not spill. Repeat five to ten times.

You can read about some longer breathing practices in Chapter 5.

Visualisations

Imagine being a mountain that remains calm throughout a storm, or the sea looking wild and ferocious on the surface but deep down calm and still. Using such images helps you to feel grounded and empowered. Check out the similar but longer mountain meditation in Chapter 6 as well.

Lake meditation

Imagine sitting on a bench looking out at a beautiful lake. Sometimes its colour appears blue, at other times turquoise. You and the lake are surrounded by beautiful, mighty mountains. Some are so high that you can see snow surrounding their lofty peaks.

You're looking at the lake and the water seems calm and still. Occasionally a bird flies down to pick up an insect from the surface of the lake. At other times a trout or perch jumps up from the depth of the lake to catch a fluttering insect from the surface. You see a mother duck with her ducklings swimming towards you, maybe hoping that you'll feed them. In the distance, a couple of majestic swans are cleaning their lovely white coats. The meadows around the lake are in full bloom: luscious green grass, meadow flowers in purple, yellow, pink and white; some bushes and tall, ancient trees too. The sky is heavenly blue with just a few scattered clouds and the sun is warming all creatures great and small. You can see butterflies, busy bees and other insects, and birds in the air. Deep down in the lake is another world, which is calm with more muted but still beautiful colours, and peace abides.

Suddenly a storm starts to rise up. The sky gets heavy with dark grey clouds. Soon rain is pouring down; the trees are bending through the force of the wind. The surface of the lake now appears dark grey-blue and big waves are chopping at the surface too. Deep down, however, the lake hardly murmurs – stillness and peace still abiding.

Kindly apply this visualisation to your own life. Imagine that even when all is topsy-turvy around you and you can barely cope, deep down is this place you've created through the practice of mindfulness. You can return to it, in your mind, whenever you feel the need.

Creating practice points

Throughout this book are a number of exercises that are essential if you want to discover how to control your anxiety, rather than let it control you. Longer mindfulness exercises, such as the body scan and being with the breath (Chapter 4), and staying with discomforting thoughts (Chapter 8), need to become part of your daily routine so that you reap the full range of mindfulness benefits.

In addition, maintaining the basic mindful attitudes is vitally important to changing your fundamental ways of thinking. With that in mind, please consider using the following key practice points to get yourself into good thinking habits:

- **Acceptance:** You're only human and, as such, you need to accept that you're never going to be perfect, and neither is any other person.

- **Beginners mind:** Bring curiosity to this adventure of doing things differently, of taking risks, of starting afresh many times.

- **Kindness:** Treat yourself as you'd treat a vulnerable child; soften into the experience and simply be (even if saying it is easier than doing so in practice).

✔ **Letting go:** This invitation is serious. Only by giving yourself permission to start anew, afresh and without the need to succeed, do you stand a chance of experiencing subtle changes or observations with regard to your state of mind, your state of emotions and your body (for example, tingling sensations when more oxygen is entering your bloodstream). This idea is strongly connected to the attitude of non-striving. Allow yourself to freely float into an experience without any attachment to outcome or deep insight. Just be for the sake of being.

✔ **Non-judgement:** Bring kindness and freedom from judgement to your attempt to overcome fear, which is a powerful force of life. Remember, however, that at times fear is essential for your survival.

✔ **Non-striving:** All you're invited to do is to pay attention, because you want to understand and discover. You needn't become the best meditator in town. You're practising mindfulness only out of curiosity and perhaps to find the gift of peace.

✔ **Patience:** Practise being calm and collected, and even when you don't always manage to tame the wild horse of anxiety, just remember that every moment is a new beginning.

✔ **Trust:** Kindly be aware that mindfulness has been around for a long time and millions of people benefit from it; perhaps you too can reap rewards.

All these basic mindful attitudes connect together and weave a different experience of life to the one you've been used to so far. So throughout the day, and not just when you do your formal meditation practice, see whether you can apply to all your actions and personal experiences as many of the above attitudes as possible.

As an exercise, please imagine this scenario. You're at work and your line manager rushes up to you and demands that you finish a certain piece of work within the hour. Your habitual reaction is perhaps to get irritated and say 'I don't think that's humanly possible', or to boil with anger internally and snatch the folder.

Please consider instead how you can respond mindfully. Here are some ideas, using a few of the above mindful attitudes:

✔ **Acceptance:** You can accept that she's a challenge to work with and try to make the best of it by responding, 'Let me have a look first and I'll get back to you as soon as I can.'

✔ **Kindness:** Show a sign of compassion by asking, 'Are you okay?'

✔ **Letting go:** As best as you can, don't bring old stories into the present. Try to evaluate each new challenge when it appears without adding past frustration to it.

✔ **Non-judgement:** Perhaps you notice that the manager is expecting too much, but also that she looks tired and stressed herself.

Making Peace with Your Fears

Your fears are yours and are important; don't feel that they're insignificant. Don't allow what others think of them to influence your own feelings about them. Take ownership of your fears, because that way you can allow yourself to be objective and non-judgemental and start making progress in addressing them.

Mindfulness in Pali, the ancient language of the Buddha, also means *heartfulness* in harmony with mind-awareness. Let your heart guide you when your brain is tired or confused.

Understanding that your instincts are natural

Your instinct to run away from certain situations and fight in others is completely natural. But unlike other animals, human beings have the ability to learn and to override their instincts (feeling the fear and yet knowing that not all things that frighten us are actually dangerous).

If you feel that your instincts are taking you to an unhelpful place, or that you want to try something different, you've got the power to do so – with the skills that MBCT provides.

Knowing that you can rise above your instincts

MBCT helps you to switch from reacting instinctively (for example, running away from an argument) to responding skilfully instead. MBCT trains your brain to become more discerning about when to go with the fight-or-flight response and when simply to be still, breathe and respond wisely and compassionately.

FMRI scanners can show how mindfulness meditation, when practised regularly, is like a workout for your brain. The cortex remains thicker (which improves long-term memory), your level of compassion increases (for yourself and others) and the amygdala reduces in size and activation. As many people now have the wonderful opportunity to live much longer than previously, I think that having a fully functional (mindful) brain and mind is desirable. What do you think?

The happiest man on Earth!

Matthieu Ricard, who has been called the happiest man on Earth, has the smallest amygdala ever observed in a living human by using an FMRI scanner. Matthieu is of French origin, and after finishing his PhD in physics in Paris he went to Nepal and become a monk in his mid-twenties. He's the Dalai Lama's French translator, a writer, a photographer and has been extremely keen to observe scientific proof for meditation leading to wellbeing. He has been known to spend two hours and more in an FMRI scanner while practising several meditations. Neurologists observed the changes in his brain and analysed them (he is still a scientist deep down). When he came out of the scanner he smiled, which is what he usually does and said the experience was like a lovely retreat. Not many other humans respond to being in a tight noisy tube for several hours in such a way. Other tests included hearing loud noises nearby, yet his brain showed no sign of agitation.

Most people will probably never reach his level of calmness and groundedness. But more and more research evidence shows that the brains of regular meditators show changes and that they feel less anxious and stressed.

In all likelihood, you brush your teeth, take showers and do some form of exercise. You may even eat healthily. So think about working out your brain too, so that it is fully functional right into older age and also offers you a calmer experience of life.

Accepting Anxiety as Part of Life

Anxiety is a natural part of life and an act of self-preservation; allow yourself to come to terms with that fact and understand that anxiety is a necessary emotion for survival. It can sometimes be misplaced (being frightened of a little spider, for example), but anxiety often helps us to be alert in times when we could potentially be harmed. Anxiety, like pain, has a purpose in your life. Evolution doesn't always get everything right, and we have an anxiety-prone brain, but we can teach it a little calmness by regularly meditating.

Pre-empting anxious feelings

Sometimes you feel that you're about to enter into a situation that you know is going to make you feel anxious and react in a certain way. Although preparation can help you to deal with the situation mindfully, instead of letting past experience dictate your reactions please also consider experimenting with some new ideas, such as the following:

✔ Sit with the thoughts that are anxiety-provoking for about 20 minutes. Allow them to arise in your awareness and pass by. Some will pass quickly, others hang around. Expose yourself to them. The longer you sit with them, just allowing them to be there, the more you see them for what they are: just thoughts. Read the poem 'The Guesthouse' in Chapter 8. It shows you that all human emotions are natural and may visit you from time to time.

✔ Use the breathing space exercise from Chapter 6 as an intervention when anxiety takes hold of you at a time when you need to be strong (for example, at a job interview).

✔ Remember that the past is gone and the future unknown. This moment may be the moment where change is possible. Bring to this experience curiosity, trust, non-judgement and even a sense of adventure.

✔ Ground yourself and visualise an image of strength: the mountain, the lake or a big oak tree (check out the earlier section 'Intervening mindfully').

Changing what can be changed

If you know that you can make your situation better for yourself in order to prevent anxious moments from arising, create an environment of harmony that protects your emotional peace and supports you in challenging times.

Here are a few suggestions, but please add your own in your diary:

✔ Set aside time to tidy your room so that it doesn't become too cluttered.

✔ Read poetry mindfully or listen to music that calms your mind.

✔ Carry out a mind-movie meditation (see Chapter 6).

✔ Engage in mindful cooking or baking.

✔ Call or visit a friend and just connect for the sake of friendship.

✔ Watch a wonderful sunset, night sky or some other aspect of nature.

✔ Feed your soul with all that's joyful for you: stroking your cat, having a long bath or going to the cinema.

✔ Book a touch-therapy session for yourself (for example, massage, reflexology, Indian head massage, facial, or one-to-one yoga or Pilates).

Allowing what can't be changed

Bring awareness to the fact that you can't control every aspect of life. You'll never be able to change certain things (for example, trains being late, other people being in a bad mood, payments arriving late, things breaking or needing repair, and so on). In such situations, just accept what you can't change as best as you can. At the same time, give compassion to yourself for challenges that anybody may find difficult.

In a recent conversation, the Dalai Lama spoke naturally about things that he still finds difficult, despite his intense meditative training. He said that as a human, your body will still weep and feel sadness when a loved one passes on. Don't try to stop being yourself or being true to yourself when life is particularly hard.

Sleeping it off

Sleep is incredibly important, because during sleep your body repairs itself. Sometimes all you need to do is have a rest in order for anxiety to slip away. However, often rest can be difficult if you've got too many anxious thoughts swirling about in your mind. So when sleeping becomes a challenge, please consider these mindful ways of allowing yourself to let go and get some much needed rest:

- ✔ Practise a long body scan before you switch off the light (see Chapter 4).
- ✔ Remember what you're grateful for, what you enjoyed today and what you're satisfied with.
- ✔ Switch on nature sounds or gentle folk or classical music.
- ✔ Drink a glass of warm milk and honey mindfully.
- ✔ Take a mindful hot bath, using aromatherapy oils such as cedar or lavender and surrounding the bathtub with natural candle light.

Remembering Helpful Lessons from the Course

Please bear in mind the following useful points that help you tackle your anxiety:

- ✔ Meditation isn't just positive thinking, although many people who practise mindfulness certainly feel that they think less negatively.
- ✔ Meditation isn't simply relaxation (although relaxing can be a welcome by-product).

✔ Mindfulness meditation isn't about trying to achieve a trance-like state; it's about focusing the mind on an anchor of awareness (whether that's a sound, image, body, breath or movement).

✔ Mindfulness meditation has to be regular to bring about noticeable change.

✔ When you meditate for your own wellbeing, you're being less selfish than when working yourself into the ground (think about it).

✔ Every moment is a new beginning, so you never have to feel guilty again. If you slip away from regular practice, just start again.

✔ MBCT is proved to help with anxiety, with many published papers and some books showing the evidence.

Certain difficult thoughts arise when you're suffering from anxiety. Please consider putting to use the following ideas for some common ones:

✔ **'How do I tell the difference between helpful fear and unhelpful fear?'** Mindfully take in the information that's causing your anxiety. If the cause is a harmless spider on the wall, let the anxiety and the spider go. If the cause is a wild dog running towards you, defend yourself as best as you can. Be mindfully discerning.

✔ **'What do I do if my anxiety causes me to lash out at people, physically or verbally? Is it my fault?'** Leave self-blame aside. The fact is that you and most other human beings sometimes feel anxious or stressed. Perhaps attempt to use mindful speech as best you can (see Chapter 11 to read about communicating mindfully).

✔ **'How do I make others understand my anxiety? How do I stop people from doing things that make me anxious?'** You can attempt to explain to your nearest and dearest that you're vulnerable to anxiety, but stopping everyone from doing things that make you feel anxious is impossible. You're the master of your own mood so gently make it your duty to be responsible for your behaviour.

✔ **'Why am I so scared about the future? Why is it so difficult to focus on the here and now?'** You need to train your mind to focus on this aim (see, for example, Chapter 4). Your life is happening only in the now.

✔ **'Why do I become such a different person whenever I'm anxious?'** Humans change when they're anxious, accessing a different 'nervous system' that should really only be switched on for survival. Have you noticed that when people fight for their life, they're least likely to think of others? The best way to stay compassionate is to practise mindfulness day in and day out and you'll feel a gradual change sooner or later.

Fear my Friend

The following poem attempts to change your perspective on fear. Kindly bear in mind as you read it that what you resist persists and may even get worse.

This poem deals with the fact that fear is part of the human experience. You are born with it and may die with it, but if you fight fear less and truly accept it as part of life – just like day and night are a part of life, for example – you may take away its thorn and maybe even be with it as you would be with an old friend.

Fear, fear you have been with me since the day I arrived

When I heard the wind blow

Forcing open the rattling old garden gate

Fear, fear you stayed close by me when I set free

My girlhood and fled into being a woman

Nestling with you in him - musky with sweat

Fear, fear you held my hand on the eve I first felt

My child starting the journey out

Into light-noise and responsibility

Fear, fear you are still here leaning against me

Oh you old friend the last one to go

My candle flickering and darkness wrapping me in

By Patrizia Collard

Chapter 15

Nurturing Hope While Living with Pain

Research shows that traditional medical pain management can be highly effective for acute (short-term) pain relief. For chronic (long-term) pain management, however, some medical interventions may cause more problems than they alleviate.

In this chapter I describe how you can use mindful interventions to deal with chronic pain and illness: mindfulness-based cognitive therapy (MBCT) can inspire confidence and improvement while you're coping with pain. I also suggest that living with an incurable or long-term condition can become much more manageable if you can accept it before looking at solutions for improvement. This statement may sound incredibly difficult to believe, but as you discover in this chapter, the saying 'what we resist, persists' unfortunately contains a lot of truth.

Your key aim is to find out how to be with and around pain while not letting it corrode your experience of life. As so often throughout this book, I invite you to be open, curious and adventurous. For this reason, I include a number of inspiring anecdotes for you to consider. Remember that your life is happening now: try to be aware of this fact as much as possible.

Be sure to consult your GP prior to making any change to your use of pain medication, whether prescribed or otherwise. Your GP will be able to guide you. Don't try and go 'cold turkey' or put too much pressure on yourself to suddenly deal with more pain than you can cope with.

Grinding to a Halt: When Pain Stops You from Living Life

Pain can appear in many different guises: you may feel heat and burning, cold and numbness, stabbing, throbbing or cutting sensations, tightness, pulling or twisting. Or what you're feeling may be completely different or cover several of these descriptions.

Pain describes a state of physical and psychological suffering or discomfort that's caused by an illness or injury. Many experts view constant pain as an unspoken epidemic. A study about pain conducted in 2004 claims that one in five Europeans suffer from *chronic* (that is, long-lasting) pain.

Michael's discovery of mindfulness

When Michael was involved in a motorbike accident, he broke his jaw and suffered serious injuries to his spine and left hand and arm. He needed reconstructive surgery to his face and had to accept living with a paralysed left arm. In addition, he is left-handed and so had to retrain his right hand to be able to write and draw (he was an interior designer and didn't want to give up his profession). He took a full year to recover and was taking painkillers, muscle relaxants and anti-depressants to cope with the intense pain he was suffering from his facial and arm injuries.

His company invited him back to work and he felt useful and connected to life again; alas, his limb pain remained. His arm and hand were completely paralysed and yet every day he woke up with hideous pain. Sometimes he could barely sleep. Soon he had to take higher doses and stronger types of pills, and eventually he developed a stomach ulcer from the regular use of pain-killers. He tried many other methods to get rid of his pain, but it didn't shift, and the longer it stayed the worse it and his depression became. Soon he was on the brink of a nervous breakdown. He split up from his girlfriend and wasn't sure that he was able to continue to work regular hours much longer.

At a pain clinic he befriended a parent of a fellow patient who told him about mindfulness and the Breathworks group (check out the later sidebar 'Moving towards wholeness in four steps' for more on Breathworks). He attended an eight-week course and now regularly engages in meditation. He says that the pain hasn't disappeared, but he's less aware, or completely unaware, of it more and more often. Also, he started to run a self-help group for people in similar situations and intends to train as a mindfulness instructor.

Here's a list of some of the costs of pain to the individual and society:

- Dependency on drugs and other people
- Dependency on self-medication (alcohol, cannabis, overeating, and so on)
- Depression and suicidal thoughts
- Financial difficulties
- High medical costs (if using private healthcare)
- Isolation
- Loss of ability to work
- Loss of purpose

Understanding the nature of pain

You can sense pain as an acute or chronic experience:

- **Acute pain:** Follows an injury, onset of disease or natural event such as childbirth immediately, and relatively speaking is short term. Acute pain can be useful because it warns you not to do certain things that may lead to deeper or lasting damage. You can see acute, short-term pain as a physical alarm bell. If you break a limb, burn your finger or have a hernia operation, pain is your guide as to what you can do while healing and what to avoid. You therefore take good care of the impaired area so that it can repair itself (which usually takes around six weeks to six months to heal completely).

    Most of the repairing happens during sleep, which is one of the reasons why sleep is so important.

- **Chronic pain:** Continual and long term, perhaps lasting for years and decades, chronic pain isn't necessarily severe or always intense but it is regularly experienced. Chronic pain can cause almost unbearable discomfort, but pain alone doesn't cause this kind of hell. The extreme struggle can arise from your desire to stop or get rid of the pain, which somehow leads to even deeper pain: you can therefore see this experience as suffering. Chronic pain is my main focus in this chapter.

As well as physical pain, humans also experience mental suffering. Physical pain is caused by external triggers whereas mental suffering is caused by worrying, non-acceptance, frustration, anger and other destructive emotions.

You can benefit from accepting this fact of life (which is no different from accepting birth and death, day and night, the seasons, and so on). Particularly with chronic pain, the dislike, the fear for the future ('how long will I suffer?', 'will it get even worse?', and so on), non-acceptance of the situation, and 'why me' and 'why now' mindsets are self-created and self-perpetuated. These sensations are referred to as *suffering*. The discomfort caused by suffering can become habitual and create so much tension that you experience yet more physical pain due to tightness, stress chemicals floating around your system and bad body posture. This discomfort can appear worse than the pain you originally experienced from an injury or illness. If you routinely trigger your stress response and inadvertently flood your body with chemicals such as cortisol and adrenaline, your experience of suffering and stress shoots through the roof (check out Chapter 14 for more details).

If suffering takes over your every waking minute in a vicious cycle, like a nightmarish merry-go-round, it can become a hated companion and account for approximately up to two-thirds of your whole chronic pain experience.

Looking at different types of pain

Research over the last 50 years or so has completely revolutionised the conception of pain in medicine. Previously, physicians didn't realise that people have different experiences of pain, even when suffering from the same injury or illness.

Now people understand that pain involves body *and* mind. For instance, pain

- ✔ Is subjective – each individual experiences and processes it differently.
- ✔ Is a disagreeable sensation.
- ✔ Is an uncomfortable emotion.
- ✔ Can be caused by real or possible tissue damage.
- ✔ Can be caused by changes to the nervous system even without obvious physical injury or disease.

In many cases certain diseases, such as arthritis, gout and cancer, cause the pain experience directly. Tissue is inflamed, joints are degenerated, and tumours are growing and pressing on other sensitive areas; any such pain you experience is linked directly to the illness. This is known as *physiological pain*.

In contrast, *neuropathic pain* is experienced by your nervous system. Medical examinations usually can't 'see' this type of pain. Its causes are manifold: damage to nerves or the spinal cord and even the brain. The problem occurs when medicine can't detect anything and yet the pain is still very much present.

Research indicates that the central nervous system can become so hypersensitive that a little pain feels like a huge invasion. Often neuropathic pain is disguised in sensations that you don't normally see as being a symptom of pain, but nonetheless pain of this nature is horribly real:

- ✔ Burning sensations
- ✔ Coldness
- ✔ Electric-shock type feelings
- ✔ Itching
- ✔ Numbness
- ✔ Phantom limb pain (when an extremity is lost or paralysed and yet causes you terrible pain)
- ✔ Pins and needles

Studying the effects of pain on memory

Intense and long-term pain alters the way that the brain remembers and recognises experiences and events. When pain is perceived, in an instant the mind produces a memory pathway. These pathways include the following:

- ✔ What caused the pain
- ✔ Which rules you need to follow to avoid further pain in the future
- ✔ Fear of returning to work, because you may exacerbate your condition or be seen as weak
- ✔ Avoiding exercise because it may increase or prolong the pain
- ✔ Avoiding challenges or adventures until you're well again

You can see that these rules lead to a restricted mindset. Your life can quickly become limited, lonely and without purpose. This change leads to two further problems: low mood and avoidant, anxious behaviour.

Pain may cause you to lose many things, but you still have a basic choice about how to proceed. Having withdrawn from the outside world, you can:

- ✔ Spend time focusing on the pain and undoubtedly increase your suffering.
- ✔ Wake up to the realisation that this is your life; however restricted, this is it. So perhaps the time is right to try and do things differently.

MBCT can help you change your mind, get you back in touch with your body and unearth a new relationship with pain. As a result, even if the pain is still present, you can discover how to look at it, experience it as an observer, dance creatively with it and start having a life around it, instead of the pain being your entire life.

Hurting mentally

Mental pain can occur for a whole range of different reasons, including:

- ✔ Biochemical imbalances of the brain
- ✔ Feeling that you can no longer live with the ongoing physical pain
- ✔ Other triggers, such as not feeling successful or attractive enough or being unsure about your sexuality

Mental pain can sometimes be so severe that it leads to self-harm (cutting and burning oneself), because sufferers tend to tolerate physical pain better than emotional pain. (Kindly refer to Chapter 12 for more information on dealing with emotional pain.)

Don't bottle it up

Psychosomatic pain refers to pain that shows up in the body but is caused by the mind. In other words, your psyche presents something to you physically because you may be ashamed or frightened of sharing a traumatic event.

In one case, a patient came to me with a terrible skin rash that medically didn't fit into any category commonly associated with this phenomenon: it wasn't psoriasis, eczema, an allergic reaction, and so on. He decided to participate in an MBCT course to deal with his depression caused by the terrible skin condition.

During a body scan meditation (see Chapter 4), he suddenly felt as if he was being held down by a large man and remembered being sexually abused by this person. He was in tears and we booked some individual sessions to try to work though his trauma. Soon the man who assaulted him was identified and the whole event came to the surface and to court.

The patient had been suffering from *post-traumatic stress disorder* (PTSD), which refers to symptoms that occur when a traumatic event isn't worked through but instead is suppressed. The mind needs to understand and file away negative events so that the incident doesn't constantly interrupt and disturb the individual. Otherwise, the mind retains bits of information that can float around your memory and emerge in dreams and day terrors, aggressive or depressive behaviour, or as a physical manifestation of the internal pain.

Working with mindfulness and cognitive behavioural therapy (CBT), this patient was able to reduce his PTSD. The better he became, the less his skin bothered him. Within a year, he was practically symptom-free.

Maintaining Perspective

Long-term pain can eat away all your desire to feel alive, which has repercussions on your relationships with others. Talking about your pain in public is frowned upon. When people ask how you are, you rarely answer, 'Well, I have this ongoing pain . . . and it makes me feel really miserable and alone.' You don't want to drive people away, be seen as weak or feel as if your pain is serious enough to mention.

Therefore, blocking your pain can seem like a wonderful temporary solution, like creating an online alter ego who's strong, successful, admired, and so on. But people who fall into this trap sometimes neglect their real life and real-life needs: relationships fall apart, jobs are lost and chronic diseases get even worse.

Please consider writing down in your diary what you tend to use to suppress the pain and fear you feel in relation to your illness, injury or disability.

Then endeavour to take the power back into your own hands to help yourself, refusing to listen when others or even yourself tell you to just 'man up and deal with it'. You have the right to feel free of pain and suffering and to live at ease, or to at least have an element of control when you're affected by pain.

Of course, everybody has struggles, but life can be so adventurous and beautiful too. Help yourself not to forget this fact by writing down in your diary moments of pleasure, gratitude and satisfaction you've noticed recently through your mindful observation of all aspects of your life.

Being mindful can help you to see the larger picture of life, because unsurprisingly people enduring intense pain can sometimes only think about the pain and not beyond it. This statement isn't to blame anybody, but is just an observation. If you sit with your pain for a while and allow it just to be present, perhaps you can experiment with looking at the larger picture.

Here are a few examples, but please create your own in your diary. See if you can apply any of the following to your own life:

- ✔ **Staying positive:** For example, even though you're in pain, you may be recovering from an injury/illness and that can be a moment of triumph.

- ✔ **Show appreciation:** For example, if people are caring for you, or you meet fellow patients in a clinic or support group, appreciate the bonds that you form in spite of, or even because of, the pain.

- ✔ **Being grateful:** For example, have you recently been helped or assisted by a total stranger who gave you kindness because he saw your difficulty?

Sometimes immense suffering can cause people to feel envious, become self-centred or lack compassion. But if you open your heart to the suffering of other people, you may find that you can let go of your own story. Consider experimenting with what it feels like putting your pain in a box for a little while and doing something out of the ordinary for somebody else.

Waking Up to Life: Accepting Pain

You can view pain and illness as a wake-up call to make positive changes in your life; if you're often in discomfort, maybe you need to change your routine, engage in gentle mindful movement or go for a mindful walk (see the suggestions in Chapter 6), go swimming, do stretches in the morning, and so on.

Perhaps consider looking at other habits and aspects of your lifestyle that may improve your wellbeing, such as adjusting your food choices and including fresh groceries that strengthen your immune system. Omega 3, for example (contained in linseed oils and oily fish), can help to prevent or improve osteoporosis, improve your heart muscle, de-clog arteries and reduce inflammation in the brain which, in turn, reduces depression. Alternatively, invest in seeing a holistic nutritionist who may know what food or plant can possibly improve your condition.

Finding new ways to enjoy life, including outlets for your creativity and passion, means that you've less time to focus on pain and less space for it in your life.

Kindly explore a way forward by meditating on this issue. Take a seat in your meditation corner (see Chapter 4) and start this sitting by asking yourself one simple question: 'The adventure of life – where can I find it?' Of course, reword this question so that it sits well with you.

After placing this question in your awareness, sit and begin by grounding yourself and focusing on your breathing. Perhaps, sooner or later, ideas, words, colours and images appear in your mind. Allow them to visit briefly and then let them pass by. As best as you can, don't engage in a whole story or plan at this point; simply notice the ideas that come up and allow them to pass.

When you've finished this explorative meditation, please write down in your diary everything you remember. Practise this exercise a number of times and continue to collect new insights. Eventually, when you feel ready, write down your action plan.

Here's an example:

1. **Join the local book/reading club.**
2. **Find out when the group is meeting.**
3. **Call them and ask whether I can join and how to go about it.**
4. **Make them aware of my needs (disability access, for example).**

Human beings are social animals. Finding interesting pastimes not only gives you more purpose, but also connects you to people and enables you to befriend others.

Accepting and then responding

Whenever you feel pain, the first sensible action is to accept its presence. The pain isn't going to leave just because you growl, scream, cry or deny it. By opening up to and exploring it, you may be able to work around it better and also feel more compassion for others who hurt and suffer.

The Buddha said that a wise person experiences pain in the body and does his best not to worry, wrestle and torture himself with 'why me'. As a result, the wise person feels the physical pain but is spared the additional mental pain (the suffering). The physical pain is like a single arrow that inflicts an open painful wound. Non-acceptance, suppression, ill will and other destructive emotions about the first arrow consequentially hit the wounded person like a second arrow, which penetrates the already painful wound, ripping it open even more.

Think about where you see yourself right now. Are you reacting unwisely to your pain or responding with patience and acceptance?

The practice of mindfulness (formal meditations and informal everyday exercises) explores and expands your ability to respond wisely. With time and practice, you discover more and more about how to pay attention to your body and the pain you're feeling. You become the investigative journalist who uncovers the little details that make a day more enjoyable and create less suffering.

Working out what works for you

Vidyamala Burch, the founder of Breathworks, suffered serious injuries to her back many years ago. She uses a wheelchair or crutches and experiences a lot of pain. Despite the pain, she's a lively and inspiring person, who has a rich and fulfilling life thanks to her daily practice of mindfulness. One of her key realisations was to discover that her pain experience was constantly changing. It wasn't the static enemy with which she'd previously mentally struggled. She became much more accepting of her pain as just one aspect of her life. Some of her pain was due to tension or to overuse when pretending that not much was wrong with her back.

When you accept what is, at least for this moment, you can respond to it in a helpful, creative way. Here's Vidyamala's 'mindfulness rhythm, or pacing' aspect of living creatively with her pain.

Vidyamala carries around a little timer, which rings every 20 minutes with the sound of a Tibetan Tingsha (bell, cymbals). Whenever the bell rings, she moves from sitting to standing and walks around a little with her crutches. When the next chime rings after a few minutes, she sits down again. She explains that remaining immobile for lengthy periods of time is worse for her painful back. Similarly, standing for long periods results in more pain. So alternating sitting for 20 minutes with standing for a few minutes is the best way for her to work through her days of training others. This way she can still do her work and not pay a high price afterwards, by having to lie down for several days.

Please sit down and ponder on how you can create less suffering and more adventure in your life. For this is your life and every second counts; every moment offers an experience in which you may find deep delight. But in order to experience anything, you need to open up to life and change your attitude.

Recognising what your body can still do

Even if you feel a lot of physical pain, your body isn't useless; perhaps start small and work up to doing more.

Consider coming up with your own action plan built on acceptance and compassion, wisdom and patience. Kindly use your diary and note down a few ideas.

Creating a new relationship with pain

Discover as much as you can about your pain. Discern what it's trying to tell you and how you can prepare yourself for it and help your body to respond to it.

'Anatomy of an Illness'

The story of Norman Cousins, *Anatomy of an Illness,* is available as a book (published by W.W. Norton & Company, 2005) and a DVD (produced by Dynamic Entertainment, 2004), and is highly recommended because it offers insights into illness and pain and is hugely inspiring.

Cousins was a well-known political journalist who developed a sudden illness in his spine after a visit to the USSR. He'd visited some power plants and the suspicion was that he was accidentally exposed to some form of radiation. Within days he was in a lot of pain, could no longer walk and had lost the use of his left arm.

Doctors had no idea how to stop the speedy decline. Cousins started his own research

and discovered that high doses of vitamin C and humour (watching funny films and reading humorous stories) helped to reduce the pain, and with time even the symptoms of his curious disease lessened. After watching a movie with the Marx brothers in, through which he laughed heartily, he forgot about his pain and noticed that it didn't return for hours.

He was convinced he wouldn't die, and guess what, he didn't. He got better and better and returned to normal. He overcame all odds and remained ever positive and hopeful.

Obviously, his act is a hard one to follow. But you can do it your way! As Jon Kabat-Zinn says: 'Stop merely existing and start living!'

See your pain as an indicator for your body to change something or your mind to respond in a different way, instead of seeing pain simply as an enemy. Notice the difference between the pain itself compared with tension, angry thoughts, fearful beliefs – feelings that can manifest physically. For instance, think about feeling restless, tired, exhausted, frustrated or tearful: how do these emotions register as sensations in your body?

Using Regular Coping Skills

In this section, I suggest several ways in which MBCT can be extremely helpful when you're coping with chronic pain.

Engaging in breathing practices

I suggest three mindfulness exercises that you may find helpful in dealing with pain.

You can carry out these exercises while sitting or lying down (Chapter 4 gives suggestions on being comfortable during your exercises). The more you focus on the breath, the less likely you are to focus on pain. The more your lungs fill with air and expand, the slower your heart beats, helping you to return from fear and anxiety to calmness and acceptance.

Whenever you engage in mindful movement, even the gentlest one, really listen to your body. If you feel any pain or tension, reduce the movement or don't do it at all. You can always just imagine doing it (some research suggests that even imagining a move can have a positive outcome for the body).

Breaths and movement

Please consider carrying out the following exercise, which involves breathing in and out and includes mindful movement:

1. **Lie on your back with legs stretched out, allowing yourself to be totally relaxed.** Alternatively, sit in a comfortable position, using pillows to feel supported.

2. **Inhale, and while doing so, open your toes.** Think of this action like a flower opening to the sunshine.

3. **Exhale, and while doing so, scrunch your toes as if the flower is closing.** If you tend to get cramps, perform the closing action gently.

4. **Inhale.** This time, softly point your toes away from you.

5. **Exhale.** This time, straighten your feet to bring them parallel to the floor. Roll your ankles in each direction, clockwise and anti-clockwise.

6. **Carry out six to nine repetitions of the above sequence (Steps 1 to 5).**

Knee folds

Please only do this exercise if you don't suffer from any back or leg injury:

1. **Lie on your back, legs stretched out, totally relaxed.** You cannot do this exercise in a sitting position – if you have trouble lying down at this point, skip this exercise until such a time as you find it easier to do so.

2. **Slide your feet in.** Bring them closer to the buttocks one after the other, and rest your feet on the floor, hip distance apart.

3. **Inhale.** Drop or open the knees to the side.

4. **Exhale.** Bring the knees back up.

Hip rolls

This exercise involves gentle hip rolls. Please:

1. **Lie on the floor.** You can also do the hand movements sitting down or even standing.

2. **Open your arms to the side.** Form a V-shape or T-shape.

3. **Exhale, dropping both your knees to the right.** The hips, pelvis and lower back and spine follow this movement, while the head stays soft in the centre or turns slightly to the left. During the inhalation, hold this position.

4. **Return the spine, pelvis, hips and knees back to the starting position when the next exhalation begins.** Please repeat on the other side.

   Move while exhaling and stay in position while inhaling.

5. **Relax your legs by stretching them away from you.** If doing so is uncomfortable, stay in the previous position.

6. **Lay your arms along the side of your body, bending them at your elbows to bring the forearms parallel to the floor.** Turn the palms to face the front (same direction as your toes).

7. **Inhale, opening and gently spreading your fingers wide.** While exhaling, tuck the thumb into the palm first and squeeze the other four fingers into a fist. Repeat to the rhythm of your breathing six to nine more times.

8. **Lay your arms and palms of your hands in the same position as Step 6.** Move from the wrist and with the inhalation point the hand and fingers forward and then down to the floor. When exhaling, change the direction, flexing at the wrist and hand – your fingers pointing towards your head.

9. **Make a fist, thumb in the palm, with the other four fingers gently squeezing it, and make circles with your fist.** After six to nine repetitions, change direction.

The simple co-ordination of breath and movement slowly brings back energy and may help you to start moving again. When you get up, slowly and gently, you can incorporate simple tasks such as going to the loo, getting dressed and making a cup of tea mindfully (not all at the same time, of course!).

Other suggestions

Many of the exercises throughout this book can help you cope with pain. For example, mindful walking can come naturally to you, even when you're unwell. Each step at a time brings back the wondrous gift of walking. Focus on your feet only and imprint them onto the floor as if you're making impressions of them in sand. Turn to Chapter 6 for much more on mindful walking.

In addition, try the sitting with difficult thoughts exercise in Chapter 7, where you choose one particular aspect of your pain experience – for example, the physical manifestation of pain – as your anchor of awareness. The whole exercise helps you to check out all the different feelings and subtle changes that occur throughout the practice.

When thinking about mindfulness exercises to help with your pain, check out the body scan (from Chapter 4). Kindly engage fully in the exercise and try as best as you can to find a posture that feels comfortable to you, changing position whenever necessary. Also, please be aware that you'll travel through parts of your body that are free from pain and other parts where pain is present. Wherever you are, stay only briefly and notice that many different shades of comfort and discomfort exist on this journey.

Achieving wholeness

When you think about wholeness, you may have a picture in your imagination of how you once were or possibly how you really wanted to be: strong, beautiful, fearless and loved. But no guarantee exists that you'd be happier if you resembled that perfect person. Recall that plenty of seemingly enviable humans have experienced a lot of suffering in their lives, despite their beauty, fame and wealth.

The idea of *wholeness* refers to something else entirely: you can only be whole and at peace in the present moment, because it's only in the here and now that your life is happening. Vidyamala of Breathworks (see the nearby sidebar 'Moving towards wholeness in four steps') points out that, by definition, wholeness has to include everything: pain and pleasure, wanted and unwanted. If you exclude even a tiny aspect of yourself or your life, you can't experience wholeness.

Moving towards wholeness in four steps

Breathworks founder, Vidyamala Burch, created her own formulation of mindfulness-based interventions in 2001. It's similar to MBCT and offers programmes to people living with pain, stress and illness. Her goal is to assist you to take control of your own wellbeing and live with self-reliance.

You may not necessarily alleviate all discomfort and restrictions, but you can discover how to become more aware, kind and accepting. In Vidyamala's view, mindfulness is 'not so much a technique as a particular attitude to life (and therefore to suffering)'. Anybody can become more mindful and more accepting. You aren't your condition; just somebody who lives with a difficulty and yet still has a life around it.

She identifies four stages of acceptance:

✔ **Denial:** First, you probably deny your pain and try to pretend that the pain isn't really happening, and don't admit that you may have a long struggle ahead.

✔ **Bargaining:** Second, you may admit that you have pain, but bargain with yourself and the universe to try to make it go away (for example, 'if I meditate my pain will disappear', or 'if I exercise I'll be cured').

✔ **Acceptance:** Third, you come to accept that you have to live with the problem but also that you can learn strategies and change your outlook. Your life includes pain, but that's only one part of it. Your wellbeing is no longer dependent on trying to have a perfect, fantasy life that's free of pain.

✔ **Flourishing:** Fourth, by accepting what is, you transform the energy of resistance into power for new adventures. You can even flourish, despite having an incurable illness or chronic pain.

Breathwork's prescription (just like MBCT) is to turn kindly towards the discomfort and search for enjoyment, because both experiences are part of life.

Chapter 16

Finding Purpose and Meaning When You're Older

I invite you to take a closer look at ageing and what it means to you. Finding meaning, purpose and joy can sometimes be a struggle when children move out, loved ones pass away or after you retire. Plus you may sometimes wonder whether you can tolerate and live with illness, pain and the inevitable restrictions that come with ageing: can life still be an adventure when your body is no longer as strong or healthy as it used to be? My answer is a resounding yes!

In this chapter, I show you how mindfulness helps you to find a sense of purpose when coping with old age, so that you can rise like a phoenix out of the ashes and become the new old you! You discover how mindful action in everyday life improves areas of your brain. Now that you probably have more time than previously, you can work on increasing the aptitude of your mind. To this end, I discuss maintaining specific abilities, such as memory, and a number of associated beneficial activities. Similarly, you find out what kind of mindset to be in to expand your present set of skills. You also get the chance to read about inspiring people and experiment with four new gentle mindful movements.

Continuing to find purpose in the present moment, separate from the more superficial satisfactions of power or monetary remuneration, is of central importance as you grow older.

Thinking About the True Meaning of Purpose

Ageing may well be the ultimate challenge that a person has to face in the 21st century. No absolute marker defines old age, so retirement is often used as a milestone to this last life phase of human existence. Thanks to regular food and the availability of medicine, you may spend more time as an older rather than a young person.

Many people certainly grow wise, insightful, patient and content in older age. Many more, however, feel like they no longer have any real purpose in living. If you were a highflyer at work, a sense of loss may prevail over the sense of freedom when you retire. If you used to be called beautiful and good-looking, you may become irritated when others say to you that you still look good for your age. After all, the media promotes a definite obsession with youth, which can create the desire to cling on to youthful looks. If you have to deal with physical restrictions and pain that probably never goes away, you may also feel anxious and angry.

Psychological research indicates that roughly 10 per cent of people living in the West, aged 65 and upwards, develop alcohol addiction, depression and anxiety in addition to physical illness. Perhaps, like many other older people, you hide your worries and struggle on alone when you feel very low, even though a number of helpful interventions can improve your life.

Please read the following statement and think about your reaction to it:

> *The American Academy of Anti-Aging Medicine (AAAAM), founded in 1993, announced in 2006 at their annual conference 'we are on the verge of practical immortality, with life spans in excess of a hundred years.'*

Do you even want to consider living on for another 40 years after you retire? Just sitting at home, watching TV, occasionally visiting your friends and family, and with your whole life experience shrinking year by year?

Well, as this section explains, by mindfully rethinking the concept of purpose you can instead adopt another attitude, such as, 'Let me understand life more deeply. Let me discover what I always yearned to know. Let me be courageous so that possible limitations in my body don't stop me from living life to the full.'

You may have lived much of your life on autopilot up to this point, perhaps because you initially discovered a way of processing and responding to the world and all the information you were receiving from it, and never broke free from that habit and allowed yourself to find a different way of under-standing things. When you mindfully rethink the concept of purpose, and endeavour to enter into each moment deliberately and non-judgementally – and so be truly present – you take each moment as a unique event in your life experience. You can choose to respond and be creative rather than merely reactive. Mindfulness helps you to feel more empathic, reflective and in con-trol, and less confined and exhausted. It supports you in overcoming times when you feel a sense of separation between you and the world around you, and allows you to feel more alive (that is, attentive, engaged and curious). Being mindful increases awareness and presence.

Redefining your concept of purpose

Searching for something you can offer to the world and to yourself is very important. People often have a skewed view of what having purpose is – that it has to be something tangible, a huge goal, something that can be achieved. But the fact is that even if you achieve that huge goal, more adventures and experiences lie ahead for you. Every moment is a new beginning. Every moment can be precious if you can incline your mind to perceive it as such.

Consider making it your purpose to live, to discover, to always find new and exciting things about life, to start every day afresh and to leave yesterday's problems behind.

The Austrian poet and writer Rainer Maria Rilke sums it up beautifully: 'Our task is to imprint this temporary, outdated earth inside ourselves, so deeply . . . so passionately that its essence wells up within us, invisibly.' This lovely calling asks you to leave behind some important messages you discover on your journey for the next generation.

If up to now you've never considered this question, maybe the time is right to ask yourself: 'What will I leave behind as a guide for those who come after me?' At the same time, however, you also need to remain fully present to what life now, or the people before you, can teach you.

Reconnecting to your own sense of purpose

If you've lost something that you feel defined your life – whether it is a pro-fessional or social position, the ability to perform certain skills or your own physical/mental strength and wellbeing – try to think about what made it so important. Ask yourself what gave you the skill or strength you needed to be successful, and consider that perhaps you can find this strength again but from another source. Or maybe it is still inside you, waiting to be released and used for a new purpose. The older you get the faster life seems to move on, so don't let it pass you by. Ask yourself what purpose would give your life meaning when you've entered your third (that is, post-retirement) phase of life. This may be the time to start focusing on your inner values, and maybe to even discover something about larger issues outside your life such as spirituality, politics or engaging with issues that concern the health of our planet, for example.

I invite you to make a list in your mindfulness diary of things that are unique, different or special about you, no matter how small – I assure you that this list will definitely be longer than you think! The following examples are just to help you come up with your own ideas; feel free to discard any items that don't feel true for you:

- ✔ I'm resourceful.
- ✔ I'm reliable.
- ✔ I can adapt items and make them serve a different purpose than they were meant for.
- ✔ I'm resilient.
- ✔ I'm patient.
- ✔ I'm considerate.
- ✔ I'm creative.

Please write down your own list and continue to add to it whenever you think of other points in the future. Make this list an ongoing project. Also kindly ask people who know you well what they think your strengths are.

After writing down your strengths, stand or sit upright in the 'mountain pose' from Chapter 6 and start focusing on your breathing. When you feel really settled, ask yourself this question: 'What would I like to try, what would give me joy or purpose, and how can I go about starting to move towards these aims?'

Again, write down any ideas, however farfetched. Be wild; nobody's ever going to read it unless you want them to.

Recovering from post-retirement depression

Depression has particular causes and displays certain patterns in older people. For example, falling victim to it is much more common in the years after retirement, when many people struggle to adjust to a new role and routine.

John had been the general manager of a power plant. He'd always liked a few glasses of wine with his meal and a whiskey or two after work to relax. When he retired at 67, he had no idea what to do with himself. He'd never looked forward to retirement and hadn't given it a thought until it happened. His drinking got completely out of control and he felt more and more depressed.

He didn't visit his GP about the problem until his wife threatened to leave him (after 35 years of marriage). The doctor referred John to a group where he discovered mindfulness-based cognitive therapy (MBCT). He slowly reduced his alcohol intake and developed a close kinship with a couple of other participants.

A year later, John feels like a new person. He's attending Chinese language and cookery classes and also helps out with the local Shelter group for homeless people. He teaches some of the people computer literacy. He and his wife have also discovered that they enjoy going on long walks. (He used to be too tired at weekends to do anything when he was still at work.) So every week they choose a new destination. She now says he's become really talkative and she likes this new John almost better than the old version. He's happy and can't imagine how he'd fit in a job nowadays.

Maybe you can go for it too! Try not to make excuses and give yourself a reason not to really live life. Why not leap into the unknown – right now!

Finding Positive Aspects of Life

Older age may well offer you additional or greater freedoms. You can liberate yourself from former responsibilities and restraints, and you may now have the time to strengthen and deepen emotionally meaningful relationships.

Surrounding yourself with positive people

Think about the following words of wisdom:

> Life is a theatre. The rows of seats in your theatre are reserved for your loved ones and friends. Sometimes a particular person may sit in the front row and sometimes in the back. Sometimes however the theatre may be closed or completely full.

> —Anonymous

You have options, and sometimes the wise course of action is to engage more with those sitting in the front row more or less continually – that is, the friendly, positive and proactive types. If you feel deeply in your heart that certain people nourish and inspire you, choose to meet up with them more often.

Or, you may choose to drop engagements with those who drain you and whom you find challenging. I don't mean that you feel less compassion towards those in the back row or those waiting for spare tickets. When they're in real need, you may do whatever is humanly possible to assist them, but you no longer have a duty to hang out with folks that just take and don't nourish you back.

You have so much more freedom in older age. Saying 'no, thank you' is easier when you're no longer dependent on making good impressions or no longer 'on duty'.

Widening your experience of life

Kindly think about skills that increase your cognitive functioning and aid your memory. Consider channelling your energy into a few projects that can benefit from your life experience, particularly voluntary ones that you're now able to engage with without remuneration. If you want to find out about charities and other voluntary projects, visit your local church, library, youth centre, town hall or temple, or look in local community magazines. Explore what kind of options are on offer and what they need; see what you can best apply your skills to or what you may want to simply try out.

You can benefit greatly from taking part in regular commitments; for example, you may find:

- ✔ A chance to 'stay in the flow' and in contact with the rest of society
- ✔ A sense of doing something worthwhile and positive
- ✔ A chance to meet likeminded people and forge new relationships with individuals of all age groups

In addition, consider engaging in health maintenance, mobility and gentle exercise, and perhaps experiment with exploring spirituality. Whatever your faith (or none), finding out more about others can be really interesting. Exploring the differences and similarities provides insights and wisdom. You may want to join a group, read some books on this theme or simply talk to people of different faiths.

I invite you to make a list of what you enjoy in life; if it's something that you feel you can no longer take pleasure in, write it on your list anyway. Perhaps write it in a more general or simplified form that allows you to find a way of enjoying it in a new way. Don't be afraid of writing abstract things down: for example, 'I enjoy being in love'; 'I enjoy feeling happy'. Everything is valid and nothing off-limits – this exercise shows you just how many things in life are good and have the potential to make you feel alive.

Cultivating motivation and inspiration

As you grow older and retire, time can become a somewhat contradictory beast: on the one hand, a lot more time is often available to you (perhaps too much); on the other hand, you can experience a sense of time running out.

To help simplify your thinking about time, I suggest focusing on what inspires you. Consider other people who've gone through life-changing experiences and come out the other side stronger. Perhaps the thing that seems to be restricting you, whether physically or emotionally, can be the key to you discovering something new about yourself. Plenty of people find a great purpose in life only after something terrible happens – and you can learn a lot from their experience.

The psychologists Rick Foster and Greg Hicks call the ability to transform problems and suffering into something meaningful *recasting,* which is a great, mindful way of putting it. Recasting is the ability to change painful experiences into opportunities for growing, learning and finding deeper meaning. For example, people who lose their ability to talk after a stroke begin to write stories and poems or paint instead.

When you respond to adversity (such as a chronic condition, the loss of physical abilities or the death of a loved one) wisely and mindfully, you don't just 'get on with it' or 'look on the bright side'. You give yourself permission to feel the gravity of your pain or loss, without censoring it and with an attitude of honouring what you truly feel and experience. After accepting the sorrow of what happened, you wisely and compassionately see whether you can turn the experience around and view what lies on the opposite side of the 'shadowland'. You search for opportunities or insights that may come in handy from now on. By applying mindfulness and acceptance, you can gain the strength to transform yourself purposefully, instead of becoming a slave to the sadness of loss and pain.

Here are a few well-known people who experienced their own losses or tribulations and yet went on to live their lives fully and inspire others. Read what they have to say about ageing:

✔ **Desmond Tutu (social rights activist and Anglican bishop):** 'Dream, dream, dream that we're going to have a world that's incredibly different.'

Tutu remained in South Africa throughout apartheid and came to London to celebrate independence at St. Martin's in the fields. His speech was overwhelming and full of compassion.

✔ **Leonard Cohen (poet and songwriter):** 'We are mad in love and in love we disappear.'

Cohen spent six years as a Zen monk in his sixties. When he turned 70 he found out that his accountant had 'lost' all his money and properties, so he left the monastery and started touring again in order to secure a little money for his pension, in case he decided not to spend the rest of his life as a monk. Cohen took to performing again with bravery and I had the great fortune to see him. He was fantastic and from a selfish perspective I was rather glad he was back on stage.

✔ **Jalal ad-Din Muhammad Rumi (poet):** 'The wound is the place where the Light enters you.'

Rumi was in love with his teacher and soulmate, Shams. One day upon waking his teacher had disappeared and for Rumi it was as if someone had cut out his heart. He went travelling for a long time to find his lost love. (You can read Rumi's poem, *The Guest House,* in Chapter 8.)

✔ **Dietrich Bonhoeffer (Anglican priest):** 'We must learn to regard people less in the light of what they do or omit to do, and more in the light of what they suffer.'

Dietrich Bonhoeffer belonged to the German resistance movement 'Die Rote Kapelle'. In 1943 he was arrested by the Nazis for planning to assassinate Hitler. His letters are very moving. He was executed a few weeks before the war ended in 1945.

Having read the above quotes, take a moment to consider whether you agree with anything in particular; anything that tickles your sense of adventure or that you want to try and apply to yourself. If so, please write it down and find out more about the people who shared their wisdom with you.

Enjoying a long, successful life

Have you heard of the famous centenarians of Okinawa, Japan, who live on the 'island of long life'? Their longevity is at least partially due to practising prayer and meditation and holding each moment as something valuable in their consciousness. They simply enjoy being alive. Look them up on the Internet.

And don't forget about the inspiring zoologist Sir David Attenborough, aged 86, who recently celebrated 60 years of TV broadcasting and still works hard to bring awareness about climate change to society.

Dismissing nothing, including everything

You may be inclined to ignore or dismiss certain adventures as being impossible or not worth trying, perhaps thinking 'surely, not at my age'. But no law of the universe puts an age limit on activities such as windsurfing, ice-skating, painting, hiking, skydiving, DJing or stand-up comedy. If you're up for it and able, give everything you fancy a go if it gives you gladness!

Please be really mindful when you enter the practice of movement. You may not have exercised for a long time, so you need to introduce movement back into your life gently. Only do practices that allow you to unfold with ease and without any discomfort. Check out the later section 'Accepting Limitations of All Kinds' for details on assessing your strengths and weaknesses mindfully.

Nothing is too small or insignificant and, as long as you're fit enough, nothing is completely beyond you. Your human body and spirit can be incredibly strong and adaptive, and your imagination is without boundaries.

Perhaps you wanted to do something when you were younger but never had the time or money; maybe now you do. Travel somewhere distant or do the most unusual thing. If you haven't tried it, how do you know?

A good friend of mine started playing the piano at 65; he's now a wonderful entertainer in his 70s. Another friend travelled to China after his retirement and 'fell in love with the country and its people'. Upon his return, he started studying Chinese and now, in his 70s, he speaks and writes it fluently.

Indeed, Grandma Moses started painting after the death of her husband (in her late 70s) and became a world renowned 'naïve' painter and very wealthy too (not that this was her motivation). She lived to be 101.

Allow yourself to explore absolutely everything – older age and retirement is the time to dream and be hopeful. As Billy Connolly said, aged 68:

> One of the great mistakes of our time is to act your age . . . Age is like your house number . . . outside and means nothing. Telling you to act your age, cut your hair, wear beige, stop trying to change things or stretching yourself – that's b*******.

So, assure yourself that no reason exists why you can't:

✔ Discover how to play a musical instrument.

✔ Join a choir.

✔ Expand your cooking repertoire.

✔ Engage in a new sport or pastime that you can physically manage: Tai Chi, golf, Pilates, gentle yoga, swimming, walking, mindful movement.

✔ Learn new games, such as chess, bridge or something more out there (think of some new ideas).

✔ Join a meditation group to enhance your MBCT practice.

✔ Rescue a pet from an animal shelter, or even volunteer to help out there.

Happiness does not light gently on my shoulder like a butterfly. She pounces on my lap, demanding that I scratch her behind her ears.

—Anonymous

Finding joy

Retirement is the time to be happy, to give yourself a chance to just enjoy life – the little things as much as the big things. Joy strengthens you and gives you a sense that life is still worth living.

Research shows that people who live longer and stay physically and mentally alert tend to have a network of people they connect to regularly: neighbours, friends, family or clubs where they attend regular meetings.

Being generous and helping others is another skill that improves life quality and is embedded in kindness, one of the attitudes that tends to develop when you practise MBCT regularly.

Accepting Limitations of All Kinds

When you're trying out new behaviours and skills (as I describe in the preceding sections), you need to assess mindfully any mental agility and physical fitness aspects that may hinder you and hold you up. You may even have to accept that certain goals are out of your reach, and this can bring you down emotionally.

In order to experience and engage in specific activities successfully, you need to realise what you're physically and mentally capable of, and also what's outside of your control. Life isn't a race and you don't have to get everything done immediately or do it as well as others; you're unique, which comes with its own set of strengths and weaknesses.

Many people born with limitations create meaningful and joyous lives. The recent London Paralympic Games were a great reminder that 'the sky is the limit'.

Here are some of the most common challenges you may experience in older age, with suggestions for working around them. Perhaps you can come up with your own additional ways to live around the difficulties rather than let them rule your life:

- ✔ **I can no longer keep up with my friends, so I may as well just watch TV.** Accept your limitations for now and see what's still possible for you to do. You can also expand in the future by persisting and regular practice: jogging, mindful walking, and so on.

- ✔ **I'm no longer able to do long-haul flights.** See how many destinations you can reach by train or bus that may also offer interesting and new explorations.

- ✔ **I can no longer play tennis and it was my favourite sport.** Try to explore which sport activities are similar and still doable for you: table tennis, bowls or golf. Also, treat yourself to a game at Wimbledon or watch some good matches on TV.

- ✔ **I've lost many friends and hate doing things by myself.** See whether you can get back in touch with people you've lost contact with (sometimes you can locate them through an Internet search), work on becoming a friendly and compassionate neighbour, or engage in activities where you'll meet new friends: taking a class, attending a choir or amateur dramatics, helping in a charity or doing volunteering for an organisation you support.

Experiment with seeking solitude from time to time. See whether you can find peace within this experience. You may be surprised and find yourself more connected to all things in life: nature, beasts and other beings, and most of all, yourself.

Stop running away from yourself and find ways to enjoy doing things on your own. As always, bring mindfulness and acceptance to all your new adventures. Really feel what's right for you in this moment.

You may gain useful benefits from carrying out the sitting with difficult thoughts exercise that I discuss in Chapter 7. In this meditation, you simply sit with your breath and body awareness. When you feel grounded, allow all the thoughts about your apparent limitations to arise and let them tell you why your life is no longer worth living. Just sit with them as if you're a compassionate ruler listening to the complaints of your people.

Remind yourself that thoughts aren't facts. Listen to them but try not to engage with them. After you finish meditating, write each thought on a separate piece of paper and let your compassionate mind respond to them.

An inspirational figure

Stella has been a yoga teacher all her working life and still teaches two classes a week as well as a few one-to-one clients. She'll be 87 years old soon. Stella is determined and has a real interest in life. A couple of years ago she travelled from London to New York on her own. She regularly travels by bus to Europe because it's more affordable. She goes swimming several times a week, plays bridge, paints, sings and goes to the theatre and cinema every week.

Considering that she's had to overcome cancer and other debilitating illnesses, as well as old age, this way of life may sound too good to be true. However, Stella is a real person, who lives by the mantra 'growing old isn't for sissies'. But she also has the wisdom to listen to her body, and knows when to say that she feels tired and has had enough.

She also practises mindful meditation and visualisations regularly. It's part of her diet, she says, 'like water, vegetables and friends'.

See whether you can think of somebody who inspires you by accepting what they can no longer do. Perhaps you can read the biographies of people who overcome limits to live long and fulfilling lives.

Maybe, however, you just want to create your own model of wellbeing in older age. Try to create a model of mindful living that suits you; you don't have to create a strict timetable, just a sense of looking forward to each activity or part of an activity moment by moment.

Trying to improve and develop

If you want to improve something about yourself, go for it! Make a list of things you want to work on, and develop action plans with a positive thought process of how you're going to achieve each aim. Be realistic: don't push yourself too far too fast, but also don't allow yourself to accept meekly what you can't do. Challenge yourself!

Authors Poeppel and Wagner developed a ten-point 'wheel of life' guidance that you may find useful to apply. Kindly write it down in your diary or make a list and pin it on your fridge:

- ✔ Commit to lifelong learning.
- ✔ Be in and recognise the *now* (this is when your life is happening).
- ✔ Pay attention to your thoughts and question those that are no longer valid or not helpful.

✔ Look after your external appearance: find your own style, be creative and true to yourself.

✔ Expand your life span and improve your wellbeing by paying attention to healthy eating, exercise, recreation, and so on.

✔ Learn to truly and fully accept yourself as you are now.

✔ Remember to allow life to amaze you, truly connecting to the little miracles that occur on a daily basis: a butterfly, a beautiful rose, a delicious dish, a pot of soup the neighbour brought round.

✔ Stick to your own goal posts. Even if you don't always feel like it, engage in the routines that you know give you a better quality of life (for example, an 87-year-old friend of mine goes swimming three times a week, whether she likes to or not; she knows how much better she feels when she has done it, how much more flexible her body feels, and so on).

✔ Become wiser, remembering the lessons life taught you and applying the wisdom you collected over the years.

✔ Start something new regularly.

Dismissing the notion of 'failure'

Setbacks, false starts and problems are natural and happen to everyone. They're part of the learning experience – things don't always go right the first time around, and they mostly don't go exactly how you expect them to go. So please don't write off all these experiences as failures!

You're learning all the time: finding yourself, giving yourself a break and growing from your mistakes! In fact, now that you're more likely to be the master of your time, you can mindfully acknowledge the things that went wrong, why they did and how you can begin all over with a new now.

Please consider doing the following exercise, which is a great way to assess your less successful moments in a mindful manner:

1. **Write down in your diary an example that caused you to think you had been unsuccessful in a particular action in the past.**

   For example: you tried to bake a cake and it didn't rise and tasted horrible. Did you stick to a recipe? If yes, check the ingredients again. Maybe you used the wrong flour or no baking powder. Maybe the oven was turned on too high or too low. How would you evaluate this mishap now? Could you imagine giving it another go? For every moment is a new beginning.

2. **Sit in quiet meditation.**

   Allow the items on the list to pass by, as if written on clouds in the sky.

3. **Ask yourself what insight you gained from each experience.**

   For example: 'I didn't have the desired outcome, but most things need more than one attempt. I'm not a failure for messing up one cake – that can happen even to a professional baker. Maybe I'll try again or ask a friend for an easier recipe.'

4. **Come up with a positive outcome for each experience.**

   For example: flexibility of mind, persistence, patience, trust and maybe getting in touch with a friend.

In the book *Mindfulness-Based Treatment Approaches,* Alistair Smith (who regularly runs mindfulness courses for older people) tells the story of a participant, Steven, who sent him a letter. It states: 'How does one find the words to express the gratitude for . . . changing my life from desperation to incredible hope?' He added that his wife thought of him as a nicer person to be with, that he reduced and finally stopped taking anti-depressants, and even coped with and accepted worsening physical pain. He had also started leisure activities and MBCT was part of his daily wellbeing routine. Even though he hadn't resolved all his issues (such as his physical pain), overall he was a happier human being and better to spend time with.

Here are some insights from this short story:

✔ Steven stopped being miserable and grumpy and improved his relationship with his wife.

✔ His mood lifted and he stopped taking meditation, regularly practising mindfulness meditation instead.

✔ He discovered how to accept that some discomforts can remain and that he has the option to work around them, having a life rather than merely existing.

Rediscovering your strengths

A great side effect of assessing your potential limitations honestly is that very often you discover strengths that you'd forgotten or never realised you had! Embrace these gifts, take them further and use them as inspiration to uncover even more new things about yourself – you have so much to give and so much potential! Here are some attitudes and strengths that you may develop in the autumn and winter of your life:

- ✔ **Acceptance:** Your life is happening to you now, and experiences still exist for you to discover and experiment with.

- ✔ **Calmness:** Responding wisely to a potentially difficult choice or situation.

- ✔ **Letting go:** You are what you are now – your heart and mind may still be the same, even if your body needs more gentle maintenance and care.

- ✔ **Non-rushing:** If you have all the time in the world, act accordingly. Let those who feel as if they need to rush do what they want, but find your own rhythm for living.

- ✔ **Self-compassion:** See yourself as a fallible human being who needs ongoing kindness and support. Compassion begins at home.

Your brain is able to improve its neural networks as long as it's alive and used. Concentration and patience tend to get easier with age, because you have more time available. But you do have to practise regularly and push yourself gently to your limits; as with any muscle, the brain grows only when you reach the level of slight discomfort. Setting yourself little goals gives you the motivation to discover more and go beyond what you already know.

Connecting Fully with the Life You Have Now

Whether you're 28 or 82, you're alive! See this reality as a gift not be squandered or taken lightly: enjoy the fact that you have a chance to start a different phase of your life now; no matter what you have been through, you always have a way forward open. If you live in the present moment, leaving the past behind is easier.

Simply hanging around is okay occasionally, but getting stuck and listless leads to depression and sometimes addiction (alcohol, food, gambling). If you stop using your muscles, they begin to wither away after just two months. And of course, when they're weak, you have even more difficulty getting around, and so you feel more stuck.

If you just stop living and wait for a miracle to give you your youth back and a personal valet, you're going to wait for a very long time! Your later decades provide you with the opportunity to be your own master, but you need to be in the moment and also fully alive to enjoy them.

Little things giving life

The psychologist Ellen Langer carried out an experiment in a nursing home in Connecticut. A number of residents were given a few mindful activities to add to their daily routines.

They were encouraged to water a house plant, make a cup of tea/coffee and make one small decision in their daily life. Some 18 months later, this group had increased cheerfulness, alertness and higher activity levels in comparison to the other residents. Fewer of them had died than from the control group.

The German monk Father Anselm Green, who wrote *The Art of Growing Older* (Vier Tuerme GmbH, 2007), compares ageing to the four seasons:

- ✔ Spring symbolises childhood and youth.

- ✔ Summer is like being an independent adult, creating a life of adventure.

- ✔ Autumn creates new colours in nature, the sun shining less harshly. Life becomes less dazzling and more peaceful. It's the time for harvesting – that is, for consolidating all of your acquired knowledge – and yet still trying new things.

- ✔ Winter has its own beauty: peace, quietness and an invitation to slow down. Yet it's filled with possibilities: building snowmen or sitting in front of an open fire telling stories.

Setting yourself new goals and challenges

Setting goals and challenges from things you want to try out is essential: not to win and beat anybody else, but just for your own self-satisfaction.

Consider creating an action plan (see Table 16-1) to ensure that you meet other people and try stuff that you've always wanted to but never gave yourself the chance to engage in. If not now, when? What have you got to lose?

Table 16-1	Sample Daily Action Plan
Time	*Monday*
9 a.m.	Get up
10 a.m.	Breakfast
11 a.m.	Tai Chi
12 a.m.	Tea with John
1 p.m.	Lunch at club
2 p.m.	Read newspaper
3 p.m.	Telephone duty for Samaritans
4 p.m.	Volunteering at the local library
5 p.m.	Shopping
6 p.m.	Meditation
7 p.m.	Simple dinner
8 p.m.	Call one or two friends
9 p.m.	Watch film
10:30 p.m.	Get ready for bed
11 p.m.	Read
11:30 p.m.	Sleep

An action plan is only a guide. Always feel free to change or drop activities if suddenly something new and exciting or unusual comes along. Also, of course, every week and every day can be totally different.

Nowadays, many universities offer postgraduate courses and frequently retired people enroll. Counselling is a popular choice as is becoming an instructor for mindfulness courses. The participants feel that they want to learn a profession that connects them with the community and gives them the opportunity to have meaningful work/action. Many people only ever see a couple of clients a week, but age is on your side when people need somebody to listen to them and help them work out how to live a better life.

Piloting the practice of Pilates

Joseph H. Pilates was born a sickly child, with asthma, rickets and rheumatic fever, but he grew stronger and healthier the older he got. No magic was involved, but Pilates was tenacious and decided early on in his life that he'd improve his health and his life by healing his body through exercise. He studied skiing, bodybuilding, yoga, qigong and gymnastics. One of his theories was that modern living, which involved less and less exercise, was a cause of bad health. He created a huge number of practices and even equipment in order to train others in his methods. He called his teaching method *contrology*.

Pilates moved to the UK in 1912 and worked as a professional boxer, circus artiste and martial arts trainer, and even taught at police schools. During the First World War he was interned in a camp for foreigners fighting for the enemy. He made it his dream to train fellow inmates so that they'd come out of incarceration in better health than they entered. During this time, he refined his techniques so that they could be practised with barely any equipment except a yoga mat. He specifically focused on yoga and animal movements.

Eventually, Pilates emigrated to the USA and opened his own studio in New York where he continued teaching for decades to come, well into his eighties. He focused on core muscles supporting the spine and awareness of breathing. Martha Graham, the famous modern dancer, became one of his students. Pilates wrote a number of books and the practice of Pilates is still a very popular way of maintaining and regaining health today.

To see how important it is for your body to move regularly, kindly read the mindful movement practices in Chapter 6 and experiment with the new ones in the 'Moving Gently, but Mindfully' section.

Moving forward one step at a time

Your life is yours to lead; don't feel that you have to do anything by a particular point in time or for anyone else – it's down to you to improve or change your life. Those around you are sure to be happier the more you enjoy your life, but retirement is the time to come into your own and nourish yourself. Don't rush anything – just take everything one step at a time. But keep moving and, equally, just being. When you spot a stunning starry sky, pause to admire it – truly savouring the moment. Really feel the freedom you have got now and use it in abundance.

Consider sorting out your collection of photos. If you've been meaning to do so for decades, now's the time. Maybe you've had a longing to go back to places that were meaningful in your childhood. If so, arrange the trip and take a close friend to show the trees you climbed and your hiding places.

Always remember to carry a mindful attitude to anything you do. 'Here and now' is your motto – rushing is a thing of the past.

Living in the now, whatever your age

Residing more frequently in the present moment allows you to discover that your mind may be continually chattering, commenting or judging. Observing this process, you have the choice to notice thoughts and then decide whether those thoughts have any value for you. You may then realise that thoughts are just thoughts, and have no weight of their own.

You can choose to release any thought that causes inner turmoil or destructive actions. By closely observing your inner reality, you discover that contentment and joy are rarely brought about by anybody else except you and your attitude. The more you can let go of fixed expectations for the future or ruminating about the past, the better you feel.

Moving Gently, but Mindfully

I invite you to experiment with the four mindful movements in this section. You can do them sitting down and still give your body a mindful workout.

Pressing palms

This practice works on your pelvic floor and back muscles, and lengthens your spine. Please:

1. **Sit on a chair.** Place your feet parallel on the floor and rest your palms on your thighs, pointing towards the knees.

2. **Inhale slowly and, while you're exhaling, draw your belly button into your spine, at the same time pressing your palms down onto your thighs.** This movement helps you to activate your pelvic floor muscles and lengthen your spine. Keep your shoulders relaxed and avoid hunching them up.

3. **Try as best as you can to apply equal pressure on your palms.** Repeat three to six times.

Cutting wood

This practice strengthens the lower back muscles. I request that you:

1. **Sit on a chair, with your feet hip distance apart.** Bend your arms at right angles with elbows touching the waist. Your palms are facing each other, the hands and fingers are actively stretched and the thumbs are touching the palm.

2. **Move your forearms up and down, bending at the elbows, as if you're making small cutting movements.** Kindly repeat this movement ten or more times.

Opening the chest

This exercise helps you to deepen your breathing and opens your chest. It can also reverse hunched-forward shoulders and help you to feel the correct alignment of the shoulders. Please:

1. **Sit on a chair, keeping your arms by your side.** Bend your elbows to a 90-degree angle and tuck them into the waist.

2. **Turn your palms face up.** The tips of the little fingers need to be nearly touching.

3. **Squeeze your shoulder blades together with your arms open to the side.** You feel the chest opening on an in-breath. Then return your palms back to the starting position on the out-breath. Kindly repeat this exercise six times.

Flexing the spine

This practice helps you to keep your spine strong and flexible. It also stretches and strengthens the deep back muscles in the neck and chest. Kindly:

1. **Sit upright on a chair, with your feet hip distant apart and your spine and neck lengthened upwards.** Draw your belly button and your groin muscles in towards your spine (gently, not with all your strength) in order to engage your pelvic floor. Please relax your shoulders and allow your head to float on top of your neck.

2. **Inhale and, when you exhale, turn the upper body to the right.** At the same time move your right arm up and behind you, your eyes following the movement of the right hand and your head following the movement of the eyes.

3. **Move your left palm gently to the right thigh and touch it from the top and side by the knee.** Kindly hold this position for a count of three and then return to the starting position. Please repeat this movement but to the left. In total, practise three rounds on each side.

Please keep your hips still and your body weight evenly on both feet and on your buttocks. Kindly relax your shoulders. Also, always lengthen your entire spine before you twist. You can start with a tiny movement and slowly increase the range.

Chapter 17

Bringing Harmony to Your Life

Mindfulness-based cognitive therapy (MBCT) can be a positive influence on your lifestyle, productivity and relationships – both personal and professional. This chapter looks at handling different challenges that affect your daily life, dealing with other people and supporting yourself. I want to demonstrate that mindful living really is possible and that you can use mindfulness to achieve a calmer and more satisfying life. Who knows, perhaps it may even be the tool that saves the world from self-destruction.

I introduce you to applying mindfulness at home, and on the way to, from and while you're at work. Plus, I describe some helpful mindful pauses throughout the day and how you can apply mindfulness to your communication and interaction with others. Throughout, I provide loads of mindful meditations and exercises as well as lots of practical tips for you to use.

Try to cultivate a mindset of acceptance, moment-to-moment wakefulness and compassion for yourself and for all beings.

Accepting the Importance of Mindful Living

Being and living mindfully isn't a sticking plaster, a quick-fix panacea or a swift takeaway that you can use for curing problematic issues. On the contrary, mindful living invites you to be aware, kind and compassionate for the rest of your life. If more and more individuals were to work on creating a mindful society, people wouldn't need to wait for a miracle to change all the suffering on Earth. The more mindfully individuals conduct their everyday living, the better they make the world for themselves and for other people.

If you want to change the world, all you need to do is change yourself; allowing change to unfold gradually and gently and most of all peacefully. Living mindfully means applying awareness and moment-to-moment experience to everything you do on a daily basis. Eventually, meditating becomes part of your regular repertoire of going through life, while at the same time each conversation, each meal, each project and each interaction with others can be like a meditation. Be really connected to the one experience you're having in the present moment and let go of all worries about the past and the future.

Employing mindfulness meditation can enable you to bring a sense of meaning and purpose to your life, based on the understanding that everything is interconnected and therefore depends on everything else. Mindfulness practice has long moved on from medicine and psychotherapy and is now being taught to parents and in schools, prisons, the workplace, sports and even politics. I hope that it spreads like a virus, for this planet needs urgent changes now if the next generations are to survive and flourish.

Jon Kabat-Zinn, the man who first brought mindfulness into the world of medicine, is so eloquent and aware when he says:

> *There is so much suffering in the world. Who are we not to respond to it . . . a lot of our efforts go into professional training, toward developing a whole new generation of people deeply grounded in this universal dharma expression and committed to bringing it into the world in various ways as a skilful means for healing and transformation at a time that the world is crying out for kindness and wisdom.*

Dharma is a Sanskrit word that refers to the idea of a natural order of things. It refers to living in a harmonious way so that all beings can live happily and with as little suffering as possible.

Homing in on Domestic Mindfulness

Kindly experiment with applying mindfulness to every step you take throughout the day. Mindfulness starts in your heart and its application is most likely to happen when you're at home. Anything and everything can become your practice ground, with actions big and small offering you opportunities to apply awareness:

- ✔ **Mindful waking up:** See the next section for ideas.
- ✔ **Mindful use of water:** When you brush your teeth, for example, turn off the tap. Perhaps collect rainwater to water your plants.

✔ **Mindful daily hygiene:** Whenever you brush your teeth or clean your body, be really present with each detail of the activity.

✔ **Mindful cooking, eating and clearing up:** Check out the later section 'Enjoying your morning routine' for suggestions.

✔ **Mindfully relating to people who live with you:** Let kindness and compassion reside in your heart when you talk to your family, flatmates, and so on. Maybe you can sometimes just wash up the dishes they forget to clear rather than tell them too often. On other occasions, you can ask them whether they can help you clear up your dishes or clean the bathroom and show them appreciation when they do.

✔ **Mindful use of time:** Being a couch potato is a highly infectious ailment. Consider using some of your spare time to practise mindfulness or do something compassionate.

✔ **Mindful bedtime routines:** The more you train your body to expect certain routines before going to bed, the easier you're going to find deep sleep. Give yourself a good hour to switch off and mindfully experience each part of the journey of going to bed.

Waking with an open mind

The way you enter your morning sets you up with the right attitude for the rest of the day. Kindly start the day by noticing how your body and mind are feeling. On waking up, please consider focusing on gratitude for another day of life and for a number of other gifts:

1. **Lie in your bed gently for a little longer and watch your breath.** Listen to any sounds and allow your thoughts to pass through your awareness, as if you're watching a short movie.

2. **Breathe in kindness and, on breathing out, let go of any worries for the day.** Stay with your breathing and the simple joy this new day may bring.

3. **See whether you can notice any particular emotions in your body.** If so, name them. Gently ask yourself what's occupying your mind most intensely right now and then let it pass by.

4. **Open your eyes mindfully.** Enjoy whatever you see first.

5. **Stretch and wriggle your toes and fingers.** Do so mindfully of course!

6. **Breathe a few conscious breaths.** Be really aware of the areas of your body expanding and deflating.

Getting up on the right side of bed

If you tend to do your longer meditations in the afternoon or evening, still focus for a few minutes on simply tasting your breath as soon as you wake up.

First thing in the morning, begin your day by simply noting:

- ✔ How does your body feel? What emotions are present? Is your mind calm or already racing off to work?

- ✔ Notice whether you've a sense of your body feeling comfortable or tense. Are you feeling calm, anxious, annoyed or maybe just neutral? What's on your mind?

- ✔ Sit up mindfully and feel your feet connecting to the floor.

- ✔ Observe your mood now and all sensations in your body.

Enjoying your morning routine

Turn your entire morning routine into mindfulness practice. Here are some ideas:

- ✔ Bring mindfulness to getting dressed, really noticing how each piece of clothing slips on and feels on your body. Can you be mindful when you button up a shirt or blouse?

- ✔ Be mindful when you're in the shower, truly feeling the temperature of the water on your skin, the smell of the shower gel and shampoo. Mindfully dry your body and hair, with kindness and patience. Perhaps smile deep down into your body.

  If you notice that your mind is starting to make plans for the day, kindly and gently bring yourself back to this moment. A mindful bath or shower is cleansing for your body and mind and sets you up for a good start to the day.

- ✔ Make breakfast for yourself (and others) mindfully, thinking about the purpose of taking care of yourself and others now and throughout the day. This first meal of the day requires a gentle and kindly attitude to reawaken your whole system. Enjoy it with all your senses: feel the texture, enjoy the smell, the taste and how a number of different items can be combined into a glorious, tasty concoction. As best you can, eat each mouthful while being utterly awake and alert, seeing how many aspects of the ingredients are still noticeable.

- ✔ Try not to think about whatever household chores are waiting for you, and, as best as you can, engage mindfully with every action, finding an enjoyable aspect to it. Then add a little gratitude. When washing-up, for example, enjoy the warm water and the lovely smell of the liquid soap, without feeling any resentment for having to do it. Focus on the miracle that your hands know exactly how to squeeze, hold a cloth and move the way you want them to. Experiment with letting go of negative thoughts about the duty and find yourself involved in an amazing experience of temperature, bubbles, smells, textures and colours.

Flip to Chapter 6 for mindfulness master Thich Nhat Hanh's reflections on the washing-up experience.

Starting with a positive attitude

If you think about your day ahead using MBCT, you avoid panicking about all the tasks and responsibilities you have from the start and instead think about them in a productive but stress-free way.

Before you leave, if pets or other family members are in the house, make sure that you say an intentional goodbye, making eye contact and connecting to them sincerely.

Each day has the potential for many, many moments of experience. The more you step out of autopilot, the more you can notice even the smallest miracle, just like seeing the first snowdrop in spring.

Open your heart for the whole day and allow it to connect to things and people that give you a sense of wellbeing. Write them down in your diary if you find doing so useful, using colours and drawings to be even more open and receptive. Here are just a few ideas:

- ✔ The smell of coffee or fresh bread you made overnight in a bread maker
- ✔ The taste of delicious strawberries or any fruit you find enticing
- ✔ The sense of silky skin when putting on a lovely body lotion
- ✔ The joy of wearing your favourite jumper
- ✔ The love from others who notice your kindness and awareness
- ✔ An adorable cat engaged in its personal grooming

Kindly add any more ideas to your diary. Consider making this a little ritual, and when you feel a little down you can reread your notes.

> *Cats are intended to teach us that not everything in nature has a purpose.*
>
> —G. Keillor

Preparing yourself for the rigours of the day

Whatever form of transport you use to travel to work, the journey time offers opportunities for mindful practice:

✔ If you're driving a car, use a red traffic light as a reminder to be mindful on the road and not completely move into autopilot. Ask yourself whether you're still grounded and aware of your surroundings. If not, take a few mindful breaths. Can you feel your feet on the pedals and your hands on the steering wheel? Bring awareness to everything around you so that you can respond promptly should you need to.

Don't expect everything on your journey to run smoothly. Being mindful can show you something quite amazing or make you alert if danger appears out of nowhere.

✔ If you're travelling by public transport, instead of listening to music or reading the newspaper, focus your awareness on the sounds of life that are coming and going as you travel. Instead of judging sounds as pleasant or unpleasant, experiment with switching on your childlike curiosity. You could focus on voices around you, not on the content of conversations but rather the pitch of sounds, the distance or closeness of it and their length and intensity. You could focus on traffic sounds, on sounds that people make when they type on their laptops or ruffle with shopping bags or on the sound of the brakes and whatever else happens to occur. This is your sound world to explore with an open, non-judgemental mind. All sounds can become an ongoing background tapestry, and in the foreground you might want to focus on your in- and out-breath.

✔ If you work from home, try sitting down mindfully, grounding yourself and observing your natural breathing. Experiment with doing this before turning on your computer. Kindly remember that you do have choices in how you respond to situations, but only a clear and calm mind can access those choices.

Attempt to treat everything that comes up during your day in a mindful way, using the breathing space exercise from Chapter 6 whenever you feel symptoms of stress, or whenever you want or need to use this exercise.

Relaxing and enjoying yourself

Make sure that you allow regular time for just being: taking regular breaks, having conversations with the people around you, checking on whether anybody needs a hand. Perhaps you can listen to a piece of music you like for a little while, being really present when you do so: hearing all the individual instruments, the vocal changes, the lead melody and bringing to your awareness what you find so special about this piece of music.

In today's busy world, make time consciously for mindfulness, rather than hoping to find it:

✔ See whether you can think of something that you do regularly that can be reduced or left out occasionally, so that you've more time to experience life as it unfolds.

✔ Pencil in some time every week to treat yourself to something uplifting and experience it mindfully (a massage, reflexology, a visit to the hairdresser, a sauna and swim, a walk in a beautiful park or wood, or going to the cinema, theatre, an exhibition or a concert).

✔ Make room for keeping in touch with friends or family. A phone call is great because it connects you to the voice of the other person and the joy of sound. A handwritten letter or card is also lovely, though, because you increase awareness through touch and sight. Receiving one is great too, because it rarely happens except at Christmas or birthdays. Celebrate the ordinary!

Winding down

Sleep is incredibly important. Without enough, you're more vulnerable to illness (diabetes, heart disease, depression and even unwanted weight gain) and more prone to accidents. Furthermore, you'll be less able to pick up new skills or retain new mental data, and more likely to feel sleepy and irritable. During sleep, the body produces growth hormones that help to repair anything in your body that needs it. As you may have heard, some victims involved in accidents are put into artificial sleep in order to heal faster.

Frequently staying up too late, consuming drinks containing caffeine to keep you alert and using a gin and tonic to wind down when you come home can all cause sleep problems.

Here are two suggestions to help improve the quality of your sleep:

✔ **Replace the quick-fix gin and tonic:** Instead, practise meditation when you get back from work. Even a brief breathing meditation helps you to let go of whatever is still waiting in the office for you. Surely it'll be there tomorrow, so allow this thought to pass. For now, you need not concern yourself with anything but *now*.

✔ **Apply consistency:** Get good rest every night and don't try to catch up on your weekends. Really enjoy feeling rested and alert when you get enough sleep. Take notice of how you feel when you're full of beans.

Please consider following this wind-down routine (of course, adapt it to your personal circumstances):

1. **Open your front door, walk in and greet all the people and animals in view.**

2. **Change into more comfortable clothes – this is helpful not only if you want to relax, but also because your mind finds it easier to let go of work thoughts.**

3. **Have a delicious cup of herbal tea with honey and engage in a ten-minute breathing, viewing or listening meditation (along the lines that I describe in Chapters 4 and 7).**

4. **Check whether dinner is ready or whether you can fix it mindfully.**

5. **Eat at least the first few bites of your meal with mindful awareness, tasting the food, smelling it and enjoying it.**

6. **Congratulate the cook (even if that's yourself); conduct any conversation mindfully, listening and responding with kindness.**

7. **Clear up mindfully – washing the dishes, wiping the surfaces, and so on.**

8. **Think about playing a game with your partner, children or flatmates as a lovely alternative to the TV, or carry out a longer mindfulness meditation.**

9. **Two hours before bedtime, disengage from all electronic devices – reading something not too exciting or listening to music is a good option.**

10. **Give yourself plenty of time for a mindful bathroom routine.**

11. **Engage in some mindful breathing when you lie down, allowing the mind to settle completely.**

12. **Sleep like a baby.**

Employing Mindfulness at Work

No matter where you work or in what capacity, MBCT can help you remain calm and stress free as well as get the most out of your work day. While you're at work, you benefit from having a number of short interventions to hand. You can fit any of the following into your schedule, however busy:

✔ **See events as they really are, without adding drama or anxiety to them.** For example, if your boss asks you to have a document ready 'one minute ago', take a quick breathing space moment (see Chapter 6). Thereafter, rather than arguing or explaining, use however much time you require – no more, no less – to complete the task. Deliver the document in a neutral fashion, without allowing yourself to succumb to any unnecessary confrontational reactions (for example, sending it along with a sarcastically worded email).

Research shows that smiling changes your internal chemistry for the better (you produce serotonin and endorphins, which are chemicals that make you feel better and improve your immune system). You can see regular smiling as a ticket to better health, even leading to lower heart rates. The English writer Joseph Addison wrote, 'What sunshine is to flowers, smiles are to humanity'. Expressing friendliness for the benefit of others as well as yourself is something that can become part of your values (for more on this subject, check out the later section 'Assessing Your Core Values').

✔ **Send all your emails mindfully, by putting yourself in the place of the person receiving the correspondence.** Time is precious! Less is more!

✔ **Take a breathing space moment before any meeting you attend.** This way you can be fresh, alert and in the moment for everybody who's participating, including yourself.

✔ **Practise acceptance and compassion.** When you find a co-worker difficult, give that person an opportunity to talk a little about themselves. Maybe ask an invitational question, such as, 'What kind of a day are you having today?' Listen carefully and only respond in a way that is going to benefit the two of you.

✔ **Observe your body.** Every couple of hours or so, sweep through your body with a gentle body scan meditation (from Chapter 4) to check in with how you're feeling. Breathe into areas of tension, drink water regularly (not only when you notice that you're thirsty) and go for a mindful mini-walk, even if it's just to the toilet and back. Your body loves moving. While washing your hands, you can do a few gentle neck rolls and massage your face with your fingertips; and remember to smile.

✔ **Use your computer to remind you with a 'bell' sound (which you can download at** `www.insightmeditationcenter.org/meditation-timers`**) to do a short listening practice.** Also, download some screensavers for a brief viewing meditation (see Chapter 7). Alternatively, pin up pictures, paintings or posters that you like to view (for example, pictures of nature such as mountains, forests, or the ocean, or perhaps animals like cats or dogs).

Focusing on each individual task

Let this very moment of your life always be your priority. When you start stressing about the multitude of things that need doing, you create chemicals in your body that reduce your ability to utilise your creativity and focus (see Chapter 7 for lots more on stress). A gentler, less exhausting way of being is to focus on each individual task at hand; this way, you're much more likely to get the most out of your time and energy.

Please follow these steps to make a creative to-do list for yourself:

1. **Take an A4 sheet of paper, fold it in the middle and then once more so that you have four equal squares when you unfold it.**

2. **Select four different coloured pens, such as red, orange, deep yellow and green like traffic lights, or any colours you prefer.**

3. **Write in the top left square with the urgent colour red, all things that are so urgent that you have to deal with them today.**

4. **Move to the top right square, and write in orange all actions that require your attention within three days.**

5. **Cover all things that need sorting out within a week in the bottom left square in yellow.**

6. **Mark the less urgent demands that you can deal with during the next month in the bottom right square, in green.**

I suspect that almost immediately you sense relief, because you've arranged a system that, though not written in stone, offers you the possibility of mindfully working out one thing at a time, step by step. Often, the red square ends up with only a few points in it, and when you've completed those you can reward yourself and pick an easy task from any of the other columns.

If you have more than ten or so items in the red box then mindfully read them again and see whether you could move a few to another column. Be mindful and compassionate, yet also firm. Would you really lose your job or would something terrible happen if a couple of actions have to wait? This is called mindful discernment and self-compassion.

You may think that this list-making is time-consuming and may need to be repeated every day. My personal observation, however, is that within a relatively short period your brain learns to differentiate the most urgent from the least urgent so that lists may no longer be required.

This list-making reduces anxiety, switching your body system from the 'threat response' to the 'be now' response. When you no longer produce stress chemicals, more oxygen reaches your brain and you will feel more effective and satisfied.

Making sure not to overload yourself

You need to try not to overload yourself workwise, but doing so can be a real challenge. In difficult economic times, fewer people are being paid to do bigger jobs. But mindfulness can help you to cope with this extra demand without breaking down and without leaving a great pile on your desk waiting to be worked through. Mindfulness can assist you in being assertive, in being much better at managing your time and in being honest with your line manager about what you can or can't do. Here are a few suggestions to help you out:

- ✔ Recognise how much you can take on and be honest about it, with yourself and your manager.

- ✔ Realise your potential by focusing on one task until you've completed it.

- ✔ Allow yourself to delegate – find somebody whom you can trust and train to take on some of the overload, and be sure to praise them for their input.

- ✔ Develop compassion for yourself and others.

Sometimes you have to say no, or 'not now, but tomorrow'. By speaking kindly, sincerely and honestly, your words are more likely to be received with acceptance from other people.

Responding to pressure and criticism

Mindful techniques can help you deal with pressure from colleagues, unmanageable workloads, impatient clients, and so on. One particular challenge is *attention deficit trait* (ADT). For details, check out the nearby sidebar 'Paying attention to ADT'.

As you're already barely coping, ADT can cause you to go to work even when you know that you should stay in bed. As a result, you force your system to give you bigger and bigger signals of being unwell. In many cases, burn-out is the final outcome. *Burn-out* happens when you allow exhaustion to run your life and don't allow yourself enough recharge periods or rest, so you run down like an empty battery. Physical symptoms can include physical fatigue, frequent illness and sleep problems. Emotional symptoms include disillusionment with the job, the loss of a sense of meaning and cynicism towards your organisation or clients, feelings of helplessness, frustration of efforts and a lack of power to change events, strong feelings of anger against the people we hold responsible for the situation and feelings of depression and isolation. Behavioural symptoms can include increasing detachment from co-workers, increased absenteeism, an increased harshness in dealing with your team, marked reduction in your commitment to work and increased addictive behaviours.

Kindly read the bullet points in the preceding section to help you stay well in a frantic world.

Paying attention to ADT

Caused by brain overload, ADT is now prevalent in many work environments. It manifests in symptoms such as being easily distracted, lacking focus and suffering frequent irritation. You can have extreme difficulty organising your day, sticking to your timetable and setting priorities.

Your immune system gets more and more compromised and so causes you to suffer from an array of ailments such as flu, respiratory tract infections, digestive irritations, headaches and even autoimmune diseases such as lupus, fibromyalgia and chronic fatigue syndrome.

Here are a few additional skills that you can use when feeling under pressure or being criticised:

✔ Have regular breaks and go for a mindful stroll, even if it lasts just a couple of minutes.

✔ Drink a cup of tea mindfully: feel the cup's shape and surface, notice the temperature, smell and sip the beverage mindfully.

✔ Work together as a team (humans are social creatures at heart), offering little treats, fruit or other healthy snacks to your colleagues and yourself.

✔ Allow the content of any criticism to sink in gently. Ask yourself what lessons you can take from it, maybe even taking guidance and positive ideas. If you feel, however, after due consideration, that it's unfounded (in your opinion), kindly offer your perspective to the person criticising you (albeit in a calm, constructive manner) or decide to let it pass.

As so often, Shakespeare has a suitably wise quote on the subject (from *Hamlet*): 'For there is neither good nor bad, but thinking makes it so'.

✔ Surround yourself with plants, because studies show that they can help to improve indoor air. Useful air enhancers are Aloe Vera, Spider plant, Snake plant, Golden Pothos, Chrysanthemums, Weeping Fig, Azalea, English ivy, Chinese Evergreen, Bamboo Palm and Peace Lily. Most of these plants are easy to look after and really improve air quality. Plus, they can also serve as an object for a brief viewing meditation (check out Chapter 7 for details).

Knowing when you've done enough and setting up boundaries

Mindful self-compassion means knowing that creating and maintaining boundaries is perfectly fine.

Through the practice of MBCT, you can develop the confidence and inner strength to know that you've done enough for today. Kindly recognise and share with the relevant person that, for now, your load is done. You may have other arrangements for which you want to be on time or you may simply feel that your body needs to stop now. This awareness grows through practising mindfulness. The majority of people, however, who aren't trained in being more sensitive and aware, tend to focus mainly on their own agenda. As a result, stopping work can be challenging when others try to pressure you into doing more than you feel able to give at this moment in time.

A helpful technique is called the *broken record intervention*. Each time your co-worker or manager tries to convince you to do a little more or at least to complete the task in hand even though you're done for the day, please try to do the following:

1. **Breathe mindfully, ground yourself and feel like a mountain/oak tree (flip to Chapter 6 for ideas on standing strong).**

2. **Offer a meaningful but unwavering response, calmly and kindly, such as: 'I think I'll do a much better job tomorrow morning'.**

3. **Repeat the exact same answer, like a broken record, as long as it takes for the other party to understand and accept it.**

4. **Remember that your 'no' remains a polite 'no'; no more, no less.**

Making time for mindfulness practice

In today's busy world, you're going to have to make a conscious decision as to which part of your frantic life you can alter in order to create the time and space for your daily meditation practice. Here are a few tips that many people find useful:

✔ Experiment with getting up a little earlier and meditating before the mad rush begins. The early hours of the day are filled with fresh air, bird song and the rising of the sun.

✔ Consider practising first thing after returning home, so that you make a clean break from work to private leisure time.

✔ Think about cutting down a little on your Internet use, television use or reading papers.

Perhaps write an activity schedule for one week, not changing anything but just noting down how many hours you usually watch TV, sit at the computer or read newspapers and magazines. You can also write down how much pleasure each of these activities gives you, with 1 being low and 10 being excellent. The following week, decide to cut out time from those activities that give you least pleasure. All you need is about 45 minutes a day to give you the regular time you need for meditation.

✐ Add a number of shorter practices on the way to work (read the earlier section 'Preparing yourself for the rigours of the day' for some ideas) or while taking a break.

Enhancing Your Relationships

Whether you want to improve and nourish your relationships at home or at work, here are a handful of mindful principles that you can try and be aware of and implement on a daily basis:

✐ **Aim to be really present when you're with another person.** Pay attention to what people are trying to say to you, observe their body language and also the feelings and body responses you notice in yourself.

✐ **Accept others for who they are, as best as you can.** If their actions hurt or annoy you, remember that everyone is imperfect and try to criticise only the deed and not the whole person. For example, say 'I get frustrated when you're late' instead of 'you're always late'.

✐ **Bear in mind and observe other people's talents and gifts rather than only their shortcomings.** Try to give positive feedback, and when you notice something special, share your appreciation with the other person. Everybody likes somebody saying something nice to them out of the blue, because it's an unexpected gift.

✐ **Show appropriate, considerate friendliness to other people, depending on the relationship you have with each other.**

✐ **Ask whether you can help the other person with anything.** Offer kindness, generosity of spirit and real help.

Communicating mindfully

On a daily basis, you engage in verbal and nonverbal communication with others. Practising calm communication helps to decrease miscommunication, missed communication and confusion, which can so often lead to conflict and tension.

First and foremost, listen to yourself and identify your strengths and weaknesses in communication. During a conversation, use short statements at first and leave plenty of space for yourself to check that you said what you meant. If not, try again and point out to the other person that you weren't altogether satisfied with your first statement. Initially, this approach appears like discovering a new language, but with practice in the long run you save a lot of time and anguish.

I invite you to consider a situation: you want to leave work earlier so as not to be late for your partner's concert. How do you ask a colleague to step in for you? Take a few mindful breaths and ground yourself. Use fewer words and more breaks so that the other person has time to digest your request and to answer truthfully.

Here's how the conversation may go:

> 'Hi Moni, my girlfriend is playing at a gig tonight.' Pause. 'I'd like to ask you whether you can help me out.' Pause. 'I don't think I can finish these applications today. They're really urgent.' Pause. 'I'd be very grateful if you could take over so I can leave on time.' Pause.

Whatever the answer, thank Moni for listening and accept whatever help she may or may not offer. In each of the pauses, Moni may say something, or not. Take her responses into account. Even if she replies unhelpfully, see whether you can respond wisely and skilfully. The worst-case scenario is that you have to come in a little earlier tomorrow.

Mindful communication helps you to develop more honest, compassionate and flexible interaction with others.

Being mindful of your body language

Bringing awareness to the way you communicate via your body language – as in how you hold and present yourself – is another essential point to bear in mind at work and at home:

✔ **Use appropriate eye contact, so that the other person feels heard and acknowledged.** No need to stare, though, and make people feel nervous.

✔ **Allow your facial muscles to be relaxed and, when appropriate, add a gentle genuine smile.** Remember to smile with your mouth *and* your eyes.

✔ **Keep your arms and legs relaxed and open (rather than crossed), because it sends a signal of non-threat.** It also indicates that you're confident, comfortable and interested.

✔ **Breathe into areas that you notice feeling stiff, such as your neck or when your shoulders hunch up.** Let them go loose on the out-breath.

✔ **Indicate that you're really present and involved when listening: nodding and saying 'hmm' and 'I see' are helpful responses.**

Be careful, however, not to interrupt people!

✔ **Choose your words mindfully.** Leave time for the person to respond.

> ✔ **Communicate with your heart as well as your words, because some-
> times words can't express the exact nuance you're trying to convey.** Try
> to imbue your words with the feelings that have caused you to want to
> say them, and the other person is more likely to pick up your meaning.

Noticing when and why moods change

The more you check in with your state of being, the more quickly you notice
when you're feeling off-kilter. You may have had a disagreement with somebody or witnessed one, slept too little, be fighting an infection, worked too
long without a break or have a deadline that seems oh so close. And when
you're feeling off-kilter or on edge, you may need to bring more mindfulness
to your relationships with, and any communication you have with, other
people. Take as an example arriving home late and hungry and being immediately asked by the person you live with how your day was. You may want to
snap and say 'awful'. But with a little mindfulness, you may be able to say, 'I
just need a little break – could we talk in twenty minutes, please?'

When you observe that you're feeling a little upset, aggressive, anxious, and
so on, kindly take a breathing space meditation from Chapter 6.

Consider following these suggested steps:

1. **Feel into your body and notice what sensations are present.** For example, heat and tingling, heart racing, numbness, fatigue, breathlessness,
   itchiness, and so on.

2. **Scan your thoughts briefly.** Are they jumping from tree to tree like a
   wild monkey? Are they focusing on all the things that you're dissatisfied
   with at the moment, and then luring you into the past where you can
   really have a celebration of the debacle called life: the unfairness of it
   all, the state of the world, wondering whether there's any purpose and
   if so what that may be? Plus, these thoughts may also pull you into the
   future, focusing on all the battles still to fight, the tensions and challenges to survive, and then coming to terms with ageing and death.

3. **Observe these thoughts and then take a good while to connect to your
   breathing.** If thoughts arise and get in the way, gently but firmly let them
   pass by and refocus on your breath. This breath connects you more
   than anything to being alive in this moment.

4. **Notice as the onslaught moves more and more into the background
   of your awareness, leaving just you, your breath and this moment.**
   Appreciate that, in this moment, everything is kind of okay. Now you
   don't have to suffer or battle, but simply *be*.

5. **Realise that your body sensations may be appearing calmer and more
   focused.** Even if you still feel discomfort, it's most probably less raw.
   You're alive and breathing. Feel your feet firmly on the ground, linking

to three points of contact (little toe, big toe and your heel) and maybe imagine a symbol of strength and balance: a mountain, a strong animal or a big ancient tree.

Having realistic expectations and accepting the notion of change

Expectations can lead to inevitable disappointments, because they're created by you. Even though the trigger may be based on social values or external expectations (for example, by your parents), you and no one else decides whether you want to live up to expectations or whether they seem unobtainable and perhaps even unhelpful for you. Too many individuals constantly push themselves harder than they should or even want to, just because they think that this behaviour is what's expected of them. For example, your parents may have hoped that you'd always look like a television star, fully groomed and ready for a photo shoot, but on some days you might just prefer to hang out in leggings and big t-shirts. Dare instead to be yourself and be less concerned about what others expect.

Accepting the notion of change is also important, because the fact that your existence and your experience of it constantly changes is the only thing that's absolutely certain and unavoidable. You may not like this inevitable fact, but getting used to and accepting it as a fact is best, because change is going to happen continuously throughout your life.

Mindfully observing natural change is really helpful, for example:

- ✔ **In nature:** The seasons or the weather.
- ✔ **In your appearance:** From baby, to child, to adolescent, and so on.
- ✔ **In technology:** Increased computerisation and mobile phone innovations.
- ✔ **In family structures:** New family members added through marriages and couples having children.

Considering these givens helps you to get to grips with constant change in your life.

The more you can live in this moment, which constitutes your unfolding life, the less you set yourself up for disappointment and exhaustion. All beings are subject to change and unknown alterations in their life courses. If you realise that other people are struggling in the same ways that you are and you're able to provide them with compassion, you create an atmosphere around you where they'll be more likely (and may indeed desire) to reciprocate and act compassionately towards you, so enhancing your relationships with them. At the very least, this compassionate atmosphere will lead you to treat yourself more kindly.

Living for today

Here I rewrite a 13th-century poem by Rumi. This beautiful piece of writing epitomises the essence of mindfulness, summing up connecting to each moment as it presents itself and the importance of living just for today:

Take good care of Today,

Because it is Life

Life of all Life.

In its brief unfolding lies all

Reality and Truth of being alive,

The Delight of Growing,

The Magnitude of an Action,

The Elation of Strength.

Because the Yesterday is but a dream

And the Tomorrow not more than a Possibility.

Today however, if lived purposefully,

Turns every Yesterday into

A dream of Joy

And every Tomorrow

Into a Vision of Hope.

This is why you should be mindful of Today.

You gain the most benefit from changing your internal language. Talk to yourself with kindness and at least attempt to add a little dash of compassion to your communications with other people too, even if the other person is challenging in their behaviour. Instead of saying: 'How can you be so stupid and forget mum's birthday again?', for example, you might try 'I wonder whether you might want to get a birthday diary. You know how mum really appreciates a little token of love on her birthday.'

Assessing Your Core Values

Discovering what you really value and care about in life happens automatically the more you practise and develop mindfulness. For example, you may well notice that cruelty in the news becomes harder to accept and even to observe. You can also decide to revisit the core values you were taught by the people who raised you – in particular, to consider whether you still think of those core values as valuable. Have you collected some on your way of growing older and wiser? Which ones do you no longer keep in this phase of your life? What would be the most important value to teach your child or your co-worker?

As mindfulness grows and awareness unfolds, so do certain basic positive attitudes:

- **Acceptance:** Taking things and events as they are, at least initially, and then responding wisely to them. Accepting others even if they appear different in their views or looks – someone, that is, who moves in a different social sphere to you (such as a punk, a school child or a businessman) – for the simple reason that they too suffer and struggle.

- **Curiosity:** Being like a child who completely lives for each present experience and never worries about it and whether it counts as being valuable. This momentary aspect of life is worthwhile simply because it's part of the whole.

- **Generosity:** Being generous of spirit and of actions. Showing awareness when, perhaps out of fear, you occasionally bend the truth about your finances to avoid admitting that you're able to help others in need. The reverse can also be true: you may have little and give a lot. If you like to be generous, try and find a balance so that those who need your support, like your family, for instance, feel cared for and looked after too. Not because charity begins at home, but rather because everyone is part of a bigger thing called humanity.

- **Kindness and compassion:** Helping others, even if their deeds may make them undeserving, for the simple reason that they're alive.

- **Trust:** Being more in tune with the wisdom of your heart and therefore open to experiences that you may have shied away from before (for example, talking to a homeless person or a beggar).

Looking at what makes people human

Please think about what you have in common with everyone else. All humans share the same basic needs for survival (food, water, shelter), but they also yearn for companionship, kindness and purpose. If you want to apply mindfulness to all your interactions with other humans, you need to be fully present, pay attention and see what you can offer other people in need.

Every day of your life presents opportunities to share a little kindness and a little help. In mindful mode, you're more likely to feel how you may make a difference. Check out Table 17-1 for some examples.

Table 17-1	Little Instances of Kindness and Consideration	
Situation	**Being Mindless**	**Being Mindful**
On an escalator	Standing in the way of others who want to pass by	Making way
Walking into a building	Not checking whether somebody is right behind you	Holding the door open for people behind you
Using your mobile phone in public	Talking loudly about private issues	Keeping it brief and talking quietly

Please write down in your mindfulness diary how you can change some of your behaviours out of kindness and consideration for others, and without feeling like a martyr. Being thoughtful feels great, because when you're compassionate towards other people the self-compassion centre in your brain becomes stimulated too. Win–win!

Seeing how your values agree or conflict with those of other people

Almost everything is becoming more and more commercialised, including practices such as yoga, Pilates, meditation and mindfulness. Open any yoga magazine, for example, and you find adverts for mats, cushions and outfits in matching colours, as well as for the latest trendy yogi, who's slim, trim and beautiful.

Please be mindful of falling into the potential trap of thinking that you can buy values, mindfulness and peace of mind. Think about how you can use your valued resources, and remember that you can offer your time, knowledge and kind actions instead of or in addition to money. The gesture can be as small as no longer accepting plastic carrier bags in shops and bringing your own reusable ones.

I invite you to ask yourself the following questions as a way of sorting out your values and how strongly you feel them:

- ✔ Do you know what you want to stand for?

- ✔ Are you prepared to voice your deepest-held truths, even if they're against the trend of the masses?

- ✔ How do you want to express your principles through the way you live your life?

✔ Are you ready or working towards certain commitments that improve you and the world?

Please spend a moment remembering what really matters to you. Make a list of your values and pin them up on the fridge so that you and everybody in your household see them regularly. Perhaps also have them as a screensaver on your computer.

Here are a few suggestions for demonstrating that you have a big and compassionate heart:

✔ Express gratitude for all the different gifts life has bestowed on you.

✔ Perhaps give up some of your precious time and become engaged in an action that makes a real difference.

✔ Have a heart-to-heart talk with a friend.

✔ Offer a generous donation to nourish your community or gift an item that helps somebody out.

✔ Commit to developing a mindful relationship with money, even if doing so means considering changing your profession or present employer and earning less, and live more fully the life you long for and the world requires.

Making a difference

Plastic surgeon Dr Mohammad Jawad is a pioneer in skin craft and reconstruction surgery for victims of acid attacks. He lives in London and says he has it good: a lovely wife, three healthy children and a comfortable lifestyle. When he heard that 100 or more women each year are the victims of savage acid attacks in Pakistan, he felt compassion and went to his country of origin to improve the lives of as many of the women as possible.

The stories he heard were unbelievable: a 15-year-old who refused her teacher's advances and was attacked by him (he still hasn't been charged for his unbelievable crime); a woman who filed for divorce after years of physical abuse by her husband, only for him to meet her outside the court house and throw acid into her face – disfiguring her and blinding her in one eye; another woman who was attacked by her husband and his family with acid and petrol and set alight. This unfortunate woman even had to move back in with her in-laws in order to have contact with her children.

This sidebar makes for hard reading, I know, and I spell the details out so that you're encouraged to ask yourself what gifts or resources you can offer to alleviate the suffering of humanity. You may be able to teach a skill to homeless adolescents, cook Christmas dinner for people suffering from multiple addictions or adopt a granny or grandpa in an old people's home to bring light and hope to their last years.

Nothing's intrinsically wrong with being well-paid and having a good life, but think about how much more you'll enjoy it if you share some of your good fortune with less fortunate people.

Accepting the imperfection of human beings

If you feel able to offer kindness only to people who are without fault, you're going to have to wait for a long time before being kind! Part of being human is that every light side has a shadow side, so please avoid trying to separate people into the deserving and undeserving.

If you can cope mindfully with the frustration that human flaws cause, and see beyond them (for yourself and for others), you'll be able to meet the vulnerable, the fearful and the needy, and offer them your care and protection. Take a look at Table 17-2 for a couple of simple illustrations.

Table 17-2	Choosing to Respond to People's Flaws Mindlessly or Mindfully	
Situation	*Mindless*	*Mindful*
Somebody dropping litter in the street	Telling them off	Picking up the item (if it is sanitary) and putting it in the bin yourself, letting go of any negative impulses
Somebody taking up three seats in a waiting area	Telling them whether they think they own the place	Asking them whether they'd be so kind as to let you sit down

Look at Table 17-2 and use your diary to explore alternatives to other examples of inconsiderate living (for example, someone talking loudly on their mobile phone in public).

Making Mindfulness a Shared Experience

Mindfulness starts with the notion that every single person experiences suffering, fear, joy, hunger, and so on. Therefore, everyone is in this life together. For this reason, I invite you to allow all the insights and skills that you pick up by reading this book or some of its chapters to touch all everyday experiences.

Considering ways to share mindfulness with other people

The best way to share mindful awareness with others without preaching to them is to let them feel it. As the old saying says, 'actions speak louder than words'. Although often throughout this book I ask you to enter the being rather than doing mode, in this case you need to work creatively around this contradiction. Here are a few ideas:

✔ Letting people get off the train before you get on (not much doing perhaps, but really helpful!)

✔ Offering a seat to somebody just because you care

✔ Sending a lovely handwritten card to a friend, as a sign of your appreciation

✔ Bringing homemade soup or stew to a neighbour on a cold rainy day

✔ Getting a hot drink and sandwich for a homeless person

Now, I ask you to brainstorm. Consider how you can share something freely, give away something to somebody who needs it more, or help a friend or neighbour with a task they can't achieve by themselves. Any other ideas? Even if some intentions you come up with do not manifest in actions (perhaps, 'I want to help a charity or take grandpa out to the pub once a month'), keep focusing on the good. All wholesome behaviours start with an intention, and one day you may actually bring it alive. All the while, please remember you are a fallible human being, and in the next moment you can start again. This is the powerful message of mindfulness.

Living in a mindful society

Kindly imagine that you can help spread the positive effects of MBCT by simply engaging in the regular practice of mindfulness. Your optimistic and life-confirming energy inevitably affects others and has a positive influence on society at large, because every society is made up of many individuals. So the initial step is just to live and act mindfully as best and as often as you can.

If your way of living ignites enthusiasm in others and helps them find a way to express kindness to and acceptance of others, you greatly contribute in creating a mindful society just by being what you are.

Mindfulness has many positive effects on the brain, such as helping you to regulate your emotions, increasing your capacity to remember things, being able to pay attention more deeply and for longer, to mention but a few. The snowball effect of spreading mindfulness by living it is unimaginable in a positive way. Research also shows that not only your brain, but also your body benefits greatly by practising MBCT:

- ✔ Improved physical wellbeing
- ✔ Better immune function
- ✔ Quicker healing of numerous diseases
- ✔ Fewer accidents

Think about some of the improvements for society if health providers needed a little less funding because you and others stay healthy more often and for longer. Perhaps the funds could be used to:

- ✔ Improve public transport
- ✔ Increase health education
- ✔ Provide more home visits from doctors for elderly and disabled people

Please come up with your own inspiring insights and note them down in your mindfulness diary.

Part IV
The Part of Tens

To read about the ten attitudinal foundations of mindfulness, head to www.dummies.com/extras/mindfulnessbasedcognitivetherapyuk for a bonus Part of Tens chapter.

In this part...

- ✔ Expand and intensify your mindfulness journey, and build on your existing knowledge of mindfulness-based cognitive therapy by checking out a variety of rewarding courses, films and websites.

- ✔ Get to know ten completely inspirational people from the wonderful world of mindfulness, and think about how they can encourage and guide you in your own journey.

- ✔ Cast your net wide and consider visiting a variety of amazing specially designed environments in locations across the world where you can deepen your own personal connection to mindfulness.

Chapter 18

Ten Ways to Expand Your Mindfulness Experience

When you start experiencing the benefits of mindfulness-based cognitive therapy (MBCT), don't be surprised if you want to discover more and more. Mindfulness and feeling better are definitely addictive. If you find yourself infected with the mindfulness bug (this bug isn't fatal, I promise!), you have loads of ways to extend your knowledge and practice.

In this chapter I provide a group of hand-picked resources connected to mindfulness, all of which can expand and intensify your mindfulness journey. The overall selection that's available is huge, but I've personally tried and tested, attended, viewed and found really helpful these ten websites, training institutes, courses and commercial films.

Dropping by the Enter Mindfulness Website

This website (which you can access at www.entermindfulness.com) is part of my own organisation (forgive the shameless plug!) and serves as an invitation for you to delve further into mindfulness. Here you can find:

✔ Information about upcoming courses and workshops

✔ Resources to help you practise mindfulness meditation yourself

✔ Dates for individual coaching and therapy sessions

✔ News and updates about my practice and the world of MBCT

In addition, an evening meditation session takes place once a month (the venue is in London, SE23) that is suitable for people with a basic knowledge of mindfulness meditation. We practise walking meditation in the garden, as well as sitting and loving kindness meditations. Each session takes place on a Wednesday (unless otherwise stated) from 7:30 to 9:15 p.m. As if that isn't appetising enough, we serve a large variety of teas and biscuits for a final round of sharing the evening's experience.

Checking out the Be Mindful Website

This website (www.bemindful.co.uk) was created by the Mental Health Foundation (MHF) charity, which is dedicated to reducing the pain caused by mental ill health and assisting people suffering from mental health issues. MHF offers a number of services such as developing research, useful interventions for improving mental health services and campaigning to decrease stigma and prejudice connected to mental illness.

The website was one such development around three years ago. As well as offering an affordable online course, the site is a great source for information about mindfulness, focusing on topics such as:

- ✔ What is mindfulness?
- ✔ What is MBCT?
- ✔ What is mindfulness-based stress reduction (MBSR: check out Chapter 1 for more on this forerunner to MBCT)?
- ✔ How to find a course close to you.

The website shares with you how to apply mindfulness to everyday life. A large number of people have used it and experienced life-changing improvements in stress, anxiety and depression. The provided programme contains the core elements of MBSR and MBCT.

Visiting the Mindfulnet Website

The independent (that is, not affiliated with any particular governing body) mindfulness information website www.mindfulnet.org covers a wide range of resources and information about mindfulness. The organisation was created and is maintained by one wonderful and committed lady (Juliet). It's regularly updated and offers a wealth of information.

Topics include:

- Research findings

- Recommended mindfulness teachers

- Uses of mindfulness at work and in the fields of education, the judicial system, medicine and psychotherapy

- Books, video clips and other resources

- Information on upcoming mindfulness events in the UK

- A brief introduction to the brain and what happens to it when you meditate

- Videos and media clips connected to the neuroscience of mindfulness, and recent research into how mindfulness helps you become more aware of your thoughts and how it actively shapes your brain

I recommend reading up on the fascinating information on how MBCT affects your brain.

Studying Mindfulness Formally: Centre for Mindfulness Research and Practice

The Centre for Mindfulness Research and Practice (CMRP) (see www. bangor.ac.uk/mindfulness) is a self-funding establishment based in the School of Psychology at Bangor University, in north Wales.

The Centre shares a deep commitment to the promotion of mindfulness-based approaches and offers training for professionals and the general public. It offers Continued Professional Development (CPD) courses for professionals and part-time postgraduate MSc/MA programmes, and organises an annual conference around Easter time, where leading experts share their research insights and new developments.

CMRP is a wonderful place and the longest-standing centre of its kind in the UK.

Benefiting from Research at the Oxford Mindfulness Centre

The Oxford Mindfulness Centre (OMC) is an international centre of excellence within Oxford University's Department of Psychiatry (the website is at www.oxfordmindfulness.org). Its main focus is to prevent depression and increase human potential by using mindfulness therapeutically. The OMC is at the forefront of research in the field of mindfulness and has incorporated training and education in benefits of mindfulness worldwide with its partners around the globe.

Clinical trials have proved the benefits of mindfulness in preventing serious depression and emotional anguish and the OMC is exploring the implications of these findings. Research is also extended to other disorders, using brain-imaging techniques and experimental cognitive science. The goal is to determine how mindfulness really works, and which practices are best for which conditions.

The Centre is exploring the potential of mindfulness to help people build resilience for the most challenging times of their lives: children and young people at school, adults at work and at home, parenting, older adults and those who care for them when they become frail.

The people working for the OMC are highly respected pioneers in the MBCT field, and having such a place in the beautiful city of Oxford is a feast for your senses.

Taking a Mindful Breath with Breathworks

Since 2001, Breathworks (www.breathworks-mindfulness.org.uk) has taught thousands of people living with pain, stress and illness how to improve and change their quality of life. The programmes are based on key elements of MBSR and MBCT and draw on the personal experience of Vidyamala Burch, who uses mindfulness to manage severe chronic spinal pain. Breathworks offers courses in a wide range of mindfulness skills to relieve the distress associated with persistent pain, fatigue and ill health, as well as stress. You can practise mindfulness skills face-to-face, through distance learning and online (alone or with mentoring).

The Breathworks approach to mindfulness is based on accepting your experience of hurting, ill health or stress and not reacting to it as you may usually do. With mindfulness, you can discover how to perceive clearly thoughts, physical sensations, emotions and events at the moment they occur without reacting in an automatic way.

By developing a new relationship with the conditions that cause you suffering, you can start to respond in new and creative ways. Breathworks' headquarters are in Manchester, but courses are available in many different locations (UK and worldwide).

Vidyamala has written a couple of books on living with pain and illness, is a fantastic teacher and inspires everybody who hears her talk or reads her words. Check out Chapter 15 for more on Breathworks.

Attending a Mindfulness Course in Scotland

Kagyu Samye Ling (in Dumfriesshire, Scotland) was the first Tibetan Buddhist Centre established in the West and everybody is welcome! It offers mindfulness one-year training via a comprehensive course and is appropriate for beginners and more advanced practitioners of mindfulness (see `www.samyeling.org`).

Participants are taught progressive skills in mindfulness through presentations, guided meditations and tutorials. A strong importance is placed on discovering by experience, and for this reason home coursework is involved between weekends that include regular mindfulness practice, daily life exercises and journal writing:

- **Module One:** Becoming present
- **Module Two:** Working with distraction
- **Module Three:** Self-acceptance
- **Module Four:** Undercurrent and observer

This beautiful venue isn't difficult to access and the environment is highly conducive for learning. Samye Ling offers many other courses as well, so take a look at the website.

A special little oasis within this oasis is the Internet cafe. The cakes are fabulous! You can, but don't have to, connect to the outside world. The two peacocks roaming the land are something else.

Watching Spring, Summer, Autumn, Winter . . . and Spring

Korean writer-director Kim Ki-Duk created this magical film (in Korean with English subtitles) in 2004. The tale's otherworldly setting is a beautiful lake, surrounded by mountains and forests. On the lake floats a small wooden temple. Here live an elderly monk and his naughty adopted son and pupil. The viewer observes the boy's turbulent course through childhood and adolescence, which all happens in this enclosed environment.

The film's five concise chapters investigate existence: the bliss and ache of desire, joy and regret, guiltiness and reparation, selfishness and awareness, death and rebirth. The outside world and its temptations come and visit the central duo in summer when a young woman seeks treatment for an inexplicable illness and the teenage monk falls ardently in love and lust with her. The young man follows her into the city where he finds out about the human condition of attachment and loss.

Animals serve as a recurring theme within the individual sections: the boy discovers truths about inflicting suffering and having to accept punishment for it. He tortures frogs and snakes around whose bodies he cruelly ties stones. The monk then ties a heavy rock around the boy, so that he discovers what suffering he caused the helpless creatures. Few words are spoken.

The film is a masterpiece of mindfulness, because everything moves slowly and metaphors open the heart and mind of the viewer. Ki-Duk doesn't judge the deeds of his characters. Instead he achieves a sense of stillness through exhilarating images of nature and contemplative pacing, without losing sight of the burdens of the human existence. Watching the film is a truly meditative experience.

Changing Lives: Doing Time, Doing Vipassana

This film tells the story of men incarcerated for life having committed horrendous crimes. The filmmakers spent about two weeks inside Tihar

Central Prison in New Delhi and Baroda Jail in the Indian state of Gujarat. They interviewed inmates and jail officials. The film shows how a strong woman named Kiran Bedi, the former Inspector General of Prisons in New Delhi, strove to transform the infamous Tihar Prison and turn it into an oasis of peace. She'd heard from a prison guard who changed his life after discovering Vipassana (insight meditation). She hoped that meditation could have the same positive effect on the prisoners.

She invited a famous mindfulness teacher from Sri Lanka, who moved into the prison with his wife and spent ten days in silent meditation with the prisoners. They discovered how to take control of their lives and channel them towards goodness. All underwent profound change, realising that imprisonment didn't have to be the end but could be a fresh beginning towards an improved and more positive life.

The change was so dramatic that recently the Indian Government decided to apply Vipassana in all the country's prisons. Other countries are becoming interested as well. What I remember most is how the hearts of all participants opened and in the end all that remained was compassion and kindness.

You can freely view the film on YouTube, at `www.youtube.com/watch?v=b8tZX3dGSM8`.

Following One Man's Mindful Recovery: I Am

I Am is a 2011 documentary film written, narrated and directed by Tom Shadyac (director of many Hollywood films including *Ace Ventura – Pet Detective, The Nutty Professor* and *Bruce Almighty*). It explores his personal voyage of recovery after a 2007 bicycle accident.

Shadyac suffered post-concussion syndrome and experienced severe headaches and hyper-sensitivity to light and noise. After medical treatments failed to help, he isolated himself completely, sleeping in his closet and walling the windows of his mobile home with blackout curtains. Gradually his symptoms began to subside at last and the director wanted to share his inner quest in the way he knew best: through film.

Shadyac also donated much of the fortune he earned as a filmmaker to open a homeless shelter. In the film he interviews scientists, religious leaders, environmentalists and philosophers such as Desmond Tutu, Noam Chomsky and many others. The central question is: What is wrong with our way of life and can we change it? The film is about creating a connection with all beings and leading a mindful and purposeful existence.

With his gentle humour, Shadyac comes across as an exceptionally likeable character. Earnings from the documentary go to the Foundation for I Am, which supports various charities.

Chapter 19

Checking Out Ten Inspirational People

....

....

In this chapter I introduce you to ten inspiring people from the world of mindfulness. They're personal favourites of mine who 'held my hand' on my way to becoming more mindful. Narrowing the list down to ten was difficult, but I chose people who left a wonderful footprint in my heart: some of them know that they did so and others don't.

In many ways, this chapter is an homage to all the people who supported and encouraged my journey into mindfulness. I hope you discover some future mindfulness friends to encourage and guide you, too.

Thich Nhat Hanh: Spreading Mindfulness and Peace

Thich Nhat Hanh (pronounced *Teek Nut Hun*) is a Vietnamese Zen master, scholar, poet and peace activist. He's published more than 85 titles, 40 of which are available in English. His first text of importance on mindfulness is entitled *The Miracle of Mindfulness*. It was originally written as a letter from exile in France to one of the monk brothers who'd remained in Vietnam.

The school that Hanh had founded in Vietnam in the 1960s was intended to help rebuild bombed villages, educate children and set up medical stations for both sides engaged in the conflict. The letter encourages and supports the brothers to continue to work in a spirit of love and understanding. It reminds them of the essential discipline of mindfulness, even in the midst of extremely difficult circumstances.

When Hanh was writing the letter in Paris, to where he'd gone in exile after receiving threats on his life, several supporters from different countries were attending the Vietnamese Buddhist Peace Delegation. Naturally, Hanh thought that people in other countries could also benefit from reading this letter. He suggested that the translator (an American volunteer) translate it slowly and steadily, in order to maintain mindfulness; thus, only two pages a day were translated. Hanh encouraged the translator to be aware of the feel of the pen and paper, of the position of his body and of his breath in order to maintain the essence of mindfulness while doing this task. When the translation was completed, it was typed and a hundred copies were printed on a tiny offset machine squeezed into the delegation's bathroom.

Since then, that little book has travelled far. It has been translated into several other languages and distributed on every continent in the world. Prisoners, refugees, healthcare workers, psychotherapists, educators and artists are among those whose life and work has been touched by *The Miracle of Mindfulness* (Random House, 1991).

Denied permission to return to Vietnam, Thich Nhat Hanh spends most of the year living in Plum Village, a community he helped to found in France (www. plumvillage.org). Check out Chapter 20 for more on this lovely place. Plus, you may want to read another Hanh book, *Peace Is Every Step: The Path of Mindfulness in Everyday Life* (Rider, 2008).

The Dalai Lama: 'My Message Is Love'

His Holiness, the 14th Dalai Lama, was born in a small village called 'the roaring tiger' in 1935. His parents were farmers and he had 15 brothers and sisters, 9 of whom died young. He was just 3 years old when he was chosen to be the next incarnation of the Dalai Lama. First he was taken to Kumbum Monastery where he lived a rather sad life, not understanding what had happened to him or what was expected of him. In 1940 he moved to the Potala Palace in Lhasa, the capital of Tibet, where he was enthroned as the spiritual head of his nation and his family were given a farm nearby.

His life was planned out for him. He needed to study twice a day for a total of two hours and then was allowed to play, but from the age of 13 he had to do the same duties as any adult monk. The topics of education he covered included healing, Sanskrit, philosophy of religion and languages.

His Holiness is the spiritual leader of the Tibetan people. He repeatedly points out that his life is guided by three major commitments: the promotion of basic human values or secular ethics in the interest of human happiness, the fostering of inter-religious harmony and the welfare of the Tibetan people, focusing on the survival of their identity, culture and religion. He appreciates his role because it gives him the opportunity to benefit others.

Recently, in January of 2013, the 'Mind and Life' conference (`www.mindand life.org`) met for the 26th time, where scientists and Buddhist scholars discuss topics such as meditation and its effects on the brain. The Dalai Lama attends the conference every year and this year he donated $1,000,000 for essential research and activities.

See Chapter 11 and consider checking out these books for more about the Dalai Lama: *The Dalai Lama's Little Book of Inner Peace* (Harper Collins, 2002) and *Ancient Wisdom, Modern World: Ethics for the New Millennium* by Tenzin Gyatso (Little, Brown and Company, 1999).

Jon Kabat-Zinn: Mindfulness in Medicine

The molecular biologist Jon Kabat-Zinn had a vision, which came into his awareness while on a retreat. He pondered whether mindfulness could be applied to the secular environment of medicine and psychotherapy. The answer was a resounding yes! He developed mindfulness-based stress reduction (MBSR) in the 1970s at the Center for Mindfulness in Massachusetts (check out Chapter 1 for more on Jon and MBSR).

His goal was to make the Eastern philosophical teachings and meditations available as life-enhancing skills for everyone. He saw his calling as connecting meditation and medicine, by offering people the chance to reconnect to their lives through the simple act of being, and letting go of doing, for brief periods every day. When you gain insight into what you truly are (whole, complete and good enough) you often experience a deep sense of freedom and healing. In short, by accepting yourself and your lot just as it is, you remove a lot of the causes of suffering. Like the Dalai Lama, Kabat-Zinn says 'my religion is kindness', a notion he follows in his teachings, books and engagement with others.

You can find out more in Jon Kabat-Zinn's books, *Full Catastrophe Living, 15th edition* (Dell Publishing, 2006) and *Wherever You Go, There You Are, 6th edition* (Piatkus Books, 2006).

Ram Dass: Expressing Gratitude

Richard Alpert was originally an American professor of psychology (see www. ramdass.org). He set up the Hanuman Foundation (www.hanumanfdn. org) in 1974, which shows people how to embody and celebrate love and service to humanity. Every day, he said, can become a spiritual, special practice. He emphasises the importance of gratitude, because it connects people to one another and offers mutual support. He believed a truly grateful life would bring peace and harmony.

Appreciation feels good and shows you how every person on the planet is connected. Discovering how to appreciate every single thing that happens as a potential source of insight and growth is the key ingredient of a joyful existence.

Dass wrote a great book called *Still Here: Embracing Ageing, Changing and Dying* (Riverhead Books, 2001) in which he explains how caring for his sick father repaired their early unhealthy relationship. When you've lived for half a century or more, it becomes difficult to ignore the subtle changes in health and appearance that occur with age, and facing these themes discussed in the book with awareness is important for everyone.

He invites you to have gratitude and concern for others and believes that true freedom can only be achieved through accepting dependence on others. His book *Be Here Now* (Crown Publications, 1971) is the one that perhaps best describes his transformation and new outlook on life, and you can read more of his work in *Grist for the Mill* (Celestial Arts, 1995).

Eckhart Tolle: Living Moment to Moment

Eckhart Tolle was born in 1948 in Germany and now lives in Canada. His best known books are the *The Power of Now* and *A New Earth,* which are written in English. In 2011, *Watkins Review* named him the most spiritually influential person in the world. Tolle shares that he suffered from depression, until he experienced at the age of 29 an 'inner transformation'. He travelled around thereafter being unemployed, 'in a state of deep bliss', before becoming a spiritual teacher.

The bestselling *The Power of Now* (Hodder), which was first published in 1997, shows how you can find a way out of psychological suffering. The more you find out how to be fully present and interact wisely with others, the more you experience loving relationships and true purpose in life. *The Power of Now* and *A New Earth* had sold an estimated three million and five million copies respectively in North America by 2009. In 2008, approximately 35 million people participated in a series of ten live webinars with Tolle and television talk show host Oprah Winfrey. Tolle has never identified himself with any particular religion.

At a two-day retreat in Findhorn, Scotland (a great place that I discuss further in Chapter 20), he talked about meditation and how mindfulness was a useful way to truly connect to the now.

Melissa Myozen Blacker: Teaching Mindfulness

Melissa is a Zen priest in the US. She studied anthropology and music and later did an MA in Counselling Psychology. Since 1993 she's worked at the Center for Mindfulness, founded by Jon Kabat-Zinn, at the University of Massachusetts Medical School. With her husband David, she formed a Zen community called Boundless Way Zen.

She shares that mindfulness-based stress reduction (a forerunner of MBCT; see Chapter 1) is a beautifully designed and secular approach to help you fall 'awake' to your life. People who'd never considered going to a Zen centre before can benefit in a life-changing way from being introduced to meditation.

She says that to focus on being fully awake and grounded are maybe the most important principles to engage with in the work of mindfulness. She's a wonderful and inspiring teacher.

To find out more about Melissa Myozen Blacker, check out her book (written with James Ishmael Ford), *The Book of Mu: Essential Writings on Zen's Most Important Koan* (Wisdom Publications, 2011).

Buddha Maitreya: Living the Path

Buddha Maitreya (check out www.buddhamaitreya.co.uk) was born and brought up in Japan. While attending a meditation course, he experienced something particularly intense that he calls 'enlightenment'. In this moment, 'he saw the absolute perfection and beauty intrinsic in all things and all beings, the essence of life'. He completely dedicated his life there and then to becoming a meditation teacher.

Maitreya completed an MA degree in Buddhist Theology and then left Japan, spending time in Thailand, India and Nepal. In England, he based himself in Nottingham, creating the Pure Land centre in 1973 (you can find out more about it online, at www.buddhamaitreya.co.uk/garden.html). Pure Land is one of the most beautiful gardens in the UK and is praised in many garden tours and guides. Even if you don't want to discover meditation, you can simply spend a mindful day in amongst nature there.

The serene garden contains traditional Japanese garden elements such as water, golden carps, bridges and bamboo, blended with a 'dash of English plants and elements'. The result is a perfect example of 'East and West in radiant harmony'.

Buddha Maitreya has published a number of CDs with meditations, such as *Perfect Relaxation and Meditation with Maitreya* and *Nature's Heart*, available online at www.buddhamaitreya.co.uk/shop.html.

Rick Hanson: Examining the Mindful Brain

Rick Hanson (www.rickhanson.net) is a fantastic teacher of neuropsychology and of how meditation affects the brain. I first met him six years ago via Skype after he'd given the most amazing lecture on the physiological changes in the brain due to long-term mindfulness meditation. I eventually invited him to present as the main speaker at a conference I organised at the University of East London, entitled 'Mindfulness and Well Being: from Spirituality to Neuroscience' in 2009. He'd just finished his first book *The Buddha's Brain,* in which he explains how contemplation and meditation can form and shape your brain to such an extent that it can deepen and improve your relationships, help you stay calm when you're facing a 'storm' and experience a life of more confidence and purpose.

Meanwhile, Rick has been busy and published another book called *Just One Thing: Developing a Buddha Brain One Simple Practice at a Time* (New Harbinger, 2011), in which he presents 52 powerful yet down-to-earth ways to strengthen your own brain and enjoy a more adventurous life. Also, you can sign up to receive his free monthly newsletter *Just One Thing* (New Harbinger Publications).

Rick travels to Europe once a year and I recommend that you attend his lectures if you can! He manages to explain neuropsychology in such a wonderful way and you don't need to be an expert to understand it.

Jenny Ronayne: Studying Autism

I first met Jenny some 20 years ago, shortly after my own son was diagnosed with autism: she'd set up the Lewisham Autism Support Group. She was an inspiration. She studied psychology and her intention was to discover more about this fascinating subject: she hoped to undertake research in the field, disseminate information and raise awareness of autism spectrum disorder (ASD).

Our paths crossed again when I started lecturing at the University of East London and Jenny, who'd taught me so much, was suddenly a student of mine. For her MA thesis, she looked at how mindfulness interventions may help people with ASD reduce anxiety.

In addition, she has founded an organisation called ASPECT: Autism Spectrum Counselling and Training. ASPECT (www.aspectcounsel.co.uk) offers in-house training and consultancy to organisations such as schools, Local Education Authorities and charities. She's currently interested in combining mindfulness techniques with a behavioural therapeutic approach, and is developing a research project to investigate whether this is effective in reducing anxiety levels in individuals with ASD.

Kristin Neff: Focusing on Self-Compassion

When I met Kristin recently, it was like a meeting of souls: as in my case, her son has autism too. Plus, I'd lived in the Far East and she'd travelled to Mongolia five years before with her son to try and find healing. *The Horse Boy* is the story that describes their journey, and how it affected her and her son deeply (see www.self-compassion.org).

Kristin is a wonderfully committed researcher, writer and lecturer, and her main focus is self-compassion and, of course, mindfulness. She became interested in Buddhism in the late 1990s and has been practising meditation ever since.

While doing her post-doctoral work, she decided to conduct research on self-compassion, a wonderful concept that hadn't been examined by empirical research up to then. With her colleague Chris Germer at Harvard, she recently created an eight-week programme on self-compassion skills called 'Mindful Self-Compassion'. In 2011 she wrote a book on the same topic: *Self-Compassion: Stop Beating Yourself Up and Leave Insecurity Behind* (Hodder & Stoughton).

Chapter 20

Surveying (Almost) Ten Inspirational Places to Visit

In This Chapter

▶ Visiting inspirational locations

▶ Attending mindfulness retreats

*J*ust as negative places can bring you down, so positive locations can be a huge encouragement on your mindfulness journey. As I describe in Chapter 4, setting up your own dedicated meditation space in your home is vitally important, but visiting specially designed and prepared environments is a great help too.

In this chapter I introduce you to several places that run courses and hold retreats that can deepen your connection to mindfulness and to mindful communities. I know this to be true, because that's precisely what they did for me!

Plumbing the Heights of Mindfulness at Plum Village

Mindfulness master Thich Nhat Hanh (see Chapter 19 for a brief biography) lives in Plum Village in the Dordogne, southern France (www.plumvillage. org). It's open to visitors from around the world who want to attend a mindfulness retreat. I can certainly recommend that you visit to hear what Thich Nhat Hanh has to say. The proceeds from the fruit of hundreds of plum trees are used to assist hungry children in Vietnam.

If you want to experiment and try Plum Village out you can stay for just a day, but most people visit for at least a week. You practise mindfulness throughout the day and in all daily activities: eating, walking, working, meditating, studying, exercising, and so on. If you hear a bell ring, you stop (along with everyone else), relax and focus on your breathing.

Plum Village has one so-called lazy day per week, without any planned activities or scheduled meditations, when you can just see how everything unfolds naturally. You can forget about time and be mindful in whatever occurs. You could write or do some light reading. It can also be a time for contemplation – giving you room to think about how your practice is developing. Often, you find insight and new inspiration on this day. Alternatively, you could just hang out with the friends you've made at Plum Village.

How much you donate for one day at Plum Village is largely up to you, though £50 seems to be the minimum amount most people give.

Attending Quiet Days at the London Insight Meditation Society

The London Insight Meditation Society (LIMS: www.londoninsight.org) offers one-day retreats (often in North or Central London) and you don't need to be a Buddhist to attend. Often, you're joined by over a hundred co-students. LIMS invites incredible speakers such as Rick Hanson (check out Chapter 19 for more information), Stephen Bachelor, Christina Feldman and Sharon Salzberg.

The days start at a reasonable time and don't finish too late. If you attend, you do a lot of sitting and walking meditations and invited guest speakers give a couple of talks. The low course fees (a day course costs around £17 to £25) only cover the hiring of the room, so you're requested to give a donation of between £10 and £50 for the teacher before you leave.

Everybody brings something vegetarian for lunch, which is put out on a buffet table and shared with all. The days remain in silence apart from the questions directed to the teacher and the whole day is an enriching experience.

Finding a Home from Home at Findhorn

My wonderful spiritual guide and teacher Astrid told me about the Findhorn Foundation in the late 1970s (www.findhorn.org). She'd been diagnosed with breast cancer and was convinced that regularly visiting Findhorn helped keep the disease at bay. To be honest, Findhorn mesmerised her.

Nobody asks you for your religious denomination or why you've come: you're just expected to help run the place and take good care of the gardens and land mindfully. For example, before cutting a vegetable for dinner or lunch, you thank it for feeding you.

Founded in 1962, Findhorn, located in Scotland, really does talk the talk and walk the walk – it is a mindful community that respects the Earth and all beings. The place itself is stunning, and so are the people you meet. You can visit for a week, a month or a year – the members of staff try to accommodate your preferences.

Findhorn offers many different courses. One such course run here is called Coming Home to the Garden, where you're invited to learn hands-on gardening over a week. The meditations on the course explore the connections between our inner and outer gardens. You can pay anything between £95 and £295, which covers all costs (including accommodations and meals) for courses such as this. Another course is Music Experience Week, which weaves music through the whole week, celebrating different spiritual traditions and introducing you to the dances of universal peace and sacred harmony songs. This course is more expensive and ranges between £475 and £800 (all inclusive).

Channelling Your Inner Bruce Lee at Shaolin Monastery

If you want a truly exotic mindfulness journey, and have the time and money, you can visit the legendary Shaolin Monastery in China (check out www. shaolin.org.cn/EN/index.aspx). Founded in the 5th century, this monastery is the birthplace of the famous martial art of *Shaolin Kung Fu*. The monastery practises Buddhism and asserts that you need to conquer the mind before you conquer anybody else.

When I visited in 1991, I expected to see the monks breaking bricks or metal rods with their bare hands. Instead I found 400 or more men and boys in yellow robes sitting in deep meditation. The senior monk explained, 'When you can control the mind you will also know when you need your body, a potentially lethal weapon, for defence. You never attack, only defend; and only if this is the last option.'

Visiting Shaolin, which lies in a beautiful valley, was certainly one of the experiences that propelled me into my meditation practice. Various holiday tour companies can arrange for you to spend periods of time at Shaolin, where you can meet the grand monks, practice deep meditation, find out about traditional Shaolin medical practices such as massage and cupping, attend lessons and discussions, watch Kung Fu shows and Shaolin monks training, and a variety of other activities. Accommodation is fine, but not splendid, though in general my experience is that the organisers try very hard to make your experience extraordinary.

If you want to make the most of your visit, April is the best time to go.

Exploring the Buddha's Teachings at Gaia House

Gaia House (www.gaiahouse.co.uk) is one of the loveliest meditation retreat centres in the UK, located deep in the Devon countryside, and is amongst the best-known Insight meditation retreat centres (a community for laymen rather than monks) in the UK. The retreats are to a large extent held in silence, though you're invited to speak and ask questions after the daily Teaching Talk in the evening.

Gaia House has a strong connection to the environment and green issues (Gaia means 'living earth'). The main meditations you experience are sitting and walking.

At Gaia House, you can go on a personal retreat (which costs approximately £37 per day) or on one of the many special topic retreats such as Meditation and Yoga, MBCT, Buddhism without Beliefs, Loving Kindness, and many more. A normal day starts with a practice before breakfast and ends with the last session at 9.30 pm. During the day, you receive full instruction regarding the practices, and in the evening you listen to a Dharma talk, during which teachers invite reflection on the teachings of the Buddha in relation to everyday life and your retreat experience. Usually you share a room with one or two other people and you're also asked to offer one hour of your time for keeping the lovely place clean. Duties can include bathroom and toilet cleaning, washing-up, cooking, gardening, and so on. The food is simple, and vegetarian.

Gaia House offers five different rates: a four-day retreat, for example, costs between £100 and £200. The fee you pay to go on the retreat covers only the costs of running the retreat. In addition, at the end of the retreat you're asked to give a voluntary financial contribution to the teacher.

Gaia House is in great demand, so I recommend that you book a year ahead. My favourite time is the late spring/early summer when hundreds of baby bunnies are hopping about all over the place!

Retreating to the Countryside at Trigonos

Trigonos (www.trigonos.org) is a beautiful retreat centre situated in the village of Nantlle (pronounced 'Nant-lay' in case you have to ask directions!) in Snowdonia, North Wales. Although quite remote, the journey itself offers immense beauty and tranquillity. You can book single or double rooms and the vegetarian food is simply amazing. The lake surrounded by the land is beautiful and you can even swim in it (in the summer).

You can hire the whole place in order to run your own retreat – Trigonos can accommodate 29 people in a mixture of single and twin rooms. Full board includes breakfast, lunch and dinner, morning coffee or tea with biscuits, and afternoon tea with homemade cake and a fruit bowl.

The cost of a room ranges from £64 to £88 per night.

Enjoying the Food (Mindfully!) at The Abbey

The Abbey (www.theabbey.uk.com), near Oxford in the village of Sutton Courtenay, England, is an astonishing venue – a Grade-1 listed building whose earliest parts date from the 13th century. The spiritual life here began in the ecumenical Christian tradition and has evolved to embrace other traditions as well. Core values at The Abbey are compassion, inspiration, creativity, contemplation and prayer. The residential community expresses these values through living together and they make you feel welcome, at home and at ease.

The Abbey offers a wide range of courses that change annually – check their website for a calendar of events. One attraction is their special collection of material relating to the life and work of Mahatma Gandhi; The Abbey hosts a yearly gathering of his followers.

I've attended a number of yoga and compassion retreats here. My favourite course is the annual Yoga, Pilates and Mindfulness weekend retreat with Helen Stephenson and Dr David Brown (a scientist and Buddhist practitioner). Both teachers weave together the teachings of yoga and meditation by the open fire in the Great Hall. Then, after lunch you have a couple of hours to yourself so you can venture out into the village or explore the numerous fine paths nearby that are good for the walking meditation.

The Abbey offers a number of meeting rooms, a meditation room and single and double accommodation. Full board ranges from £100 to £170 per day.

The vegetarian food provided is so delicious that you don't want to stay here while trying to lose weight!

Getting the Best of Both Worlds: West-Östliche Weisheit, Benediktushof

This beautiful centre for spirituality, near Wuerzburg in Germany (see www.willigisjaeger-foundation.com for details), was founded by Willigis Jäger, who's a Benedictine monk and a Zen master. The centre offers different types of retreats throughout the year. Its particular focus is on combining Eastern spiritual practice with the wisdom of Christianity, although you need have no religious affiliation to attend. *West-Östliche Weisheit* means 'Western and Eastern wisdom'.

The breadth of courses at West-Östliche Weisheit is praiseworthy. Zen and Contemplation, Paths of Judiasm, Paths of Yoga, Meeting Your Voice and Sufi Mystik are just a few of the courses on offer at the time of writing.

Three years ago I attended a week-long retreat led by Jon Kabat-Zinn and Saki Santorelli. The centre was in the process of completing a traditional Zen Garden and I had the great privilege of observing the gradual transformation from my balcony. The experience is still deeply etched into my heart.

If you're considering spending a guided retreat here, please check which language will be used for instruction, because most are held in German.

Single room and all meals cost £60 per day. The cost for teaching is not included.

Visiting The Well at Willen

The Well at Willen (www.thewellatwillen.org.uk), near Milton Keynes in England, is a multi-faith community surrounded by stunning grounds. The Well welcomes all visitors, irrespective of their beliefs and traditions, and the community includes Quaker, Catholic and Buddhist traditions. The Well offers retreats and prayer meetings. Residing at The Well is Helen Stephenson, an experienced and fully trained MBCT teacher and trainer. She teaches with myself on advanced mindfulness trainings, but also offers yoga and pilates courses.

Five guest rooms are available at The Well, but most participants stay at nearby hotels or come for the day, which costs £50.

Index

About the Author

Dr Patrizia Collard discovered meditation, Buddhism, yoga, Qui Gong and Tai Chi when living and working in Hong Kong and China for nine years. She returned to the UK in 2000 and continued her voyage into mindfulness at the Centre for Mindfulness Research and Practice at Bangor University in North Wales. A circle closed magically, for her first job as a university assistant lecturer had also been at Bangor University.

Patrizia feels very fortunate to have worked and trained with some of the most inspiring teachers in the field. To mention but a few, they included Jon Kabat-Zinn, Mark Williams, John Teasdale, Christina Feldman and Rick Hanson. Nowadays, Patrizia trains students at the University of East London and both educators and psychotherapists in mindfulness-based cognitive therapy and has had opportunities to work in many settings all over Europe: the UK, Ireland, Austria, Germany, Slovenia, Spain and Greece.

Patrizia is an accredited cognitive behavioural therapist and integrative psychotherapist and coach, and she works with organisations, groups and individuals. Over the 25 years of her ongoing experience in the field of psychotherapy and training, she has qualified in many different approaches and is thus able to offer unique treatment combinations tailored for the needs of each client. In her former life, she studied acting, literature and art – skills that come in very useful at times when communicating ideas is both critical and essential.

Patrizia is a member of many governing bodies (BABCP, UKCP, Association for Coaching, Austrian Association for Behaviour Therapy, Institute for Health Promotion and Education and Obsessive Action) and is therefore always in touch with current developments in her fields of expertise.

Last, but not least, Patrizia enjoys writing fiction (poetry and short stories) and professional and self-help books. For six years she was interview editor of *Counselling Psychology Quarterly,* has co-authored four books and is the sole author of three. Some of her poems have been published too.

She lives in London and Vienna.

Dedication

This book is really for you, the reader. I do hope that MBCT will help you enjoy the adventure of life, and more deeply.

Author's Acknowledgements

I wish to thank my son Dan for all his support, Toby for his smiles and laughter, Tybalt the cat for bringing me into the moment whenever he feels like it, and my love and joy Bernhard.

Publisher's Acknowledgements

We're proud of this book; please send us your comments at http://dummies.custhelp.com. For other comments, please contact our Customer Care Department within the U.S. at 877-762-2974, outside the U.S. at (001) 317-572-3993, or fax 317-572-4002.

Some of the people who helped bring this book to market include the following:

Acquisitions, Editorial, and Vertical Websites

Project Editor: Steve Edwards

Commissioning Editor: Sarah Blankfield

Assistant Editor: Ben Kemble

Development Editor: Andy Finch

Copy Editor: Kim Vernon

Technical Editor: Helen Stephenson

Proofreader: Kerry Laundon

Production Manager: Daniel Mersey

Publisher: Miles Kendall

Cover Photo: ©iStockphoto.com/ Sergey Galushko

Composition Services

Sr. Project Coordinator: Kristie Rees

Layout and Graphics: Carrie A. Cesavice, Jennifer Creasey

Proofreaders: Lindsay Amones, Melissa Cossell

Indexer: Sharon Shock

Brand reviewer: Jennifer Bingham

FOR DUMMIES®

Making Everything Easier!™

UK editions

BUSINESS

978-1-118-34689-1

978-1-118-44349-1

978-1-119-97527-4

MUSIC

978-1-119-94276-4

978-0-470-97799-6

978-0-470-66372-1

HOBBIES

978-1-118-41156-8

978-1-119-99417-6

978-1-119-97250-1

Asperger's Syndrome For Dummies
978-0-470-66087-4

Basic Maths For Dummies
978-1-119-97452-9

Body Language For Dummies, 2nd Edition
978-1-119-95351-7

Boosting Self-Esteem For Dummies
978-0-470-74193-1

Business Continuity For Dummies
978-1-118-32683-1

Cricket For Dummies
978-0-470-03454-5

Diabetes For Dummies, 3rd Edition
978-0-470-97711-8

eBay For Dummies, 3rd Edition
978-1-119-94122-4

English Grammar For Dummies
978-0-470-05752-0

Flirting For Dummies
978-0-470-74259-4

IBS For Dummies
978-0-470-51737-6

ITIL For Dummies
978-1-119-95013-4

Management For Dummies, 2nd Edition
978-0-470-97769-9

Managing Anxiety with CBT For Dummies
978-1-118-36606-6

Neuro-linguistic Programming For Dummies, 2nd Edition
978-0-470-66543-5

Nutrition For Dummies, 2nd Edition
978-0-470-97276-2

Organic Gardening For Dummies
978-1-119-97706-3

FOR DUMMIES®

Making Everything Easier!™

UK editions

SELF-HELP

978-0-470-66541-1

978-1-119-99264-6

978-0-470-66086-7

LANGUAGES

978-0-470-68815-1

978-1-119-97959-3

978-0-470-69477-0

HISTORY

978-0-470-68792-5

978-0-470-74783-4

978-0-470-97819-1

Origami Kit For Dummies
978-0-470-75857-1

Overcoming Depression For Dummies
978-0-470-69430-5

Positive Psychology For Dummies
978-0-470-72136-0

PRINCE2 For Dummies, 2009 Edition
978-0-470-71025-8

Project Management For Dummies
978-0-470-71119-4

Psychology Statistics For Dummies
978-1-119-95287-9

Psychometric Tests For Dummies
978-0-470-75366-8

Renting Out Your Property For Dummies, 3rd Edition
978-1-119-97640-0

Rugby Union For Dummies, 3rd Edition
978-1-119-99092-5

Sage One For Dummies
978-1-119-95236-7

Self-Hypnosis For Dummies
978-0-470-66073-7

Storing and Preserving Garden Produce For Dummies
978-1-119-95156-8

Teaching English as a Foreign Language For Dummies
978-0-470-74576-2

Time Management For Dummies
978-0-470-77765-7

Training Your Brain For Dummies
978-0-470-97449-0

Voice and Speaking Skills For Dummies
978-1-119-94512-3

Work-Life Balance For Dummies
978-0-470-71380-8

FOR DUMMIES®

Making Everything Easier!™

COMPUTER BASICS

978-1-118-11533-6

978-0-470-61454-9

978-0-470-49743-2

DIGITAL PHOTOGRAPHY

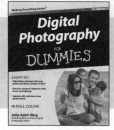

978-1-118-09203-3

978-0-470-76878-5

978-1-118-00472-2

SCIENCE AND MATHS

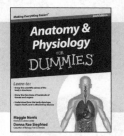

978-0-470-92326-9

978-0-470-55964-2

978-0-470-90324-7

Art For Dummies
978-0-7645-5104-8

Computers For Seniors For Dummies, 3rd Edition
978-1-118-11553-4

Criminology For Dummies
978-0-470-39696-4

Currency Trading For Dummies, 2nd Edition
978-0-470-01851-4

Drawing For Dummies, 2nd Edition
978-0-470-61842-4

Forensics For Dummies
978-0-7645-5580-0

French For Dummies, 2nd Edition
978-1-118-00464-7

Guitar For Dummies, 2nd Edition
978-0-7645-9904-0

Hinduism For Dummies
978-0-470-87858-3

Index Investing For Dummies
978-0-470-29406-2

Islamic Finance For Dummies
978-0-470-43069-9

Knitting For Dummies, 2nd Edition
978-0-470-28747-7

Music Theory For Dummies, 2nd Edition
978-1-118-09550-8

Office 2010 For Dummies
978-0-470-48998-7

Piano For Dummies, 2nd Edition
978-0-470-49644-2

Photoshop CS6 For Dummies
978-1-118-17457-9

Schizophrenia For Dummies
978-0-470-25927-6

WordPress For Dummies, 5th Edition
978-1-118-38318-6

Think you can't learn it in a day? Think again!

The *In a Day* e-book series from *For Dummies* gives you quick and easy access to learn a new skill, brush up on a hobby, or enhance your personal or professional life — all in a day. Easy!

Available as PDF, eMobi and Kindle